T0240845

Beginning Ractive.js

A Practical Introduction to Ractive.js
using Real-World Examples

Alex Libby

Apress®

Beginning Ractive.js

Alex Libby
Rugby, Warwickshire, United Kingdom

ISBN-13 (pbk): 978-1-4842-3092-3   ISBN-13 (electronic): 978-1-4842-3093-0
https://doi.org/10.1007/978-1-4842-3093-0

Library of Congress Control Number: 2017962046

Copyright © 2017 by Alex Libby

This work is subject to copyright. All rights are reserved by the Publisher, whether the whole or part of the material is concerned, specifically the rights of translation, reprinting, reuse of illustrations, recitation, broadcasting, reproduction on microfilms or in any other physical way, and transmission or information storage and retrieval, electronic adaptation, computer software, or by similar or dissimilar methodology now known or hereafter developed.

Trademarked names, logos, and images may appear in this book. Rather than use a trademark symbol with every occurrence of a trademarked name, logo, or image we use the names, logos, and images only in an editorial fashion and to the benefit of the trademark owner, with no intention of infringement of the trademark.

The use in this publication of trade names, trademarks, service marks, and similar terms, even if they are not identified as such, is not to be taken as an expression of opinion as to whether or not they are subject to proprietary rights.

While the advice and information in this book are believed to be true and accurate at the date of publication, neither the authors nor the editors nor the publisher can accept any legal responsibility for any errors or omissions that may be made. The publisher makes no warranty, express or implied, with respect to the material contained herein.

Managing Director: Welmoed Spahr
Editorial Director: Todd Green
Acquisitions Editor: Louise Corrigan
Development Editor: James Markham
Technical Reviewer: Phil Nash
Coordinating Editor: Nancy Chen
Copy Editor: Karen Jameson
Compositor: SPi Global
Indexer: SPi Global
Artist: SPi Global

Distributed to the book trade worldwide by Springer Science+Business Media New York, 233 Spring Street, 6th Floor, New York, NY 10013. Phone 1-800-SPRINGER, fax (201) 348-4505, e-mail orders-ny@springer-sbm.com, or visit www.springeronline.com. Apress Media, LLC is a California LLC and the sole member (owner) is Springer Science + Business Media Finance Inc (SSBM Finance Inc). SSBM Finance Inc is a **Delaware** corporation.

For information on translations, please e-mail rights@apress.com, or visit http://www.apress.com/rights-permissions.

Apress titles may be purchased in bulk for academic, corporate, or promotional use. eBook versions and licenses are also available for most titles. For more information, reference our Print and eBook Bulk Sales web page at http://www.apress.com/bulk-sales.

Any source code or other supplementary material referenced by the author in this book is available to readers on GitHub via the book's product page, located at www.apress.com/9781484230923. For more detailed information, please visit http://www.apress.com/source-code.

Printed on acid-free paper

This is dedicated to my family, with thanks for their love and support whilst writing this book

Contents

About the Author

Alex Libby is a Digital Ops / MVT developer, working for a global distributor based in the United Kingdom. Although Alex gets to play with different technologies in his day job, his first true love has always been with the open source movement, and in particular experimenting with front-end frameworks and libraries. To date, Alex has written a host of books on subjects such as jQuery, HTML5 Video, SASS, and PostCSS. In his spare time, Alex can often be found putting on shows at his local theater, or out and about on his bike (and with his camera).

About the Technical Reviewer

Phil Nash is a developer evangelist for Twilio serving developer communities in London and all over the world. He is a Ruby, JavaScript, and Swift developer; Google Developer Expert; blogger; speaker; and occasionally a brewer. He can be found hanging out at meetups and conferences, playing with new technologies and APIs, or writing open source code.

Acknowledgments

Writing a book can be a long but rewarding process; it is not possible to complete it without the help of other people. I would like to offer a huge vote of thanks to my editors, but in particular Nancy Chen and Louise Corrigan, and with Phil Nash as technical reviewer – all three have made writing my first book for Apress a painless and enjoyable process, even with all of the edits!

I've also asked for help on StackOverflow, so my thanks also to those who responded, and help provide answers – in particular, Joseph, who has the patience of a saint and has been particularly helpful.

My thanks also to my family for being so understanding and supporting me while writing – it requires a lot of late nights alone, so their words of encouragement (and also from Nancy and Louise) have been a real help in getting to the end and producing the finished result that you now have in your hands.

Introduction

Beginning Ractive.js is for people who want to learn how to build real-world, interactive applications, using the RactiveJS template library.

Originally created by the United Kingdom's *Guardian* newspaper to produce news applications quickly for its online site, guardian.com, it has matured into a fully fledged, easy-to-use library for creating sites, where time is short, and results must be produced quickly.

Over the course of this book, I'll take you on a journey through the library, showing you how easy it is to construct templates, take care of events, and manage data updates automatically using the library. We'll cover such diverse topics as animation, data-binding, event management, and more – each will provide a solid grounding in the use of Ractive, with lots of simple exercises, culminating in a full-size project to produce a basic e-commerce shopping cart and template page that you can use in your future projects.

Beginning Ractive.js is targeted to those who are familiar with HTML, JavaScript, and CSS, and want an alternative to some of the larger, more cumbersome templating libraries such as Angular – where we don't have time to learn a whole new technology! I'll also include lots of tips on how to use the library, and provide links to help with getting accustomed to using Ractive throughout the book.

PART I

Getting Started

CHAPTER 1

■ ■ ■

Getting Started with Ractive

Hands up if you can remember the early days of the Internet, surfing pages on dial-up connections that were slow, prone to drop-outs, and struggled with anything more than just plain text on a white or gray background? Sound familiar…?

It's a good bet that the pioneers of the Internet never envisaged that we would use a geeky language such as JavaScript to shop online, play games, or conduct our financial affairs online. Yet some of the world's most popular companies conduct all of their business online: it would be hard to find a regular user of the Web who hasn't bought something from the likes of Amazon.

It's easy to forget though that visual experiences presented by the likes of Amazon require significant effort to perfect: effort that takes time and money to achieve. There is a good reason for this though – I will let you into a little secret: the Web is not a great platform for building applications. I should quantify this admission though: it's great for displaying static content, but when it comes to creating interactive content that responds to our input – well…it can be painful, to say the least!

To put this into context, let me ask you a question: if you had to develop an online display that displayed the number of emails you had, how would you update it? Keep this in mind, as throughout the course of this chapter, I will introduce you to another way of working, and show you – to badly misquote that oft-used saying from *Hitchhiker's Guide to the Galaxy*, the answer is not always 42!

Introducing Ractive

Let's follow up on that question I posed at the end of the previous section – how would you update that display? To keep it simple, let's assume you have to update this content:

```
<span>Hello Alex! You have 24 new messages.</span>
```

As a developer, it's likely you may come up with one or more of the following answers:

- Use React, jQuery (or from a more practical perspective, JavaScript)
- Target specific elements in the code
- Make use of a template system
- Use a sledgehammer to crack a nut

Okay – I must confess: that last option is really in reference to larger libraries such as Angular! These are perfectly valid libraries in their own right, but their complexity makes it analogous to using a sledgehammer to crack that proverbial nut.

© Alex Libby 2017
A. Libby, *Beginning Ractive.js*, https://doi.org/10.1007/978-1-4842-3093-0_1

If we've been using them successfully for so long, why are they not ideal? In short, all of these options require extra work that isn't necessary. If we take jQuery for example, then mixing template and logic code isn't good practice; we can change the content, but it is prone to error if the code isn't changed correctly.

Altering our code to target specific elements or to use a template system is an improvement; we still have to deal with extra elements and the performance issues created from disposing of them. At this stage, a developer might consider using a framework such as Angular or Ember to do the heavy lifting, but this is not without cost. Once we get past the simple "Hello World!" demos, the learning curve is almost vertical, and the resulting code is often more complex than it should be. Okay – I might be exaggerating a little, but you get the idea...

So – what can we do? Well, there is an alternative – enter Ractive. Developed by the interactive team from the U.K.-based *Guardian* newspaper, this library shares some philosophies with Angular, but with some notable differences:

- Ractive only cares about the UI – it doesn't force you to have to use predefined routers or back-end functionality, unlike other frameworks.

- Angular uses "dirty checking," which checks every watcher if it thinks the view model has changed; Ractive uses a dependency tracking system that only changes the dependencies of a specific element.

- Angular (and others) traverse the DOM to set up data-bindings based on attributes set in code. Not only must we deal with non-validating tags throughout our code, it also increases the work the browser has to do to traverse the DOM.

- Ractive takes a different approach – strings are compiled in the same manner, but a lightweight parallel DOM is set up to manage updates. Allowing the template to be parsed before the browser allows Ractive to set up everything it needs to update the DOM, before updating the real thing. This makes it more performant, as most of the work is already done before changes are made to the DOM.

Okay – enough talk: let's move on and turn our attention to more practical matters! Throughout the course of this book we will explore how Ractive can be used to create fully interactive applications, but without the excess baggage of other libraries; hopefully this book will show you that we don't have to always use libraries "because that's what we've done before", and that Ractive is a worthy contender for your next application. It's time we made a start on that journey; the first step is to download and install Ractive, but before we do this, there are a couple of housekeeping tasks we need to take care of first.

Creating a Project Folder

Before we get started, there are a couple of tasks we need to perform:

- Go ahead and create a folder called `ractive` on your PC or Mac; this will be your project folder for all exercises in this book.

- We need a text editor too – you may already have a suitable one installed; if not, my personal preference is the cross-platform shareware application Sublime Text, which is available from `https://www.sublimetext.com/3`.

Now that we have that out of the way, let's get cracking with installing Ractive for use.

Downloading and Installing Ractive

Okay – with the housekeeping out of the way, we can now focus on getting Ractive installed!

Installing Ractive is probably a misnomer – if you're expecting a set of steps or a lengthy process, then I am sorry to disappoint: installing Ractive is as simple as adding this line into your HTML markup, at the appropriate point:

```
<script src='https://cdn.jsdelivr.net/npm/ractive'></script>
```

For most applications, this will suffice; it is better practice to reserve this for use in production environments, and use a local version for development. Ractive is also published regularly to NPM, so it can also be downloaded or linked to using any of the URLs as listed in Table 1-1.

Table 1-1. *URL links for obtaining Ractive.js*

Version	URL
latest, stable	https://unpkg.com/ractive
CDNjs	https://cdnjs.com/libraries/ractive
NPM	npm install --save-dev ractive
Bower	bower install --save ractive

If, however, you prefer to keep content locally, then you can install Ractive using npm – we will cover this in more detail in the next section, *Compiling using Node.js*. You can also use the Yarn package manager to install Ractive – the package details are listed at https://yarnpkg.com/en/package/ractive.

For the purposes of this book, we will assume use of a local copy of Ractive; in the meantime, let's turn our attention to installing Ractive using Node.js.

Compiling Using Node.js

For those of you who prefer to work with an existing Node.js installation, it is possible to install a version of Ractive that works with Node.js. However there are a couple of limitations though, which will affect how we use Ractive:

- When using Ractive through Node.js, we lose one of its key features – the parallel DOM is not available when using Node.js, so two-way binding is not possible. Instead, we must do it manually – we can use methods such as ractive.set() to change our data, or ractive.toHTML() to render the current template as HTML.

- The method to precompile templates also changes – for this, we need to use ractive.parse(). This is easy to do as a task using Gulp; we will explore this in more detail later in this chapter, in *Working through our first demo*.

For now, let us assume the limitations are not an issue for us, and go through installing Ractive with Node.js in more detail.

Installing Node.js

Installing Ractive using Node.js is very easy – for the purposes of this book, I will assume you do not have Node.js installed, so let's go ahead and follow these steps:

INSTALLING NODE.JS

1. We'll begin by installing Node.js – go ahead and browse to `https://nodejs.org` to download a version suitable for your platform.

2. Next, fire up the installer and run through each step of the wizard; it is sufficient to accept all defaults for the purposes of this book.

3. Once completed, go ahead and launch the Node.js command prompt, then change the working directory to our newly created project area.

4. We now need to update the NPM package manager to the latest version – at the prompt, type `npm install npm@latest -g`, then press Enter. Once this is complete, we can enter `npm -v` at the prompt to verify a newer version has been installed, as shown in Figure 1-1.

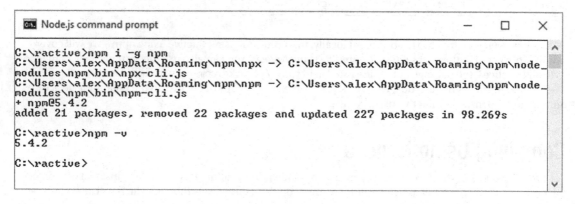

Figure 1-1. *Confirming the version of npm installed*

Configuring Node.js for Use with Ractive

Now that Node.js is installed, we can go ahead with installing Ractive; our first step is to set up a very basic `package.json` file, which is effectively a set of instructions that NPM follows, when installing packages.

For further information, please refer to the NPM documentation at `https://docs.npmjs.com/files/package.json`.

This isn't obligatory, although not running this step will generate an error; creating a package file now makes it easier to reinstall Ractive at a later date. Let's make a start:

CONFIGURING NODE.JS

1. We can now install Ractive using npm – first, fire up a Node.js command prompt, then change the working directory to our project folder area.

2. Next, go ahead and enter the following, then press Enter: npm init.

3. This will walk us through creating our package.json file – go ahead and enter the information as provided in the screenshot shown in Figure 1-2.

```
name: <my-awesome-package> testing-ractive
version: <1.0.0> 1.0.0
description: Package to test using Ractive with Node.js
entry point: <index.js>
test command:
git repository:
keywords:
author: Alex Libby
license: <ISC>
```

Figure 1-2. Details for creating a package.json file

4. Node.js will then display a summary of your entered text; if all is OK, press Enter to commit this to file.

With a package.json file created, let's install Ractive – npm will automatically add an entry into our package.json file (Figure 1-3).

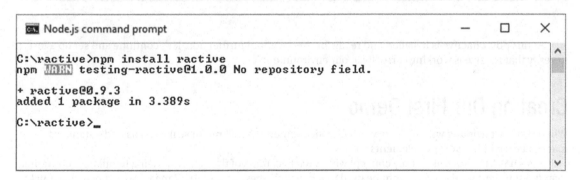

```
Node.js command prompt                          —    □    ×

C:\ractive>npm install ractive
npm WARN testing-ractive@1.0.0 No repository field.

+ ractive@0.9.3
added 1 package in 3.389s

C:\ractive>_
```

Figure 1-3. Installing Ractive

If we open up the package.json file that is located in our project area, we can indeed see that NPM has added an entry for Ractive, which will be 0.9.3 or newer (Figure 1-4).

```
1  {
2    "name": "testing-ractive",
3    "version": "1.0.0",
4    "description": "Package to test using Ractive with Node.js",
5    "main": "index.js",
6    "scripts": {
7      "test": "echo \"Error: no test specified\" && exit 1"
8    },
9    "author": "Alex Libby",
10   "license": "ISC",
11   "devDependencies": {
12     "grunt": "^1.0.1",
13     "path": "^0.12.7"
14   },
15   "dependencies": {
16     "ractive": "^0.9.3"
17   }
18 }
19
```

Figure 1-4. *Exploring our package.json file*

At this point Ractive is installed and ready for use – without further ado, let's continue and set up a test to verify that Ractive is working correctly in our environment.

Creating Our First Demo

When you start working with Ractive, you will notice something that might strike you as odd – standard markup tags within <script> elements?

Yes – it is true, but this is a key concept within Ractive; think of the HTML as being template code, rather than the standard markup you might be used to seeing on pages. To see what I mean, let's knock up a quick test to prove that we have a working page that uses Ractive (Figure 1-5).

Figure 1-5. *Our first demo*

Let's create our code:

CREATING A TEST RACTIVE FILE

1. Browse to http://cdn.ractivejs.org/latest/ractive.min.js, and save a
    copy of this file into a subfolder marked js, within our project area.

2. We will add a custom font to provide some styling to our demo – it's not obligatory,
    but does help show how we can style standard elements on a page, as opposed
    to styling elements in a Ractive component (we will explore this later in the book).
    The font we will use is Roboto; a copy is available in the font folder of the code
    download that accompanies this book, or you can download it from https://www.
    fontsquirrel.com/fonts/roboto. (If you want to use a standard font such as
    Arial or Helvetica, then this will work just fine.)

3. In a new document, go ahead and add the following code, saving it as
    testractive.js in our project area:

```
<!doctype html>
<html lang='en-GB'>
<head>
  <meta charset='utf-8'>
  <title>Beginning Ractive: Test to see Ractive working</title>
  <link rel='stylesheet' href='css/teststyles.css'>
</head>
<body>
  <h1>Ractive test</h1>
  <div id='container'></div>
  <script id='template' type='text/ractive'>
    <p>Hello, {{name}} - you are now using Ractive for the first time!</p>
  </script>
```

```
    <script src='js/ractive.min.js'></script>
    <script src="js/testscript.js"></script>
  </body>
</html>
```

4. In a separate file, save the following code as `teststyles.css`, into a subfolder called `css` within our project area:

```
@font-face { font-family: 'robotoregular'; src: url('../font/Roboto-Regular-
webfont.woff') format('woff'); font-weight: normal; font-style: normal; }

body { font-family: robotoregular, sans-serif; font-size: 14px; }
```

5. The magic of our demo comes in the next file – add the following code to a new document, saving it as `testscript.js` in the `js` subfolder within our project area:

```
var ractive = new Ractive({
  el: '#container',
  template: '#template',
  data: { name: 'reader' }
});
```

6. Save the file, then preview the results in a browser – if all is well, we should see the text shown in the screenshot at the start of this exercise.

In many cases we will simply use a local copy of Ractive to compile our code, or use the CDN link, if we're working on the production version of a project. However we can also use Node.js to compile our code – this is more suited for those of you who might already use Node.js within your development workflow. There are two ways to achieve this – either using the command line, or a task runner such as Gulp.

Compiling Code Using Node.js

When compiling code using Node.js, the method we use will depends on whether we simply want to compile our code, or tie it into an automated process that performs other tasks, such as adding vendor prefixes to style sheets. If all we want to do is test compiling our Ractive code, then we can run a manual task using this process:

COMPILING CODE USING NODE.JS

1. Add the following code to a new file, saving it as `testractive.js` at the root of our project area:

```
var Ractive = require('ractive');
var ractive = new Ractive({
  template: 'Hello, {{name}} - you are now using Ractive for the first time!'
});
ractive.set('name', 'reader');
console.log(ractive.toHTML());
```

2. Fire up a Node.js command prompt session, then change the working directory to our project area.

3. At the prompt, enter `node testractive.js` then press Enter; Node.js will go ahead and compile our code and render it on-screen, as shown in Figure 1-6. You may see a message about running Ractive in debug mode (see Figure 1-8), along with some links for help and support; these can be safely ignored.

```
Hello, reader - you are now using Ractive for the first time!
c:\ractive>_
```

Figure 1-6. *The output of compiling using Node.js*

Although the code looks a little different to how we created our first example, it uses the same principles during compilation. A key point to note is that when compiling or running Ractive-compiled code, we will by default see debug messages that are piped to the command line (Figure 1-7).

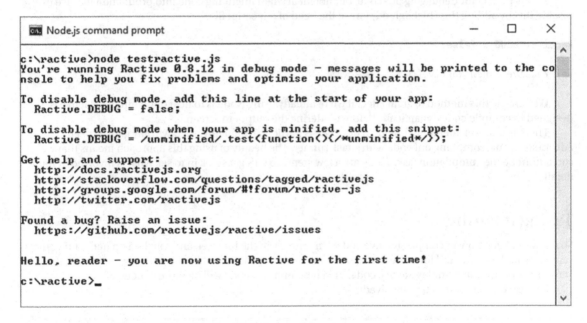

Figure 1-7. *Compiling Ractive code using Node.js*

We can see similar messages shown in the browser when running our first demo, as shown in Figure 1-8.

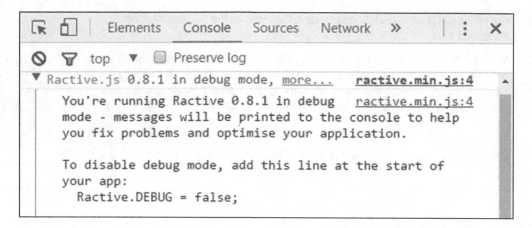

Figure 1-8. *In-browser debug messages*

This is perfect for debugging our code, but not ideal when migrating code into production use; we can disable this by adding this (highlighted) line at the head of our script file:

Ractive.DEBUG = false;

```
var ractive = new Ractive({
```

We can use this method to great effect if we're already using Node.js to host our content – Ractive is designed to compile code dynamically before rendering the output to screen.

There is one consideration though: if our code is particularly lengthy, then we may gain a speed advantage by precompiling our code with a task runner. The beauty of using this approach means that we can automate the compilation task. There are a few steps, so let's get stuck in to see what is involved in more detail.

Taking It Further

So far, we've seen how to compile Ractive code dynamically in the browser, and touched on performing the same task at the command line. The first of these methods is great for smaller sites, but up to a point; if we start to really develop complex Ractive code, then precompiling code will be more beneficial.

Let's take a look at the steps involved:

PRECOMPILING RACTIVE CODE USING NODE.JS

1. Fire up a Node.js command prompt session, then change the working directory to our project area.

2. At the command prompt, enter this command, then press Enter – this will install the Grunt task runner: `npm install grunt --save-dev`.

3. Once Grunt is installed, enter this command and press Enter: `npm install path --save-dev` (this installs Path, which is used to locate our templates).

    Note: you can install the commands shown in steps 2 and 3 with one command if preferred; for this use `npm install grunt path`.

4. Copy the contents of the folder marked `node compile` to our project area – if all is well, we should have this folder structure present (Figure 1-9).

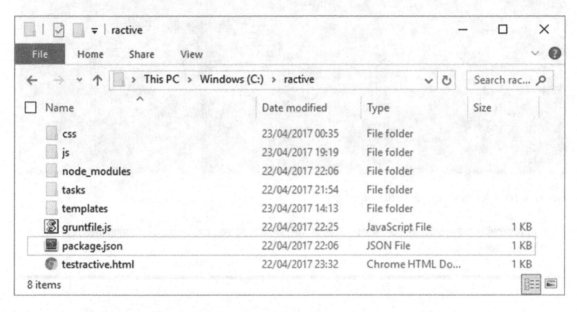

Figure 1-9. *Folder structure for compiling with Node.js*

5. At the command prompt, ensure the working directory is still set to our project area, then enter `grunt` and press Enter.

6. This will compile our template files within the `templates` folder, into a valid˙ JavaScript-based source map of Ractive templates.

7. Browse to `templates.js` within the templates folder, then copy and paste the contents of this file into the top of `testscript.js`, which is located in the `js` folder (Figure 1-10).

```
C:\ractive\js\testscript.js - Sublime Text                                    —    □    ✕

File   Edit   Selection   Find   View   Goto   Tools   Project   Preferences   Help

      testscript.js                  ✕

1   var templates = {
2     testtemplate: {"v":4,"t":[{"t":7,"e":"p","f":["Hello,
3   }
4
5   var ractive = new Ractive({
6     el: '#container',
7     template: templates.testtemplate,
8     data: { name: 'reader' }
9   });

    Line 1, Column 1                              Tab Size: 4          JavaScript
```

Figure 1-10. *Changes made to testscript.js*

Try previewing the results in a browser – if all is well, we should see the same welcoming message as in our earlier demo.

Exploring Our Node Demo in Detail

Although the end result should be the same, the sharp-eyed among you will have noticed a few key changes to the code – it's worth detailing these:

- The biggest change is in testractive.html – we've completely dropped the inline <script> block; this has been converted into a separate template file, which we've compiled into a source map of template code.

- Staying with testscript.js – we can see the addition of code at the top; this is a source map, which details each Ractive template, and what should be inserted into the container. To ensure we reference the right template, the template: option has been updated to point to the right template.

- We have two grunt task files present in the folder – one is at the root, while the other sits in the tasks folder. This isn't strictly necessary for our demo, but shows how you can split out tasks; the contents of any task file present in tasks folder will be loaded into the main grunt file and executed as part of that file.

- Our demo has a templates folder – inside this you will see a mustache file (*.mustache). This contains the template that has been hived off from the original markup; inside this same folder we have the template.js, which is the compiled source map code for our demo.

At this point, it's worth asking ourselves one simple question: is there any benefit to using Node.js, over and above the standard CDN link or a local copy? In short, the answer will depend on your requirements: clearly there is no point in setting up a Node.js-based compilation process if your project is a simple, lightweight affair!

The use of Node.js really comes into its own if we have lots of templates to compile; we've seen how it starts to produce a source map list of each template. Although our demo only used one, we would see entries for each template file present in that folder. We can also extend the Grunt task file to incorporate other tasks (recommended), such as adding vendor prefixes, or even writing the results of our Ractive compilation into `testscript.js` that we use in the final solution. We may even go as far as adding a watcher, to automatically run each task when required.

■ **Note** Ractive can be installed from a variety of different sources, including NPM. For the purposes of this book, we will use a local copy; please feel free to use NPM or a different source if you prefer.

That is something for the future: this gives you a flavor of what is possible, if you decide to use Node.js to compile your code. But – before considering that, we should least understand something of how Ractive works. The key to how this library works is in the `testscript.js` file, so let's dive in and explore the inner workings in more detail.

Understanding How Ractive Works

Cast your mind back to step 5 in *Creating our first demo* – yes, it might seem a long time ago, but the block of code in that step is where most of the magic happens within Ractive. As a library, Ractive follows the **MVVM**, or **Model – View – Viewmodel** architecture – in short, we provide the data for the **Model**, define the template (or **View**), and let Ractive manage the data (**ViewModel**) interaction automatically (Figure 1-11).

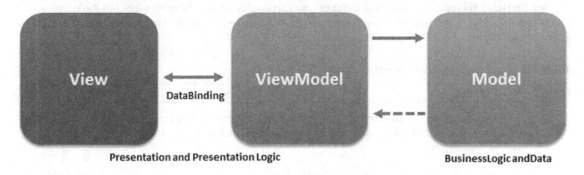

Figure 1-11. *A representation of the MVVM model – source: Wikipedia*

Let's strip back our HTML markup to show the critical elements of our demo:

```
<h1>Ractive test</h1>
<div id='container'></div>
<script id='template' type='text/ractive'>
  <p>Hello, {{name}} - you are now using Ractive for the first time!</p>
</script>
```

The markup highlighted is our template code, or placeholder for our data – this represents the View part of our demo. In the main, this is standard HTML markup, but with two differences: the use of {{name}} and that our markup is within <script> tags, not the other way round.

The curly brackets form the placeholder for each piece of data we need to insert: Ractive uses the Mustache templating library to format where data should appear on the page. Simply put, we set up a reference to each placeholder (or delimiter) within our Ractive configuration; Ractive inserts the relevant data into the appropriate slot during compilation.

We'll cover using the Mustache library in more detail in Chapter 2, *Creating Templates.*

The second key concept is the placement of HTML markup within <script> tags – it's easiest to think of these as building blocks, with the markup being the content within each block. We make reference to each template and its destination container within the Ractive configuration.

With the template in place, we created our Ractive configuration – we first of all added in links to the Ractive library and our script file (standard I know, but nevertheless still important!):

```
<script src='js/ractive.min.js'></script>
<script src="js/testscript.js"></script>
```

Within the script file is our Ractive configuration – as a refresher, this is ours from our first demo:

```
var ractive = new Ractive({
  el: '#container',
  template: '#template',
  data: { name: 'reader' }
});
```

We first have to create a new Ractive instance – we can do this several different ways, but the simplest is to use new Ractive(), and to pass in configuration options as we see fit. We've started with three common options, which are el, template, and data (Table 1-2).

Table 1-2. *Basic configuration options for Ractive*

Option	Purpose
el	Used to define the destination for our compiled content – we can use an element ID, selector class or HTML element as the identifying element, such as these examples: el: 'container' el: '#target' el: document.getElementById('container')
template	Defines the markup that is to be used as the basis for our template; this is parsed by Ractive, before the compiled results are inserted into the element defined in el. This can be of type string, array, object, or function.
data	This specifies the data we should use during the compilation process.

In many cases, these options will be sufficient for compiling our code. There will be occasions when we will need to specify additional options within our configuration object - Ractive has an exhaustive list of settings that we can use, so let's explore these in more detail.

Defining Our Configuration Options

Although the three options we've covered will suffice for some projects, there will come a point when we need greater control over how Ractive operates. To achieve this, we can use any one of the options available for use – these are split into six categories, beginning with the Data category.

Data

The Data category defines the configuration options we will use when defining our Ractive instance; a summary of the options available are listed in Table 1-3.

Table 1-3. *The Data category of configuration options*

Option	Type	Purpose
adapt	Array	Ractive uses adaptors to communicate with other libraries such as Backbone; these can be specified by name or through the adaptors object.
adaptors	Object	Ractive maintains a registry of available adaptors it can use in a key: value hash; we use the adaptors property to register an adaptor.
computed	Object	Ractive can use computed properties when specifying certain options; we can use the computed property to store these calculations.
data	Object or Function	The data to bind to the template at initialization.
isolated	Boolean	Normally set to true by default – setting this to false will prevent components from accessing parent data and registries.

It's worth noting that only the isolated property has a default setting; all others are set as per our development requirements. We will cover these settings in more detail throughout this book.

Placement

With our data defined, we now need to place it on the page – the options for doing so form the Placement category (Table 1-4).

Table 1-4. *The Placement category of configuration options*

Option	Type	Purpose
append	Boolean or anchor	This property controls whether the data is appended or replaced. It is set to false by default, so content will be replaced by default.
el	Various	Defines the element that should be used in the DOM, when rendering content. Can be set as a Nodelist, HTMLElement, or String.
enhance	Boolean	If set to true, Ractive will try to reuse existing DOM elements on the initial render of an instance. Normally set to false by default.

Binding

Once our data is defined and inserted, we can start to control how we manage it, using options from the Binding category; a summary of the options available is listed in Table 1-5, but we will cover these in more detail in Chapter 3, *Binding Data*.

Table 1-5. *The Binding category of configuration options*

Option	Type	Purpose
lazy	Boolean	Controls whether to use ES5 accessors only (for modern browsers), or normal Ractive methods. This is set to false by default.
twoway	Boolean	Controls whether two-way data-binding should be enabled - this is set to true by default.

Parsing

When working with templates, there are some settings we need to set, such as the types of delimiter to use; we can do this using the Parsing group of configuration options (Table 1-6).

Table 1-6. *The Parsing category of configuration options*

Option	Type	Purpose
csp	Boolean	This controls whether to inline functions for expressions – setting this value to true will affect how the template is served, so this is normally set to false by default.
delimiters	Array	; these are set by default to ['{{', '}}'].
preserveWhitespace	Boolean	Sets whether whitespace should be preserved when code is parsed – this is false by default.
sanitize	Boolean or Object	Set to false by default, this controls whether to remove specific elements and event attributes when parsing code.
staticDelimiters	Boolean	Set the value for to be used for static (one-time binding) delimiters.
staticTripleDelimiters	Boolean	Set the value for to be used for static (one-time binding) triple delimiters.
stripComments	Boolean	Removes comments from code when parsing, if set to true.
tripleDelimiters	Boolean	Controls what should be set for triple delimiters, when parsing code.

Templating

The Templating group of configuration options can be used to control how templates are configured, such as which components, decorators, or events should be applied.

We can create components to add predefined functionality to a Ractive instance (such as controlling a third-party plugin such as Vibrant.js), or by adding extra styling through the use of decorator plugins. With events, these can be controlled directly in our Ractive instance, or can be added through the use of plugins such as creating a custom click handler. A summary of the templating options are listed in Table 1-7.

Table 1-7. *The Templating category of configuration options*

Option	Type	Purpose
components	Object	A key:value hash of components to include for use in a specific Ractive instance.
css	String	Used to specify what CSS styling should be used on components.
decorators	Object	A key:value hash of decorators to include for use in a specific Ractive instance.
events	Object	A key:value hash of events to include for use in a specific Ractive instance.
noCssTransform	Boolean	Prevents transformation of component CSS styles.
partials	Object	We can create partials, or blocks of code for reuse; use the partials object to store details in a Ractive instance.
template	Various	Specifies the template to use in our Ractive instance, as a String (or if pre-parsing, Array or Object).

Transitions

Over the last two decades, we've come a long way since the days of the tacky marquee element – anyone remember those? Thankfully Ractive, like other libraries, supports more advanced animations; we can specify our configuration using any of the options from the Transitions group (Table 1-8).

Table 1-8. *The Transitions category of configuration options*

Option	Type	Purpose
complete	Function	A function to call when all intro animations have completed; this will be called as soon as a Ractive instance is set, if transitions are set.
easing	Object	A key:value hash of easing functions to use in transitions within a specific Ractive instance.
interpolators	Object	A keypath:value hash, or list of elements to use as interpolators for animating values.
noIntro / noOutro	Boolean	Do not apply transitions on render / unrender– set to false by default.
transitions	Object	Transitions to include for use by the template, within a specific Ractive instance.
transitionsEnabled	Boolean	Set to true to allow transitions to operate in a Ractive instance.

Phew – there's a real mix of options available that we can use! We clearly won't be able to use them all in one go (and neither would we), but you will over time begin to use a number of these options regularly.

To help with this, we can set a default configuration that applies to all Ractive instances used in a project – this set once, apply everywhere approach will help save time, as long as we use the right settings. It's a useful technique to master, so let's make a start in seeing how it works.

Setting Default Options

As a library, Ractive is very flexible, with a long list of options available for controlling which data should be used, and how it will be rendered on a page. Over the course of this chapter, we've worked with one instance of Ractive; we may need to specify multiple instances, each with its own separate list of options.

Specifying options for each Ractive instance can be tedious, if each instance shares identical options; instead, we can specify a list of options as a default configuration, which will be used on any future instances. Let's take a look at an example:

```
Ractive.defaults.delimiters = [ '[[', ']]' ];

// uses the delimiters specified above
var ractive1 = new Ractive({
  template: 'Hello [[reader]]'
});
```

Notice how we don't have to specify the option in the configuration if we want to use the default that has been set; we can easily override this option as needed:

```
// uses the delimiters specified in the initialization options
var rative2 = new Ractive({
  template: 'Hello //reader\\',
  delimiters: [ '//', '\\' ]
});
```

In this instance, the delimiters specified in the configuration object will override those set as default in the Ractive.defaults property. The exception to this is for plugins, which are registered directly on the Ractive object, and that initialization or extend options are combined with the defaults, rather than replace them.

We will cover this difference and more, when we explore creating plugins in Chapter 7, *Building Plugins*.

Setting Advanced Configuration Options

It is worth noting that we are not limited to using static values when setting configuration options; we can use a more advanced method of specifying functions that resolve when our Ractive instance has been initiated.

We can achieve this in various ways – the detail of this falls outside the scope of this book for now, but it is worth exploring when you are more accustomed to using Ractive in your development workflow. To give you a taster of what can be achieved when specifying which template to use, we can set a function to resolve to a value, based on the return value of another option:

```
var ractive = new Ractive({
  template: function ( data ) {
    return data.am ? '<p>Good morning</p>' : '<p>Good afternoon</p>';
  },
  data: {am: true }
});
```

In this example, I've specified a Boolean-based data value am, to signify that it is morning; if this were set to false, then it would show "Good afternoon" instead.

It's worth noting that this is only a theoretical example to show how you can choose between the two – it's more likely that you would set an appropriate greeting based on the browser's time, not as part of this configuration. For example, you might use it to specify which currency format should be displayed: true for dollars, and false for euros. We can switch between the two, using a mustache to ensure the values are formatted correctly. There are other examples available on the website – the scope of what is possible is only limited by your imagination!

For more details, please refer to the documentation on the Ractive website, which is available at `http://docs.ractivejs.org/latest/advanced-configuration`.

We're almost at the end of setting up Ractive, but before we move onto learning about each of the core concepts of this library, we need to cover one last question: if things go wrong, how or where do you get support?

Getting Support

"Help! How do I do this....?"

That's a question I've heard a thousand times in almost 20 years of supporting users as an IT professional – I never tire of it. I get a great sense of satisfaction being able to help others, and give back; there are times though that I wish some of my users would try to remember how to do something, once they've asked the same question for the 100th time! But I digress...

That said, an important part of learning how to use a new library or framework is where to get support if you need it; there are a few places where you can find help:

- **StackOverflow** – there is a Ractive-tagged section for general questions at `http://stackoverflow.com/questions/tagged/ractivejs` – this is perfect if you want to ask for help on resolving an issue, where it isn't a bug or feature change.

- **The Ractive.js mailing list** – hosted at `http://groups.google.com/forum/#!forum/ractive-js` – this list is available for sharing ideas or tips, ask for help, or show the world your projects.

- **GitHub issues** – if you do come across a bug or want to see if a new feature could be implemented, then these should be logged on the GitHub pages at `https://github.com/ractivejs/ractive/issues`.

- **@RactiveJS on Twitter** – regular notices are posted on Twitter; for those of you who want to subscribe, the handle is @RactiveJS, or they can be viewed online at `http://twitter.com/RactiveJS`.

The great thing about open source technologies is that there is usually a good group of people who are willing to help others. It is worth noting though that you are likely to get a better response if you can try to follow these simple pointers where possible:

- Use the latest version of the library where possible – it sounds silly I know, but there are times where this doesn't always happen, so you will miss out on something that has already been fixed. Granted, it may be necessary to try with an older version, but hopefully only to confirm if a feature is broken in a more recent version.

- Give as much detail as possible, highlighting any points in bold or italics where appropriate – if you say "it's not working" isn't likely to get much help; after all, how are people to know what the problem is, if there isn't any detail?

- Make sure your subject line is concise, relevant, and it is clear where to look, if you post a URL to a problem. No one likes trying to solve an issue if the subject isn't clear, or they have to hunt to find the location of the problem!

- Do provide screenshots if you can, and they're relevant – there are occasions when that old adage "a picture can paint a thousand words"; sometimes displaying a screenshot can make it easier to explain what the issue is.

- Do be courteous and don't assume you know the answer – there may be times when the answer is obvious, but this won't always be the case. It's far better to let the assigned person work out how best to fix it as your solution may not fit in with the overall design of the project.

Above all – do ask if you need help: developers will spend countless hours designing a project, and there is nothing worse than someone abandoning their use of that project because they didn't feel up to asking a simple question! I always maintain that there is never a silly question, only a sensible one that hasn't been asked the right way, and that others will always help as long as you do ask that question in the appropriate way.

Summary

The discovery of a new technology opens up a wealth of opportunities - we're about to start a journey through the world of RactiveJS, so before we embark on that journey, let's take a moment to review what we've covered in this chapter.

We kicked off with a brief introduction to Ractive, and explored some of the benefits of using Ractive as a different approach to some of the more well-known frameworks such as Angular. We then turned to learning how we can obtain Ractive, either via CDN or through using Node.js.

Next up came a look at our first demo, which we completed using the CDN and Node methods, before getting accustomed with how it works. We then rounded out the chapter with a look at some of the settings available for configuring Ractive, ready for use in our projects.

Let's move on - we must start somewhere, so there is no better place than with creating basic templates, which is the subject of the next chapter.

CHAPTER 2

∎ ∎ ∎

Creating Templates

We've downloaded and installed Ractive – so what's next? Well, Ractive is all about creating templates quickly and easily – there is no better place than getting started with creating them!

Ractive prides itself on being a library that doesn't offer an opinion on how you should construct your sites; after all, it isn't that we want to control, right...?

Over the course of this chapter, we'll work our way through each of the core elements that we can use in the Ractive library – this covers templates, elements, mustaches, references, and more. We'll go through each part in detail, to understand what role they play, how to set them up, and create some simple examples, so we can see them in action as a precursor to later in the book.

Understanding the Parallel DOM

At first glance, you might be forgiven for thinking that Ractive code looks very similar to a mix of standard HTML markup and JavaScript (or even jQuery) based code. If this is the case, then I can imagine you are probably asking yourself – what makes Ractive different, and more attractive to use?

Well, the answer to this – at least in part – is how Ractive manages updates to the DOM. Typically, when updating elements using JavaScript, you would cache objects as much as possible, and to reduce the number of updates to the DOM. It works, but it is still slow!

Ractive takes a different approach – it creates a virtual, or parallel DOM, to which updates are first applied. When we initiate a Ractive instance, we are creating a fragment that contains a number of properties; these are illustrated in Table 2-1.

Table 2-1. *Properties of a Ractive fragment*

Property	Function
contextStack	The context stack in which mustache references should be evaluated.
root	A reference to the Ractive instance to which it belongs.
owner	The item that owns this fragment (in the case of the root fragment, the same as root).
items	The items belonging to this fragment.

© Alex Libby 2017
A. Libby, *Beginning Ractive.js*, https://doi.org/10.1007/978-1-4842-3093-0_2

Each fragment will contain details of elements, nodes, and any mustaches (or placeholders) we create – Ractive parses them into an array or object, before adding them to the virtual DOM and then updating the physical DOM. So, if we had code such as this:

```
<div class='gallery'>
  {{#items}}
    <!-- comments get stripped out of the template -->
    <figure proxy-tap='select' intro='staggered'>
      <img class='thumbnail' src='assets/images/{{id}}.jpg'>
      <figcaption>{{( i+1 )}}: {{description}}</figcaption>
    </figure>
  {{/items}}
</div>
```

...it would automatically be parsed into this:

```
[{"t":7,"e":"div","a":{"class":"gallery"},"f":[{"t":4,"r":"items","i":"i","f":[" ",{"t":7,"
e":"figure","a":{"intro":"staggered"},"f":[{"t":7,"e":"img","a":{"class":"thumbnail","src":
["assets/images/",{"t":2,"r":"id","p":4},".jpg"]}}," ",{"t":7,"e":"figcaption","f":[{"t":2,
"x":{"r":["i"],"s":"❖0+1"},"p":4},": ",{"t":2,"r":"description","p":4}]}]}],"v":{"tap":"sele
ct"}}," "],"p":1}]}]
```

It looks unintelligible to say the least! This string of characters contains all of the DOM updates that are required – this includes data-binding, proxy events, and transitions.

It's not intended to be read or even edited, but to use as few bytes as possible; this helps Ractive to determine exactly where changes must be applied to the physical DOM, so the number of updates is kept to a minimum.

If you want to really understand what happens, then take a look at the source code, which is available at https://github.com/RactiveJS/Ractive/tree/master/src.

This is just a brief overview of what happens – in most cases, the parsing and updates are handled automatically by Ractive, but it is nevertheless still useful to have an appreciation of what happens during compilation. Let's put some of this into practice, and begin to use Ractive in anger: we'll start with creating templates.

Creating Templates

When developing a project or working with a new technology, we clearly must somewhere – with Ractive, there is no better place than with the templates that we create.

Put simply, templates in Ractive are nothing more than snippets of HTML; it is important to understand that these must be well-formed (Ractive's parser is not as forgiving as HTML), but that they won't necessarily be valid HTML in their own right. Although this may seem like an odd concept to grasp, it shouldn't be considered an issue as such; code will only become valid HTML, when it has been compiled by Ractive.

Leaving this aside for the moment, there are some noticeable differences between Ractive and standard HTML; these are listed in Table 2-2.

Table 2-2. Differences between HTML and Ractive

Type of functionality	Differences when compared with HTML
Mustaches	Ractive templates contain mustaches, or placeholders for data; they will look like {{...}}, where ... represents the data reference. We saw how to change the delimiters used in our configuration, as indicated in Chapter 1, *Getting Started*.
Event directives	When working with elements in a Ractive template, we may add events; these look like attributes, but are not rendered to the DOM in the same way. Instead, they are intercepted at compilation, and used to provide event binding instructions, such as in this example: `<button on-click='@this.submit()'>Submit!</button>` We'll cover event directives in more detail within Chapter 4, *Handling Events*.
Transitions	In a similar vein, transitions allow us to specify how elements should behave, once introduced to the DOM, and are subsequently removed. These look like attributes, but are not treated in the same way – they act in a similar fashion to event directives. `<div fade-in>This element will fade in gradually when it renders</div>` We'll cover transitions in more detail within Chapter 5, *Animating Content*.
Decorators	Decorators within Ractive are used to decorate elements – these look like attributes, but are never added to the DOM: `<div as-ace-editor>This element will be turned into an Ace Editor.</div>` We'll cover decorators in more detail within Chapter 2, *Creating Templates*.

Okay – so what do these changes mean in practice? This is one of the great things about Ractive: we don't need to add lots of extra markup, which helps to maintain a gradual learning curve, and page weight down. At a basic level, elements work very much in the same way as standard HTML, with only minimal changes required to apply styles. Let's dive in and take a look.

Adding Elements and Decorators

Take a look at this code, based on a demo we created back in Chapter 1:

```
<!doctype html>
<html lang='en-GB'>
<head>
  <meta charset='utf-8'>
  <title>Beginning Ractive: Styling Elements</title>
  <link rel='stylesheet' href='css/teststyles.css'>
</head>
<body>
  <h1>Ractive test</h1>
  <div id='container'></div>
  <script id='template' type='text/ractive'>
    <p>Hello, {{name}} - you are now using Ractive for the first time!</p>
    <div style-width="{{x}}rem" style-height="{{y}}rem" style-border="{{z}}rem solid #000"
    style-backgroundColor="#d3d3d3" style-padding="{{a}}rem">This is some text inside a
    box</div>
  </script>
```

```
  <script src='js/ractive.min.js'></script>
  <script src="js/testscript.js"></script>
</body>
</html>
```

Try running the example demo from the styling elements folder in the code download that accompanies this book. When previewing it in a browser, it looks like Figure 2-1.

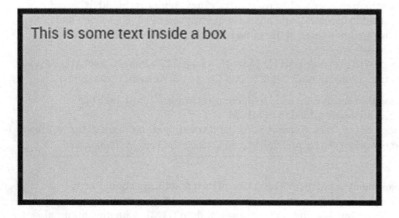

Figure 2-1. *Example code in Ractive*

If we examine the code, most of it is standard HTML – this includes tags such as <title> or <script> elements. There are a couple of key differences:

```
<p>Hello, {{name}} - you are now using Ractive for the first time!</p>
```

```
<div style-width="{{x}}rem" style-height="{{y}}rem" style-border="{{z}}rem solid #000"
style-backgroundColor="#d3d3d3" style-padding="{{a}}rem">This is some text inside a
box</div>
```

Both lines are standard HTML elements that contain mustaches to format where data should appear in our code. They both the use the format that we saw back in Chapter 1, but with one key difference: the first contains mustaches to locate data, whereas the second line uses mustaches to style our HTML markup. But hold on, I hear you say – sure we would simply use our CSS style sheet to apply styles to elements in our code, right...?

Styling Elements Using Ractive

Well – not always! In an ideal world, we would, but there are occasions when we have to add styles inline (such as within a plugin). Ractive is no different; we can make use of the two attributes in Table 2-3 to facilitate quick changes to properties.

Table 2-3. *Different style attributes available in Ractive*

Attribute	Used to...
style-*	Apply changes to individual style properties – it can take the form of `style-property-name="value"`, or `style-propertyName ="value"`. If style-property-name is used, then this is converted to camel case.
class-*	Effect changes to elements by applying or removing classes to individual elements. Class changes are applied or removed, based on the truthiness of the value applied to a class.

It's worth noting that values are not processed as expressions, but plain text; it means we have to use mustaches to insert values at compilation. To see how this works in practice, let's work through our example.

In the demo at the top of this section, we created a `<div>` element with a number of inline styles; for this to work, we need to initiate values within our Ractive object, which we can see in the `elements.js` file, thus:

```
var ractive = new Ractive({
  el: '#container',
  template: '#template',
  data: {
    name: 'reader',
    x: 20,
    y: 10,
    z: 0.3,
    a: 0.5
  }
});
```

If we explore the code using a DOM inspector, the styles are clearly displayed, as shown in Figure 2-2.

Figure 2-2. *Viewing compiled styles*

Ractive has compiled our values into valid CSS; at face value, it looks like perfectly reasonable code. However, there are at least two issues that warrant changes.

Notice how our style has appeared as element.style in Chrome? This gives us no indication as to what element this is applied to (okay, I know the affected element is highlighted, but that's not the point here – I'm talking about the lack of a named class or ID).

The nameless style attribute has multiple properties assigned to it – by themselves, they are appropriate for this type of element, but when we use multiple entries together, it begins to clutter our code with unnecessary markup.

This is a perfect example of what we should **not** do when using these style-* attributes in Ractive; they are designed for quick changes of single items, where using a style sheet would be impractical. As a rule of thumb, if we have more than two elements, then ideally the styles should be in a style sheet. Not a hard and fast rule, but it certainly makes for cleaner code!

Improving Our Code

So – to improve our code, we should consider the following:

- We're updating several properties in one go, so ideally we should reconsider our use of style-property-name, and apply a class name instead;

- Are we changing too many properties in one go? With a little care and application, can we adjust our styling such that we can reduce the number of changes that need to be made using Ractive? Any that don't can be added as a standard class in our style sheet.

With this in mind – take a look at the reworked version within the styling elements - fixed folder, from the code download that accompanies this book; we can already see some changes to our code (Figure 2-3).

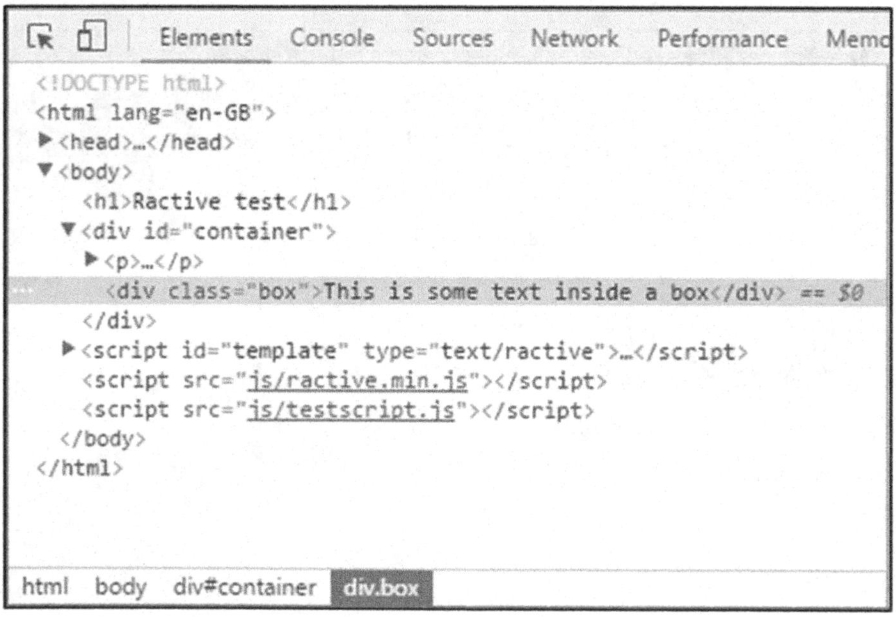

Figure 2-3. *Updated markup*

This is reflected in our amended styles, which now use a defined class (Figure 2-4).

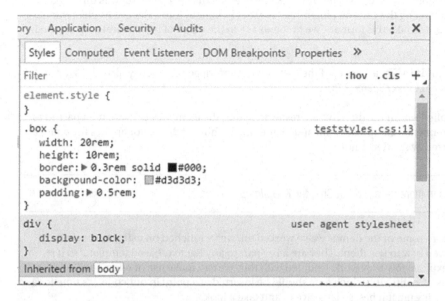

Figure 2-4. *Updated styling example*

When running the code, we won't see any changes to the rendered output (a good sign – we've not impacted our demo). However a peek under the covers will reveal two changes:

- We've created a class called .box within our style sheet;
- The inline style-* attributes have been replaced with a single class-* attribute; Our Ractive name has been updated with a box class attribute, which directs Ractive to use the .box class at compilation (Figure 2-5).

Figure 2-5. *Editing properties with Ractive DevTool*

■ **Tip** To get the updated code, I used the Ractive Dev Tool for Google Chrome. It's available from http:// bit.ly/2poR6HV, and is a great way to see changes made on the fly (as shown in Figure 2-5, without having to edit files. To get it working, click on any element within your Ractive container such as the highlighted one shown in Figure 2-3; you will then see the component details as illustrated in Figure 2-4. You can of course view the files manually if desired!

It is worth noting though that we are not limited to simply applying styles – we can take it further by adding a decorator. Decorators can be used to apply behaviors to elements on a page, such as turning a <div> into a tooltip, or integrating the Chosen plugin for <select> element into a Ractive implementation. A decorator within markup will take this format – we prepend as- to the name of our decorator, as shown in this tooltip example:

```
<span as-tooltip="'A tooltip is a piece of helper text that appears when you mouseover a
particular element'">tooltips</span>.</p>
```

Any arguments supplied within the directive are resolved within the element's context, then passed to the decorator; if these arguments are updated, the update method within the decorator applies the changes, provided they are supported by the decorator.

We will explore decorators in more detail within Chapter 7, *Building Plugins*.

Okay – let's move on. In some of the demos we've worked on, we've touched on using mustaches, although not really explored how to use them. They are a key part to any Ractive-based template, so it is worth spending time to explore how they work. Coupled with this, we can make use of references – we can consider these as a means of identifying which data should be inserted at a point in our code. It's time for a little background 101 on using mustaches, so let's dive in and take a look.

Understanding Mustaches

If I were to mention the word "mustache," you would be forgiven for thinking this was a reference to a man's facial hair; it's not – it's simply a way of locating data on a page, using a template. Sorry to disappoint...!

This is a very simplistic description though – mustaches in a Ractive context can be one of two things:

- A snippet of code from within a template, which is enclosed using mustache delimiters, such as {{name}};

- The object within our parallel DOM that is set to listen for changes, and is responsible for updating the real DOM.

Ractive uses the Mustache templating library (available from http://mustache.github.io/); it's lightweight, easy-to-read syntax makes it very easy to learn. There are a host of ways to manipulate data using mustache extensions, but for now, let's take a look at the core concepts with which we should be familiar.

Table 2-4. *Core Mustache concepts*

Type of mustache	Purpose
Variables	This is the most basic type of mustache – if we have a variable such as {{name}}, Ractive will look for this in the current context to resolve it. If it cannot find it there, it will move through each parent context until it is found; if nothing is found, then nothing is displayed.
Comments	There may be instances where we want to include comments in a mustache – particularly if it helps explain a complex design. To do this, add a bang before the comment text:

<h1>Tomorrow {{! this will be ignored }}.</h1>

The text within the delimiters will simply be ignored. |
| Custom delimiters | By default, the delimiters used in Ractive are double or triple curly brackets. We can change this if desired – this can be done using a mustache: |

```
{{foo}}
  {{=[[ ]]=}}
[[bar]]
```

...or setting appropriate values for the `delimiters:` or `tripleDelimiters:` attributes in our configuration:

```
var ractive = new Ractive({
  el: someElement,
...
  delimiters: [ '[[', ']]' ],
  tripleDelimiters: [ '[[[', ']]]' ]
});
```
 |
| Sections | These are blocks of markup that are rendered, based on the value being referenced – for example, this might be an array of names, or the properties of an object. Sections start with a pound, and end with a slash, as shown: |

```
{{#animals}}
  <b>{{type}}</b>
{{/animal}}
```

Ractive will check the #animal key in the current context; it will render content if any values are found, or not display anything if the key is empty or not present.

Note: Sections and #each blocks look very similar, but are not the same.
A section can render a block of different types of markup based on what is stored within it – this can include array items, objects, or plain text. In comparison, #each blocks will only iterate through each item in the iterable; they work on a keypath : value pairing basis. These blocks also support the conditional {{else}} and {{elseif}} options, whereas these are not available in standard sections.

For more details, please refer to the documentation on the main site at https://ractive.js.org/api/#sections. |

(continued)

Table 2-4. (*continued*)

Type of mustache	Purpose
Partials	These begin with a > sign – they can be considered as form of includes, or template expansion. These are stand-alone files that normally end with a `.mustache` extension.

For example, let's assume we have a template that includes this partial (highlighted):

```
<h2>Names</h2>
{{#animals}}
    {{> type}}
{{/animals}}
```

If our partial file, type.mustache, contains this:

```
<strong>{{type}}</strong>
```

...then this can be thought of as a single, unified template:

```
<h2>Types of animals:</h2>
{{#animals}}
  <strong>{{types}}</strong>
{{/animals}}
```

For more details, please refer to the documentation on the main site, which is available at `https://ractive.js.org/plugins/#partials`.

Although Ractive maintains 99% backward compatibility with the Mustache library, it adds a host of other features. For example, how about applying a little logic within a mustache, such as converting a given number? For this, we'd use a mustache such as this: `<p>{{ num * 100 }}%</p>`. This isn't supported within standard Mustache, so is worth getting to know it (and the other Mustache-based features), once we're more familiar with Ractive.

The Ractive-specific extensions are detailed at `https://ractive.js.org/api/#mustaches`.

The missing 1% compatibility that Ractive is not able to offer is due to how Ractive manages strings. Unlike other templating libraries, Ractive turns data strings into a DOM, which has to be reprocessed to a string to test compliance. It means that some features such as lambdas are lost in translation, but they are not critical to the operation of Ractive.

Okay – let's change tack: in many of our examples, we've assigned specific names to each mustache, but there's more to this than just using a naming convention! In order to use references effectively, it's worth understanding some of the principles behind how they work in more detail.

Working with References

If we are creating mustaches for our template, then deciding which data to insert is only part of the story; we must also decide how we reference that data.

What do I mean by this? Well, when creating mustaches in Ractive, we can't simply give it any placeholder name and let Ractive take care of resolving it at compilation. For one, this is likely to become messy, if we don't give some thought to a suitable naming convention! If we take care over our naming, we can reduce the risk of duplicating names, or creating more mustaches than is necessary.

To make this story complete, we must consider how we use references. In a Ractive context these are the names given inside the double delimiters; for example, this could be {{animal}} or {{language}}. This is important, as a reference can sometimes be satisfied by a value that already exists. Ractive will work its way up through each context within the stack until it can either resolve the name, or nothing is found (similar to the "event bubbling" concept familiar to developers).

The only constraint we must work to is that our reference must be resolved to a valid keypath – we'll dig into what this means in more detail shortly, but for now, it's enough to know that if we have {{animal}} in our markup, we must see a reference to it in our Ractive instance:

```
ractive = new Ractive({
  el: myContainer,
  template: myTemplate,
  data: {
    animal: {
      type: 'lion'
    }
  }
});
```

Our code shows a reference to animal – but how can we tell if our code will resolve correctly?

The key to this is to think of each Ractive instance as a tree, with branches – the branch we're interested in is data; this contains our reference to animal. Let's explore the steps taken internally by Ractive to resolve this data; although this happens automatically, it is nevertheless beneficial to understand how this works, so that we can debug issues in our code.

Resolving References

When creating a Ractive instance, we must give consideration to the context of our reference. This is something I've referred to throughout the course of this chapter – take a look at Table 2-4 on page 3, as an example. There is a reason for this: a context in Ractive has special meaning. It refers to the subsection that contains your data – in this example:

```
{{#user}}
  <p>Welcome back, {{name}}!
    {{#messages}}
      You have a total of {{total}} messages, of which {{unread}} are new.
      You last logged in on {{lastLogin}}.
    {{/messages}}
  </p>
{{/user}}
```

We have one top-level context, which is user; within this, we have a second one in the form of messages:

```
ractive = new Ractive({
  el: container,
  template: emailTemplate,
  data: {
    user: {
      name: 'Alex',
      messages: {
        total: 17,
```

```
        unread: 3
      },
      lastLogin: 'Sunday'
    }
  }
});
```

The code in the section example contains a HTML template, in the form of #user, which is devoid of data. Within our Ractive instance, we have a top-level context, in the form of user. Inside this, we have one keypath (or route) – name. This contains the value Alex - if our mustache contains a reference to user.name, it will resolve to this value without problem.

This is where it gets a little more complicated – what if our reference to name had been under the messages context instead of where it is now? Well, the same principle applies: we move down the tree to a branch that is one level lower:

```
data: {
  user: {
    ...
    messages: {
      total: 17,
      unread: 3,
      name: 'Alex'
    },
```

Here I've removed the top-level keypath to simplify matters: our route down is a little longer. The secret to working out contexts is to look for the open and closed curly brackets – we start with user, but follow this with messages. This gives us three possibilities in what is a two-level context stack. The one we're after is name, so this would be user.messages.name; we can reference the other two using user.messages.total or user.messages.unread, which will resolve without issue.

■ **Tip** To visualize the route, try replacing the indents with arrows. For example, the total keypath would be user → messages → total (as highlighted in the code extract).

In many cases, we can access data using standard references; there are occasions though when we may find we need to reference content that isn't accessible using the standard methods. There are a few special references we can use for this purpose; let's go through them in more detail.

Using Special or Restricted References

When using Ractive, we may find we have a need to reference a property, irrespective of whether it exists. Typically this would throw an error when using jQuery or vanilla JavaScript.

However, within Ractive, we can use restricted references – these are designed for this purpose; they are not a standard part of the Mustache library, and are specific to Ractive. A summary of the three different types that are available is listed in Table 2-5.

Table 2-5. *Restricted references in Ractive*

Type of reference	Purpose

Restricted	This is perfect for resolving values immediately, such as the current state of a checkbox – our checkbox doesn't yet exist on the page, but we need to specify if it is selected or cleared:
	
	`{{#selections}}`
	` <label><input type='checkbox' checked='{{.selected}}'> {{productdesc}}`
	` </label>`
	`{{/selection}}`

Ancestor	If we want to reference a value that is not within the current context, but is located at a different level, we can prefix our reference with one or more ../ before the name. This helps to avoid any conflicts, if the same reference name is used elsewhere, but for a different purpose.
Root	If the reference we need is at the root of our data hierarchy, we can use ~/ as a shortcut, rather than multiple instances of ../ as a prefix.

For more details, please refer to `https://ractive.js.org/api/#special-references` in the main documentation.

If we stay with the theme of "unusual" references, there are some others we should be aware of when referencing content that doesn't really exist within our data. We can use these in the same way as any other data reference, except when using data-binding – a summary of these references is listed in Table 2-6.

Table 2-6. *Special references in Ractive*

Reference	Purpose
@index	The current iteration index of the repeated section that contains the reference. for example, `{{#each animals}}{{@index}}{{/each}}`
@key	The current key name of the object iteration section that contains our reference. for example, `{{#each sports}}{{@key}}{{/each}}`
@keypath	The keypath to the current context e.g., `foo.bar.baz` in this mustache: `{{#foo}}{{#with bar.baz}}{{@keypath}}{{/with}}{{/}}` If the current context happens to be a mapping in a component, the keypath will be adjusted relative to the mapping.
@rootpath	The same as `keypath`, except not adjusted for components.
@global	The current global object for this environment, for example, window in a browser, or global in node. This reference can be used with two-way binding, but note that if something outside of Ractive changes a value, Ractive won't know unless you tell it to update.
@this	The current Ractive instance, for example, the current component or the Ractive root. You can access any properties or methods available on a Ractive instance with this; it also works when using `@this.get('...')` in a binding to update a target keypath.

Okay – let's change tack: we've covered how references play a part in our templates, but what about accessing them through our Ractive instances. For this we need to use keypaths; let's explore what these are and how to use them within Ractive in more detail.

Interacting with Ractive Instances Using Keypaths

Over the last few pages, we've touched on two key concepts within Ractive – mustaches and references. These describe both the placeholders we use, and the data we need to insert: but what about how we access that data?

At first thought, this might seem odd, but an important part of interacting with a Ractive instance is through the use of keypaths – these can appear in a Ractive instance, as indicated in Figure 2-6.

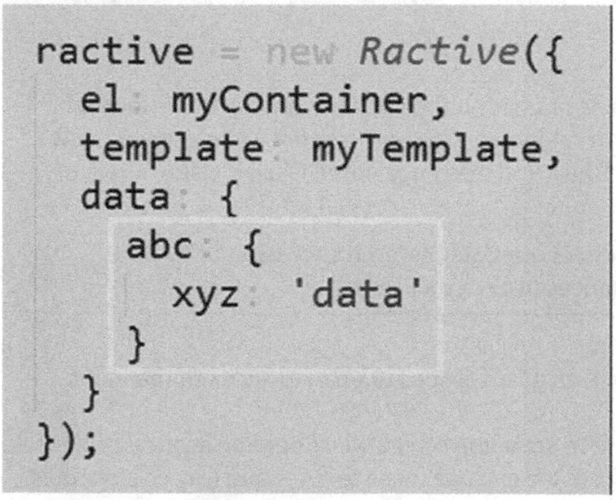

```
ractive = new Ractive({
  el: myContainer,
  template: myTemplate,
  data: {
    abc: {
      xyz: 'data'
    }
  }
});
```

Figure 2-6. *Keypath in a Ractive instance*

To be clear, the keypath itself is the reference to the data we want to include – this can take one of two forms:

- Simple – we can retrieve the key pair value using `ractive.get('abc')`; this returns { xyz: 'data' };

- Compound – we can go one step lower, and call just the value; we can do this using `ractive.get('abc.xyz')`, which will return `'data'`.

A similar principle applies if we're using arrays, although we can use a slightly different format. Consider this extract of code:

```
data: {
  list: [ 'x', 'y', 'z' ]
}
```

We can get the values within the array, using dot notation, using either of these two methods:

```
// Array notation
ractive.get( 'list[0]' ); // returns 'x'

// Dot notation
ractive.get( 'list.0' ); // also returns 'x'
```

A word of note – if we had tried to access a value within the array, but used the name of an object that doesn't exist, then it will throw an undefined error:

```
ractive.get( 'listing[0]' );  // throws error – listing does not exist; should be list[0]
```

This aside, notice something about how we obtained that data – more specifically the direction we took? This sense of travel is referred to as a **downstream keypath** (reference to corresponding data) or **downstream keypath** (data back up to its reference). This is illustrated in Figure 2-7.

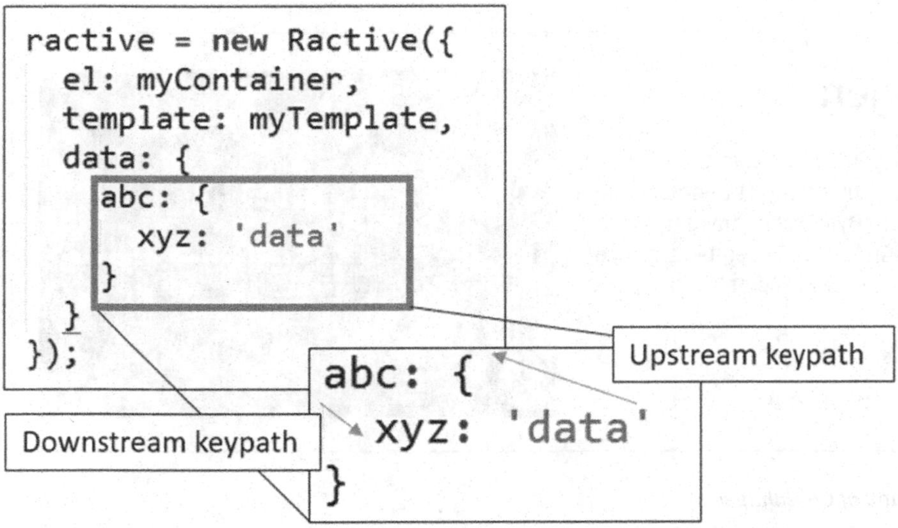

Figure 2-7. *Types of keypaths, based on direction*

Over the last few pages, we've covered the basics of references, mustaches, and keypaths; how about taking things even further? Instead of just including what is effectively static data, we can introduce logic into the equation (sorry – pun intended!), and make use of expressions to calculate values during compilation. It's a useful technique to master, so let's take a look.

Applying Logic with Expressions

Up until now, we've worked with mustaches (or placeholders), that help us to insert static content into our markup. This works well, but only touches on a small part of what we can do – how about formatting the content, for example? What happens if the values change? Can we be sure we retain a consistent format if we make any changes?

Clearly using static content isn't sufficient – we can take things further by introducing expressions into our templates. These can be as simple or complicated as needed – for example, we might want to display numbers as "X.X million," rather than a string of digits. We might instead want to format prices with an appropriate currency – or even convert a base number to a country-specific currency value!

These are just some of the options we have open to us – this is just the tip of the iceberg though, as we can introduce other JavaScript libraries, such as Moment. There's nothing better than exploring this as a demo, so with this in mind, let's dive in and take a look at the first of two examples for using expressions in Ractive.

Introducing Copenhagen

Before you ask – no, I have not lost the plot and suddenly changed the theme of this book: the title of this section is a reference to the subject for our next demo.

We're going to knock up a quick introduction to my favorite city, Copenhagen, Denmark. It might not be the cheapest place to visit, but it is definitely worth going for the wonderful hospitality alone! For this exercise, we will use information from Wikipedia, along with a suitable image from Wikimedia; the numbers will be formatted using expressions within our Ractive object. When completed, we will end up with something akin to the screenshot shown in Figure 2-8.

Copenhagen

Copenhagen, or København (in Danish), is the capital and most populous city of Denmark. The City of Copenhagen (Byen København) has a population of 763,908 (as of December 2016), of whom 601,448 live in the Municipality of Copenhagen.

Source: Wikipedia / Wikimedia

Figure 2-8. *Description of Copenhagen*

For this exercise, we'll reuse some of the code from the previous demo, and replace the appropriate code with our new version:

CREATING EXPRESSIONS

1. First, let's save a copy of the previous exercise into a new folder – this includes a copy of the css, font and js folders; label this new folder as expressions.
2. Open up a copy of expressions.html from within the expressions folder, and delete all of the lines between the two <script> tags – replace them with the following code:

```
  <h1>Copenhagen</h1>
<p>{{city}}, or København (in Danish), is the capital and most populous city
of Denmark. The City of {{city}} (Byen København) has a population of {{
format(population) }} (as of December 2016), of whom {{ format(inCopenhagen)
}} live in the Municipality of Copenhagen.</p>
<div class="image"><img src="img/nyhavn.jpg"></div>
<span>Source: Wikipedia / Wikimedia</span>
```

3. Save this file. Next, go ahead and open a copy of the `expressions.js` file from within the `js` folder; delete the `data: { }` block, and replace it with this code:

```
var ractive = new Ractive({
  el: '#container',
  template: '#template',
  data: {
    city: 'Copenhagen',
    population: 763908,
    inCopenhagen: 601448,
    format: function ( num ) {
      if ( num > 1000 ) return ( Math.floor( num / 1000 ) ) + ',' +
      ( num % 1000 );
      return num;
    }
  }
});
```

4. We now need an image – for this exercise, I'm using an image of Nyhavn from Wikimedia; a copy of this is available in the code download that accompanies this book, within the `img` subfolder. Save this into a new folder called `img` within the expressions folder we created in step 1.

5. Open a copy of the `expressions.css` file that is within the expressions folder in our project area; replace all of the existing styles with this code:

```
@font-face { font-family: 'robotoregular'; src: url('../font/Roboto-Regular-
webfont.woff') format('woff'); font-weight: normal; font-style: normal; }

body { font-family: robotoregular, sans-serif; font-size: 0.875rem;
padding: 2rem;}
p { width: 19rem; float: left; }
span { font-style: italic; margin-top: -1.5rem; position: absolute; }
h1 { margin: 0; padding: 0; width: 12rem; }

#container { border: 1px solid #000; width: 40rem; clear: both; border-radius:
0.4rem; padding: 1rem; }

.image { padding-left: 20rem; margin-top: -2rem; }
```

6. Try previewing the results of our work – if all is well, we should see the information displayed about Copenhagen, as shown in Figure 2-8, at the start of this exercise.

Although our code may appear simple, it touches on some key points when using expressions – let's review what we've covered in our demo in more detail.

A copy of the code for this exercise is in the download that accompanies this book, within the expressions folder.

Exploring What Happened

A first look at our code may scare some, but in reality, it's not complicated – the magic in our demo is added in steps 2 and 3. If we reproduce the code from step 2:

```
<h1>Copenhagen</h1>

<p>{{country}}, or København (in Danish), is the capital and most populous city of Denmark.
The City of Copenhagen (Byen København) has a population of {{ format(population) }}
(as of December 2016), of whom {{ format(inCopenhagen) }} live in the Municipality of
Copenhagen.</p>
<div class="image"><img src="img/nyhavn.jpg"></div>
<span>Source: Wikipedia / Wikimedia</span>
```

Much of our code is standard HTML markup – code that many developers will have seen thousands of times before. However, take a closer look at this extract:

```
...of whom {{ format(inCopenhagen) }} live...
```

What's going on here? Put simply, this is an expression – in this instance, we're formatting what will become a population total that will have a comma as a thousand separator.

This will make more sense when we look at the code from step 3:

```
data: {
  country: 'Copenhagen',
  population: 763908,
  inCopenhagen: 601448,
  format: function ( num ) {
    if ( num > 1000 ) return ( Math.floor( num / 1000 ) ) + ',' + ( num % 1000 );
    return num;
  }
}
```

Here, I've extracted the key part – our format function. We take the value from the format placeholder (or mustache), and assign it to num. A check is performed on num – if the value is over 1000, we split it and insert commas after every third digit (reading from right to left). It's worth noting that the maths in the function is a little more complex than this, but the detail isn't critical for our purposes; it's more important to know that we can add in a suitable function to calculate a value from within our Ractive instance.

So – to finish the function: the values from the population and inCopenhagen references are reformatted through this function, giving 763,908 and 601,448 respectively. Adding in a function in this manner means we don't have to worry about how content is formatted; as long as our references / keypaths resolve, then providing we supply valid numbers, we know our content will be formatted correctly.

Taking It Further

Adding in functions, as part of any expressions we create, opens up some real possibilities – formatting currency values is a perfect example of how we can manipulate our data in this way. But going in with all guns blazing, means we will likely end up in trouble if we're not careful! There are a few tips we should consider to help maintain order:

- If we find ourselves regularly using an expression such as formatting a price in dollars, we can add it to the default configuration for Ractive, so we don't have to define the function each time. This is great for making use of external libraries, such as the JavaScript-based date library, moment.js. We'll cover this in more detail in Incorporating external libraries and expressions.

- Ractive will support most expressions, with the exception of three – we can't use assignment operators, such as a=b, include functions (these must be in the Ractive instance instead), and new, delete or void operators cannot be used.

- If you've used Mustache before, then you may have come across the implicit operator – this is a neat trick for referencing items within an array that is specified in our Ractive instance. In short, instead of including values that refer to each array element, we can simply do this:

```
<script id='template' type='text/ractive'>
  {{#type}}{{.}}{{/type}}
</script>
```

- Assuming our Ractive instance is correctly configured, then it will render the contents of the type array on screen automatically. To see this in action, head over to a CodePen I've created https://codepen.io/alexlibby/pen/ZKojRq; try adding in items under the array:

```
"type": [
  [0, "Exclusive"],
  [1, "Open "],
  [2, "Co-Broke"],
  [3, "Limited"],
  [4, "Shared"]
  ...add more items here....
],
```

The code will be automatically compiled by Ractive, and the new values rendered on screen.

■ **Note** We can equally use this in place of a full stop; they both refer to the current data context. In short, this renders each keypath/value pairing stored within the type data block. Both . and this have the same meaning in Ractive; this works equally well in standard references, not just within expressions!

We're not limited though by what we can write as a function – in many cases, it's not worth the effort to craft something, when others may have already created useful function libraries we can use. There is no sense in trying to reinvent the wheel, so rather than expending lots of time and effort, we can simply plug their libraries into our Ractive instance, and reference them as part of our project. A good example of this is the Moment and Moment Timezone libraries, available from http://momentjs.com, and used for manipulating dates and times. I feel a demo coming on, so let's dive in and take a look in more detail.

Incorporating External Libraries and Expressions

Over the course of the last few pages, we've touched on using expressions within Ractive mustaches; although this begins to break down the notion that we're limited to using static content, we can definitely expand our horizons further.

To achieve this, Ractive allows us to add in support for external libraries, such as the aforementioned library, MomentJS.

The beauty of Ractive is that we can even add it to Ractive's default configuration; this saves us time, as we don't have to keep specifying this within each Ractive instance. For example, the Moment library has a function to subtract a number of days from a given calendar date. The function would look like this:

```
moment().subtract(2, 'days').calendar();
```

Let's imagine that we are continually entering this calculation – for example, we might use this in a travel calendar, where return trips cannot be made for a minimum of 48 hours. Instead of writing all of that, how about we set up a helper function:

```
var helpers = Ractive.defaults.data;
helpers.minStay = function(timeString){
    return moment(timeString).subtract(2, 'days').calendar();
}
```

We can then reference the function by calling `helpers.minStay(timevalue)`, which is a lot easier to use!

Setting Time Zones in Ractive

This is just one option open to us – to help understand how we might use this, we first need to incorporate an external library into our Ractive object; there's nothing like a demo to see this in action. For this next exercise, we'll use the Moment time / time zone libraries available from `https://momentjs.com/`. Figure 2-9 is a screenshot of our finished article.

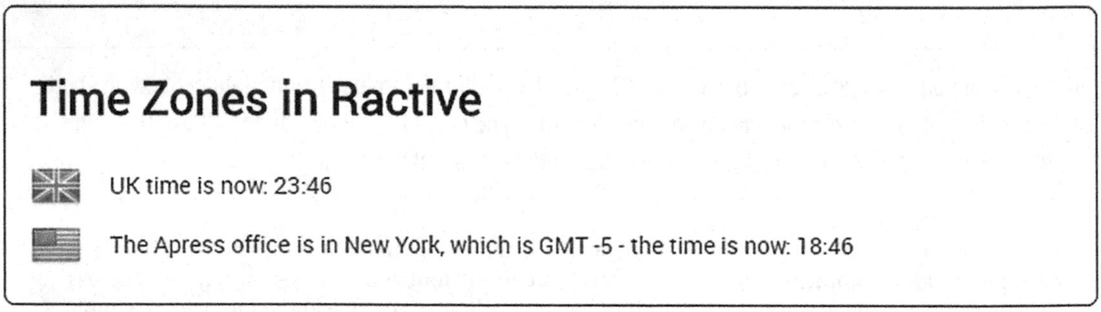

Time Zones in Ractive

 UK time is now: 23:46

 The Apress office is in New York, which is GMT -5 - the time is now: 18:46

Figure 2-9. *Setting timezones with Ractive and Moment*

Let's get started on our demo:

DISPLAYING TIME ZONES USING EXPRESSIONS

1. We'll start by setting up our base project – for this, take a copy of the previous exercise folder, and save it as `expressions - third-party`.

2. We need to download copies of the Moment and Moment Timezone libraries; these are available from `http://momentjs.com/downloads/moment.js` and `https://momentjs.com/downloads/moment-timezone.js` respectively. Download both into the `js` subfolder of the `expressions - third-party` folder.

3. Next up, we need to modify our markup; for this, edit a copy of `testractive.html` from within the `expressions - third-party` folder, and replace the template script block with this code:

```
<script id='template' type='text/ractive'>
  <h1>Time Zones in Ractive</h1>
  <div id="uktime">
    <div class="flag"><img src="img/United-Kingdom-icon.png"></div>
    <div class="timeZ">UK time is now: {{uk}} </div>
  </div>
  <div id="nytime">
    <div class="flag"><img src="img/United-States-icon.png"></div>
    <div class="timeZ">The Apress office is in New York, which is
    GMT -5 - the time is now: {{ny}} </div>
  </div>
</script>
<script type="text/javascript" src="js/moment.js"></script>
<script type="text/javascript" src="js/moment-timezone.js"></script>
```

4. Save the file. Our styling needs adjusting, so for this go ahead and open up `teststyles.css` from within the `css` subfolder, then remove all but the `@font-face`, `body`, `p` and `#container` styles.

5. We can now add in the following styles, saving the file with the same name:

```
.flag { width: 50px; }

#uktime, #nytime { display: flex; }

.timeZ { line-height: 32px; }
```

6. We need two suitable icon images – for this, I used the `United-Kingdom-icon.png` and `United-States-icon.png` icon files from `https://www.gosquared.com/resources/flag-icons/`; you can either use these, or others if you have a particular preference.

7. We're almost done – the biggest change is in our script file. Find and open up
    `exp-thirdparty.js` from within the `js` subfolder in the `expressions -`
    `third-party` folder and replace it with the following code:

    ```
    moment.tz.add('America/New_York|EST EDT|50 40|0101|1Lz50 1zb0 Op0');

    var london = moment().format("H:mm");
    var newYork = moment.tz(moment(), "America/New_York").format("H:mm");

    var ractive = new Ractive({
      el: '#container',
      template: '#template',
      data: {
            uk: london,
            ny: newYork
      }
    });
    ```

Save the file with the same name as before – we can now preview the results of our efforts in a browser. If all is well, we should see something akin to the start of this exercise.

This demo opens some real possibilities – granted, we may have to limit ourselves to using JavaScript libraries for compatibility; there is so much available on the Internet, that the world is literally our oyster!

A copy of the code for this demo can be found in the exp-thirdparty folder within the code download that accompanies this book.

Before we go rushing in headlong though, it's important to understand the core principle behind this demo, so let's pause for a moment to review our code in more detail.

Understanding Our Demo in More Detail

Go ahead and open the testractive.html file from within the `expressions - third-party` folder; on or around line 11, we will see this block of code:

```
<h1>Time Zones in Ractive</h1>
<div id="uktime">
  <div class="flag"><img src="img/United-Kingdom-icon.png"></div>
  <div class="timeZ">UK time is now: {{uk}} </div>
</div>
```

There is nothing particularly special about this code; the {{uk}} we've inserted is a standard mustache that we'll use as a placeholder for locating the UK time. We then repeat this block again from line 17, but this time with a {{ny}} mustache for displaying the time in New York.

The real magic though happens in the `exp-thirdparty.js` file – a peek inside shows this code:

```
moment.tz.add('America/New_York|EST EDT|50 40|0101|1Lz50 1zb0 Op0');
var london = moment().format("H:mm");
var newYork = moment.tz(moment(), "America/New_York").format("H:mm");

var ractive = new Ractive({
  el: '#container',
  template: '#template',
  data: {
    uk: london,
    ny: newYork
  }
});
```

So – what is happening here? We start with adding a definition for our time zone; this is a dependency for configuring Moment Timezone. We then define two values – the `london` variable is to set to the local time of the user's browser, while `newYork` is to store the adjusted time for New York. We then make use of both values within the data configuration – Ractive will automatically update both values if we refresh the browser window.

The beauty about this is that we keep our configuration code within `testscript.js`; granted, we've linked in the two library files for Moment in the main HTML markup, but all of the hard work is done within the `exp-thirdparty.js` file, and not in multiple files.

Okay – let's move on: within our Ractive markup, we've included two `<div>` blocks, to manage the display of each time. It works perfectly well, but Ractive can manage the content better; although the text within each block is different, the markup is still identical. Ractive has a useful technique to better manage content of this nature; let's dive in and take a look at partials in more detail.

Creating Partials

Over time, our code has the potential to become unwieldy if we're not careful. Inlining code may help reduce the number of requests that the browser has to make of the server, but this is at the risk of littering our HTML markup with extraneous code and making it impossible to maintain separation of concerns.

To help with this, we can make use of partials – in the same way that each Ractive instance becomes a fragment of our overall code; a partial is a snippet of code we can insert into our templates, or even into other partials. This helps not only keep our code uncluttered and easy to read, but can also help with reducing the number of files we need to edit. If we keep the HTML markup to a minimum in the main file, we can focus on editing our script file and leave the markup alone.

Enough chitchat – let's work on a demo! We can put this theory into practice with a simple gallery effect; our gallery will showcase a mix of flowers, orchids, and cacti.

Introducing Our Gallery

As anyone who knows me personally, they will know I love seeing different flowers, but particularly orchids and cacti – what better excuse do we have then to create a gallery to show off some thumbnail shots of suitable plants?

This is a perfect opportunity to use partials: we can create a repeatable template to display our images. It would look something like this:

```
<figure class='thumbnail'>
  <img src='img/{{id}}.png'>
  <figcaption>{{description}}</figcaption>
</figure>
```

We can use this as a basis to create our gallery; our finished demo will look something like Figure 2-10.

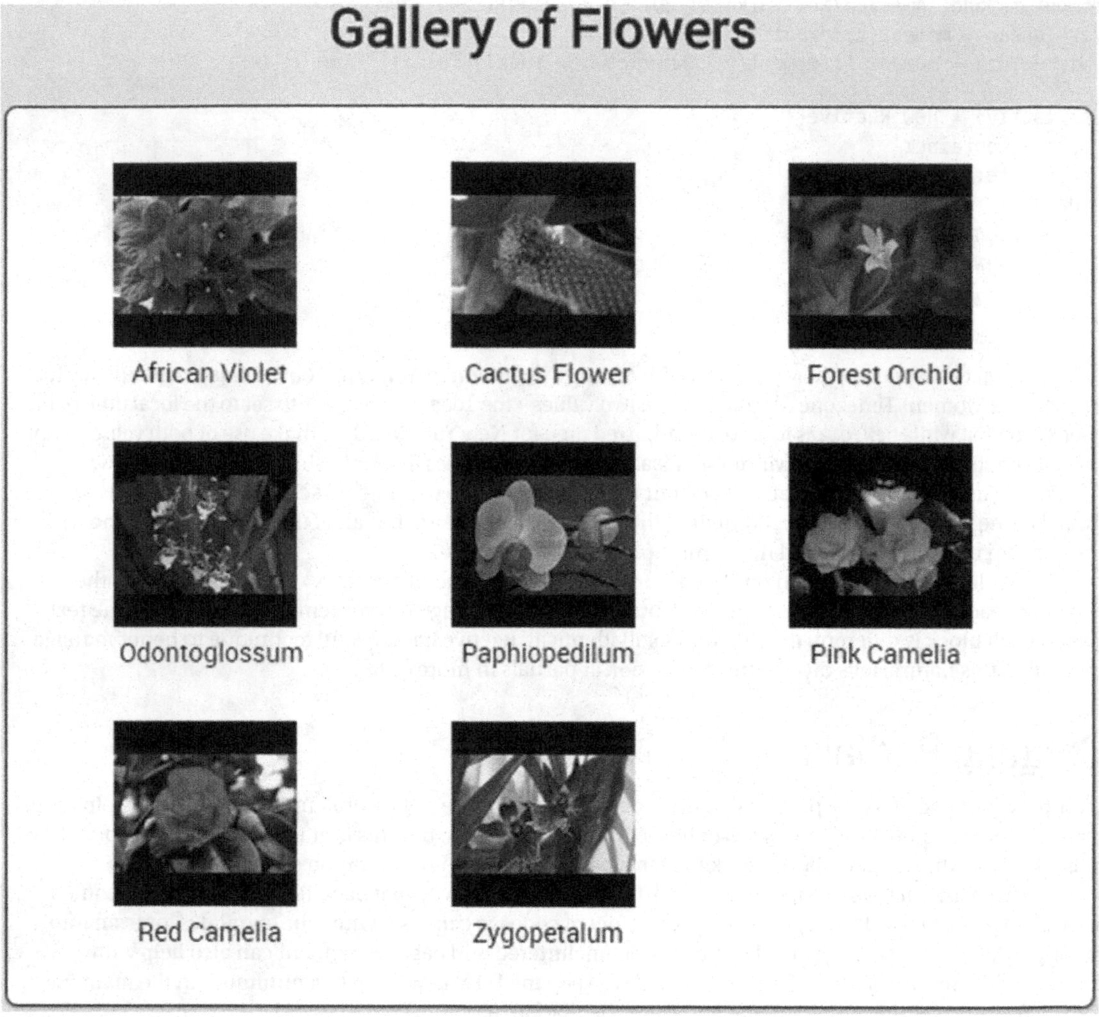

Figure 2-10. *Our finished gallery*

Let's get cracking with creating our demo:

CREATING A GALLERY USING PARTIALS

1. We'll start by taking a copy of our previous demo folder, and saving it with a name of `partials`; this will form the base for our demo.

2. Next, open a copy of the `testractive.html` file from within the partials folder, and look for the opening `<body>` tag.

3. Remove everything within the `<body>` tags, and replace it with the following:

```
<h1>Gallery of Flowers</h1>
<div id='container'></div>
<script id='template' type='text/ractive'>

  <div class='gallery'>
    {{#items}}
      {{>thumbnail}}
    {{/items}}
  </div>
</script>
<script src='js/ractive.min.js'></script>
<script src="js/testscript.js"></script>
```

4. We need to update our Ractive instance – there are a few changes required, so we'll start with adding in our mustache, or template. Add the code to the top of the `partials.js` file, within the `js` sub-folder in the partials folder:

```
var thumbs = "<figure class='thumbnail'><img src='img/{{id}}.png'><figcaption>
{{description}}</figcaption></figure>";
```
Next, alter the Ractive object in the same file, as indicated below:
```
var ractive = new Ractive({
  el: '#container',
  template: '#template',
  partials: { thumbnail: thumbs },
  data: {
    items: [
      { id: 'africanviolet', description: 'African Violet' },
      { id: 'cactusflower', description: 'Cactus Flower' },
      { id: 'forestorchid', description: 'Forest Orchid' },
      { id: 'odontoglossum', description: 'Odontoglossum' },
      { id: 'paphiopedilum', description: 'Paphiopedilum' },
      { id: 'pinkcamelia', description: 'Pink Camelia' },
      { id: 'redcamelia', description: 'Red Camelia' },
      { id: 'whitecamelia', description: 'White Camelia' },
      { id: 'zygopetalum', description: 'Zygopetalum' }
    ]
  }
});
```

5. Save the results – go ahead and preview `testractive.html` in a browser. If all is well, we should see a gallery effect similar to that at the start of this exercise.

There is more to creating partials than simply creating a `<script>` tag version; we can inline partials into HTML markup if needed, or even create partials based on an expression, such as the ones we've explored earlier in this chapter. Before we talk about these extra possibilities, let's first review what took place in our demo in more detail.

47

Exploring What Happened

By now, some of the code we're using should be a little more familiar – much of it is standard markup with a JavaScript object, in the form of our Ractive instance. However, if we take a closer look at steps 3 to 5 from the previous demo, we can see some changes; these make up our new feature – a partial.

The base for our partial is the HTML markup:

```
{{#each items}}
  {{>thumbnail}}
{{/each}}
```

Here, we've removed the contents of our template – these now form a variable in our script file:

```
var thumbs = "<figure class='thumbnail'><img src='img/{{id}}.png'><figcaption>{{descripti
on}}</figcaption></figure>";
```

To make use of this template, we've introduced a new option in the form of partials: the key here is to specify our reference from the markup (i.e., `thumbnail`), and the string template we're going to use (`thumbs`):

```
template: '#template',
  partials: { thumbnail: thumbs },
  data: {
```

Our string template will be parsed when viewing for the first time; after this, the parsed content will be stored in `Ractive.partials` to reduce the time taken for future lookups.

The best way to see the effect of compiling this code is to view it in the console of a browser – this is a screenshot our code (Figure 2-11), taken from Chrome.

```
<h1>Gallery of Flowers</h1>
▼ <div id="container">
  ▼ <div class="gallery">
    ▶ <figure class="thumbnail">...</figure>
    ▶ <figure class="thumbnail">...</figure>
    ▶ <figure class="thumbnail">...</figure>
    ▶ <figure class="thumbnail">...</figure>
    ▶ <figure class="thumbnail">...</figure>
    ▶ <figure class="thumbnail">...</figure>
    ▶ <figure class="thumbnail">...</figure>
    ▶ <figure class="thumbnail">...</figure>
    ▶ <figure class="thumbnail">...</figure>
  </div>
</div>
▼ <script id="template" type="text/ractive">
      <div class='gallery'>
        {{#items}}
          {{>thumbnail}}
        {{/items}}
      </div>
```

Figure 2-11. *Compiled code that uses a partial*

If we take a closer look at each `<figure>` tag, we will see something akin to Figure 2-12.

```
▼ <figure class="thumbnail">
    <img src="img/africanviolet.png">
    <figcaption>African Violet</figcaption>
  </figure>
```

Figure 2-12. *Our compiled partial*

We can match this up with our partial – any changes to data that we need to make can be confined to our script file, leaving the markup untouched.

■ **Tip** As a test, try entering `ractive.partials.thumbnail` into a browser console. If you dig deep enough, you can begin to see the various values that have been parsed by Ractive.

Summary

Phew – we've certainly covered a fair amount of content! It's important to get our base set up correctly, so to help with this, let's take a moment to review what we've covered throughout this chapter.

Our journey through this chapter kicked off with exploring the concept of the Parallel DOM, and how this plays a role in updating code; we then covered the core elements of a Ractive template.

Up next we saw how styles can be applied using standard CSS or Ractive decorators, before moving on to set up references and keypaths so that we can target our data correctly. We then stepped this up a notch by using the power of adding functions and expressions to our code, to help reduce the static nature of our data.

Our journey through creating templates rounded out with a look at creating Ractive partials, before putting them into good use in a gallery-based demo.

It's time to move on – with our templates now in place, it's time to start adding data, to help fill in the blanks; this will be the subject of our next chapter.

PART II

■ ■ ■

In More Detail

CHAPTER 3

■ ■ ■

Binding Data

A site without data is (almost) like a library without shelves – we may have content in the form of books and journals, but without some way of managing where it is stored and how it is retrieved, it is useless! Thankfully Ractive can automatically manage much of the interaction required, such as re-rendering of the mustaches in the template – throughout the course of this chapter, we'll explore the various techniques we can use, from managing simple form elements, through to observing changes and building adaptors that allow us to interface with third-party libraries such as Backbone. We'll start this stage of our journey with a look at how Ractive manages form elements.

Managing Data-Binding in Ractive

A question – how many times have you bought something online, from the likes of Amazon.com? Hopefully it's more than just on a few occasions: there are times when we have better things to do than trudge to the shops!

A key part of this online experience is, of course, having to fill in a form, give delivery details, and a means to pay for our goods. In most HTML-based forms, data normally goes one way – from the model to the view. In Ractive's case though, it provides bindings to allow two-way traffic from elements to the view. What does this mean? Well – now is a perfect opportunity to see it in action: let's explore this in a simple demo. Head over to `https://codepen.io/alexlibby/pen/QvRjEv` - yes, we're going to break with tradition, and run this as a CodePen, as shown in Figure 3-1.

© Alex Libby 2017

A. Libby, *Beginning Ractive.js*, https://doi.org/10.1007/978-1-4842-3093-0_3

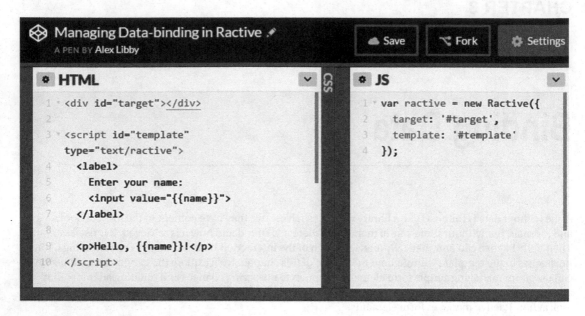

Figure 3-1. *Example of two-way data-binding*

Go ahead and enter your name into the <input> field: notice how it is added to the Hello...! text below, without having extra code to do this? This two-way binding is handled automatically by Ractive, as illustrated in Figure 3-2:

Figure 3-2. *The output of our Codepen demo*

The same applies to other form elements – try replacing the HTML markup from the Codepen we've just run, with this:

```
<div id="target"></div>

<script id="template" type="text/ractive">
  <select value='{{color}}'>
    {{#each colors}}
      <option>{{this}}</option>
    {{/each}}
  </select>

  <p>The selected colour is <span style='color: {{color}};'>{{color}}</span>. </p>
</script>
```

We need to update the Ractive instance as well, so go ahead and replace the code in the JS window with this:

```
var ractive = new Ractive({
  el: '#target',
  template: '#template',
  data: {
    colors: [ 'red', 'green', 'blue' ],
    color: 'green'
  }
});
```

Try selecting a new sentry in the select box: you will see that the statement "The selected color is…" will automatically update with the chosen color.

Okay – let's move on, and try something a little more complex this time: how about setting up something that changed the price of a product, based on choosing a specific size, such as large, medium, or small?

Understanding the Principles

Although this request may sound harder, in reality it is very easy – Ractive handles much of the updating itself, leaving us to specify which values should be set in our instance. Let's dive in and see what this means in practice, using the example of pricing for sizes of a picture frame as our next demo, as shown in Figure 3-3.

Acme Black Wooden Picture Photo Frame

- These frames are made to order and dispatched from our workshop.

- The picture moulding is made from pine and measures 15mm wide and 25mm deep

- Our frames come ready to hang or stand portrait or landscape, frame sizes 16x12 inches and above to hang only

Price: $6.96

Sizes available:  A4

Figure 3-3. *Displaying the price of a frame*

The screenshot shown in Figure 3-3 depicts a standard black wooden frame, with some marketing blurb, a size selector, and the price for that size. If we select a different size, the price automatically changes. Not convinced? Let's dive in and take a look at the code in more detail – I promise you, it's not complicated!

The demo for this in the form elements folder within the code download that accompanies this book – go ahead and open up dropdown.html; inside, we'll see the usual markup, along with this (edited for brevity):

```
<script id="template" type="text/ractive">
  ...
  <p class="sizes">Sizes available:</p>
  <select value='{{avsize}}'>
    {{#avsizes}}
      <option value="{{this.value}}">{{this.name}}</option>
    {{/avsizes}}
  </select>
  <p class="price">Price: ${{avsize}}</p>
</script>
```

This is our Ractive component – leaving aside the mustache markup, it follows the same format as any standard <select> element. The key here though is within the {{#avsizes}} section – this is a reference back to the Ractive object:

```
var ractive = new Ractive({
  target: '#container',
  template: '#template',
  data: {
    avsizes: [
      { name: 'A4', value: 6.96 },
      { name: '8 x 6 inch', value: 5.18 },
      { name: '10 x 8 inch', value: 9.88 }
    ],
    size: 'A4'
  }
});
```

We could have hard-coded each of the name : value pairs within the avsizes keypath, but that isn't the most efficient route; instead, we've used this.value and this.name. Ractive uses the #avsizes reference to iterate through the data block until it has inserted all three sizes automatically. It is one less thing for us to have to do!

How does it work though? It's a good question – although Ractive allows data to be bound to HTML elements such as checkboxes or select lists, it relies on one key factor: it automatically binds to the change event (and click event too, for IE – this is due to a bug). This means that as soon as we make a change, the model is updated automatically.

However, if we take a closer look at our Ractive instance, the presence of avsize might confuse you – it's not used directly in our template, yet, how does our demo know what price to show when we change the entry in the drop-down box? Well, we do make use of {{avsize}} – this is treated as the value attribute in the <select> element. If the drop-down value is changed, it re-binds the updated value of the <select> to avsize. We then simply render this value later in the <p> element. Our demo also makes use of ractive.observe(), to look for any changes – if one is triggered, then a message is displayed in the browser's console.

We don't even have to work any magic to extract and display the new size value – we've used the avsize value in the select element, which can simply be dropped into a suitable statement (as we have done in this demo).

To learn more about the different ways of binding to HTML elements such as radio buttons, head over to the main documentation at `https://ractive.js.org/api/api/#data-binding`.

Now – there may be instances where we want to trigger an update on change or blur only – for this, we can use the `lazy` attribute that needs to be specified in our Ractive instance. This can also accept a value that delays the trigger by x seconds, depending on the value specified in our instance.

What does this mean for us? If we're working on a project where we need a direct update as soon as we enter some information (such as updating totals in a basket if we increase quantities), then we would write something like this:

```
<input type="text" value="{{ abc }}"> {{ abc }}
```

However, there may be occasions when updating so promptly isn't necessary; a change to the DOM won't take effect until we trigger a late-firing DOM event such as change or blur. If triggering a change when we lose focus is sufficient, we can add in the `lazy` attribute thus:

```
<input type="text" value="{{ bar }}" lazy="true"> {{ bar }}
```

Irrespective of how quickly we need to trigger an update, the key point here is that Ractive automatically manages that update for us; there is no need to add additional code to force that change to happen. Ractive is able to make that update very quickly – question though: how does it manage to achieve this update so quickly?

Managing Dependencies

The answer lies in the how: Ractive maintains a dependency tracker, which lists all of the parent elements, and identifies which have child dependencies that may require updating.

This is only part of the story though – this dependency tracker maintains a concept of priority. It's best to describe how this works with an example; it's a little contrived, but it shows the basic principle behind how Ractive works.

Assume for a moment that we have a checklist that displays a number of items – we show or hide individual items, depending on how the respondent completes previous questions in the list. Seems a sensible arrangement, right? After all, there is no point in asking a question if it clearly doesn't apply to the individual! Now – what if a question from that list had a number of options: do we check each one to ensure it should be displayed?

Ractive takes a different approach – it maintains a tracker that lists each element and its dependencies; these are prioritized within the tracker. In our example, if a particular question shouldn't be displayed, then why do we even need to check if the subitems (i.e., answers / choices) need to be shown? If a question shouldn't be displayed, then Ractive simply tears down the element (question) and its children. The latter will automatically unregister themselves as dependents, before they can update themselves.

To put this into context, we can best see what might happen if we look at a Ractive instance – we can see how elements are tracked from within the console.

VIEWING RACTIVE ELEMENTS IN A CONSOLE

1. For this demo, fire up a copy of one of our Ractive exercises – for the purposes of this demo, I will assume you are using the Gallery demo from Chapter 2, and that we're using Chrome (if you want to use a different browser, then please adjust accordingly).

2. Display the console by pressing F12, or Ctrl + Shift + I – at the prompt, enter `ractive.viewmodel` and press Enter.

3. It will display a list of properties initially – we can use the right arrow to expand the list, as shown in Figure 3-4:

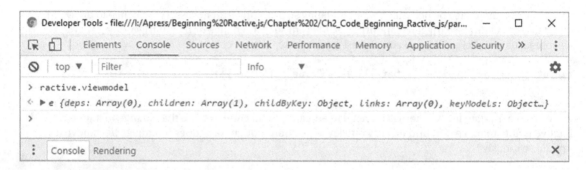

Figure 3-4. *Initial view of ractive.viewModel*

4. If we expand the list, we can begin to see (as shown in Figure 3-5), items that relate back to the demo:

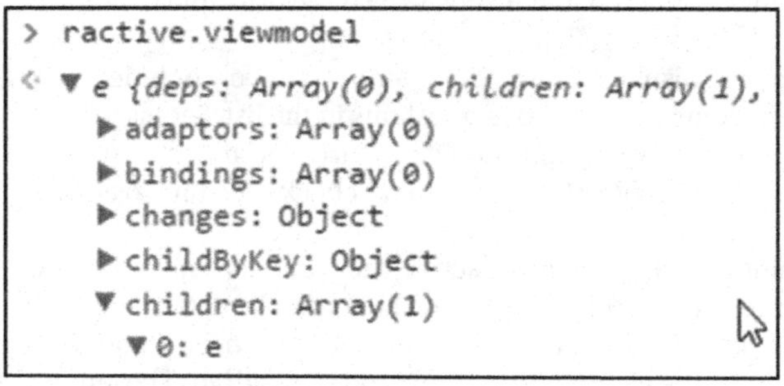

```
> ractive.viewmodel
<  ▼ e {deps: Array(0), children: Array(1),
      ▶ adaptors: Array(0)
      ▶ bindings: Array(0)
      ▶ changes: Object
      ▶ childByKey: Object
      ▼ children: Array(1)
         ▼ 0: e
```

Figure 3-5. *Initial view of ractive.viewModel*

5. Try this – from the top, click on `children | 0 | children`; Figure 3-6 shows a list of numbered items, which represent the nine images we have in our demo:

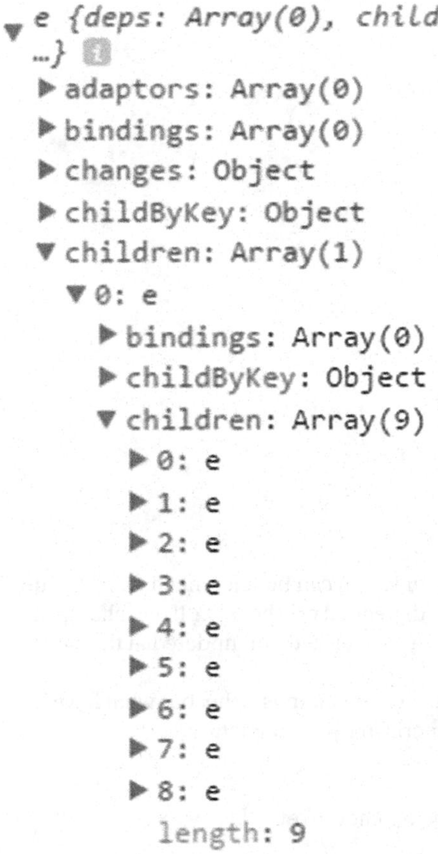

```
▼ e {deps: Array(0), children:
  ...} ℹ
  ▶ adaptors: Array(0)
  ▶ bindings: Array(0)
  ▶ changes: Object
  ▶ childByKey: Object
  ▼ children: Array(1)
    ▼ 0: e
      ▶ bindings: Array(0)
      ▶ childByKey: Object
      ▼ children: Array(9)
        ▶ 0: e
        ▶ 1: e
        ▶ 2: e
        ▶ 3: e
        ▶ 4: e
        ▶ 5: e
        ▶ 6: e
        ▶ 7: e
        ▶ 8: e
          length: 9
```

Figure 3-6. *Browsing to one of the image items*

Try exploring the rest of the list – it is not meant to be human-readable; Ractive maintains the bare minimum to allow it to track where content needs to be updated in the physical DOM. It is still worth exploring though, as we can get an understanding for how Ractive works; if you look in enough places, you should start to see other elements, such as the names given to each of the flowers within each image in the gallery.

Managing Indirect Dependencies

Take a look back at *Interacting with Ractive Instances Using Keypaths*, back in Chapter 2 – remember how we talked about the concept of up and downstream keypaths, such as the one shown in Figure 3-7?

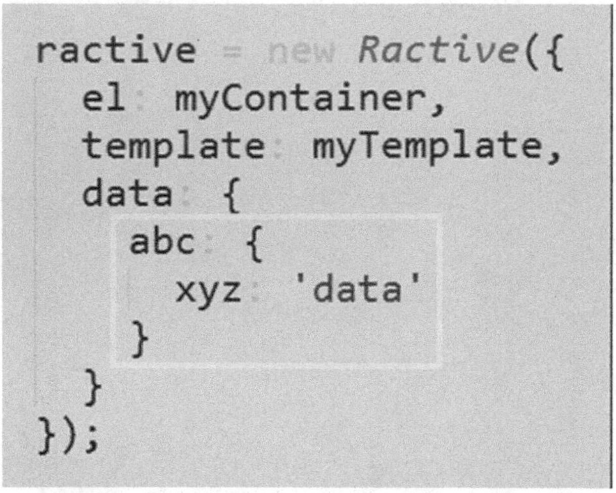

```
ractive = new Ractive({
    el: myContainer,
    template: myTemplate,
    data: {
        abc: {
            xyz: 'data'
        }
    }
});
```

Figure 3-7. *A keypath*

In the example given, xyz was a **downstream keypath** to abc, or which can be referenced using the dot notation of abc.xyz. However, what if we had had a mustache that depended on abc.xyz? If abc changed, then any indirect dependents (in this case xyz), would automatically be checked and updated at the same time.

In our first example, we do a simple update of the keypath and associated mustache, but what if we had been using an array? Take, for example, this example of a list of American car manufacturers:

```
data: {
  list: [{ name: 'Ford' }, { name: 'Cadillac' }, { name: 'Chevrolet' }],
  sort: function ( list, property ) {
    return list.slice().sort( function ( a, b ) {
      return a[ property ] < b[ property ] ? -1 : 1;
    });
  }
}
```

This will render Ford, Chevrolet, Oldsmobile – if we ran this command:

```
ractive.set( 'list[0].name', 'Oldsmobile' );
```

...this will not only update the Ford entry to Oldsmobile, but trigger a sort, as Ractive will have detected a change to the list. It means that our final result would render as Cadillac, Chevrolet, then Oldsmobile.

A small note – if we decide to use an expression in a ractive.set() statement, then we must take into account any dependencies, whether they be direct or indirect.

Why is this critical? It all boils down to when these dependencies are updated – let's take the expression{{ x + y }} as an example. We have a dependency on two objects, x and y – we'll assume for now that there are dependencies lower down the keypath.

Ractive's dependency tracker will contain objects representing these references, and not the expression itself. It means that an update to the expression will not be triggered until Ractive receives updated data for both objects. This will trigger two updates, which is an inefficient use of resources; it is better to write an update akin to `ractive.set({ x: 5, y: 10 })`, in order to avoid triggering unnecessary updates.

This concept of managing dependencies is key to Ractive; it becomes more critical if we need to work with values that are not static. Imagine we have a box, for which we need to work out its volume; it's an easy calculation, and Ractive will take care of updating it automatically. But how do we reference this in our code? Or, as we'll see later in this chapter – even monitor for any changes?

Working with Computed Properties

In our previous example, our data was static – this is fine for many instances, but there may be occasions where we might benefit from using a calculated or computed property when using Ractive.

What do I mean by this? Instead of setting a static value, we have the option to set one based on the result of a function; Ractive will automatically update this value based on any changes to its dependencies. For example, we wouldn't want to set a static value for volume, right? That wouldn't make sense – what if we changed it? Instead, we set this as a dynamic value, and let Ractive take care of updating it automatically. Let's put this theory into a practice with a demo, which will work out the volume of – well, why not a fish tank?

Calculating Volume of a Fish Tank

Mmm…working on anything aquatic is probably not what you expect in a book about Ractive – and no, there's nothing fishy going on, either! (Yes – pun intended, before you ask…). It's a great way though to show off how we can make use of computed values that automatically update, based on their dependencies.

To illustrate just how we can use computed properties, we can build a simple demo that takes the measurements of a fish tank, and work out how much water we need to fill it. For now, our demo will concentrate on rectangular tanks – the math required is simpler than that needed for working out odd-shaped tanks! A screenshot of what we're going to produce is shown in Figure 3-8.

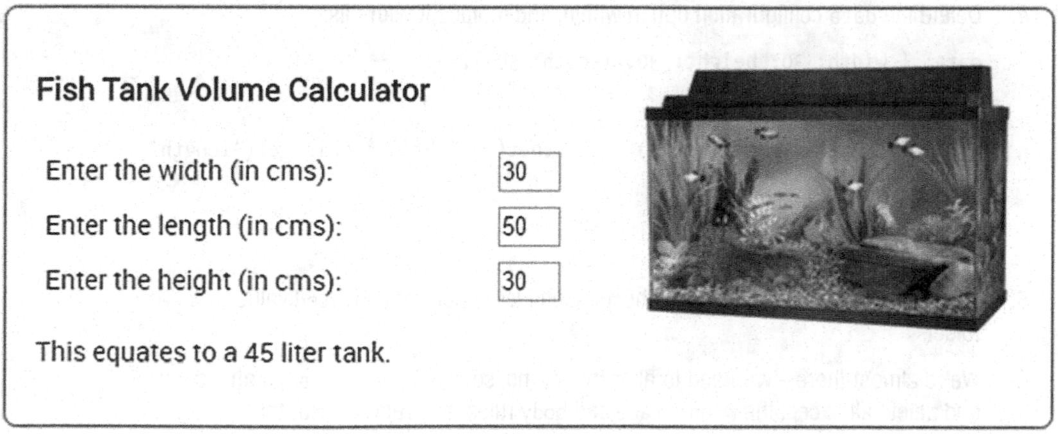

Fish Tank Volume Calculator

Enter the width (in cms): `30`

Enter the length (in cms): `50`

Enter the height (in cms): `30`

This equates to a 45 liter tank.

Figure 3-8. Our completed tank volume calculator

CALCULATING COMPUTED VALUES

Let's make a start on putting together our code:

1. We'll begin by taking a copy of the `form elements` folder, and saving it to our project area, giving it the name `computed values`.

2. Next go ahead and open up the `computed.html` file within this folder – remove the three `<script>` calls within the `<body>`, and replace with this:

```html
<script id="template" type="text/ractive">
  <h3>Fish Tank Volume Calculator</h3>
  <img src="img/tank.jpg">
  <label>
    <p>Enter the width (in cms):</p> <input value="{{width}}">
  </label>
  <label>
    <p>Enter the length (in cms):</p> <input value="{{length}}">
  </label>
  <label>
    <p>Enter the height (in cms):</p> <input value="{{height}}">
  </label>
  <p>This equates to a {{volume}} liter tank.</p>
</script>

<script src='js/ractive.min.js'></script>
<script src="js/computed.js"></script>
```

3. Save the file as `computed.html`. We need to modify our Ractive instance, so go ahead and open up `dropdown.js`.

4. Delete the `data` configuration option within, and replace it with this:

```js
data: { width: 30, height: 30, length: 50 },
computed: {
  volume: function() {
    return (this.get('width') * this.get('height') * this.get('length')
    / 1000);
  }
}
```

5. Save this file as `computed.js`, in the `js` subfolder under the `computed values` folder.

6. We're almost there – we need to alter the styling, so in `dropdown.css`, go ahead and delete all except the `@font-face` and `body` rules, and replace with this:

```css
img { position: absolute; padding-left: 20.25rem; margin-top: -4.4rem; }
label p { width: 234px; display: inline-block; margin: 5px; }
input { width: 30px; }
#container { border: 1px solid #000; width: 33rem; border-radius: 0.4rem;
padding: 1rem; }
```

7. Save the file as `computed.css` – make sure you change any reference within the HTML markup from `dropdown` to `computed`, so that our demo continues to work.

8. The last step is to replace the image – for this, I've downloaded a suitable image of a fish tank. You can use the one included in the code download for this book, or if you want to use an alternative, then it should be no larger than 200px square.

Phew – we're there! Go ahead and preview the results of the demo in a browser; if all is well, we should see a simple calculator.

We've built up the template within our Ractive instance, which is then applied to the `#container` element within our markup. Try changing the values in the input fields – you will see that the volume level rendered in the `{{volume}}` mustache will change automatically, as Ractive will recalculate the volume as soon as it detects a change has been committed in the demo.

Improving Our Code

At this stage, we have a simple but effective calculator – it's a good base for adapting for other purposes. Trouble is, I'm never one for resting on my laurels; we can do better! Before we take a look at how, there is one small topic I want to cover: if we wanted to be notified of any changes (say for example, the volume size is too great), how would we do that?

The simple answer is to use observers in Ractive – we'll cover this in more detail shortly, but to give a taste of what to expect, try adding these lines of code in immediately after the end of our Ractive instance:

```
ractive.observe( 'volume', function() {
  console.log("Volume level has changed!")
});
```

Now try changing any of the dimension values in our demo – notice how we get a message that appears in our console? Oh – and notice something else: see how similar this function is to standard DOM observers.

Tip – computed values are by default read-only. In many cases it is advisable to leave them as such; if you need to set a computed value for a project, then check out a Codepen demo at https://codepen.io/alexlibby/pen/boBdqR for an example of how to achieve this, using a slightly different syntax. This brings us nicely to our next topic – we talked about setting up code to monitor for changes to specific values; the role observers play a critical role within Ractive, so let's dive in and see how they work in action.

Observing Changes in Ractive

If you've spent any time developing in JavaScript, then there is a good chance you may have heard, or even made use of, JavaScript patterns. If however, you haven't, then there is nothing sinister about them – they are simply a way of solving problems that others have already come across and created solutions for them. Patterns take it one step further by encapsulating the solution into something that can be reused, is scalable, and has a set of rules you should follow, to make best use of the pattern.

If you would like to learn more about design patterns, then the online book by Addy Osmani is a good source – it's available at https://addyosmani.com/resources/essentialjsdesignpatterns/book/index.html.

What does this have to do with Ractive, I hear you ask? A typical pattern in JavaScript is to make models observable, using the publish/subscribe mechanism. Ractive is no different – we can implement the .observe() method to trigger notification when specific changes have been made. This is one of several methods available, which implement the pub/sub pattern – others include ractive.on(), ractive.off() and ractive.fire().

We'll cover the ractive.on(), ractive.off() and ractive.fire methods in more detail in Chapter 4, *Handling Events* – but for now, let's dive in and take a look at the observe() API in more detail.

Understanding the API Methods

It's important to note though that we can't use the standard pub/sub pattern for monitoring changes in Ractive. If our data contains nested properties, then making (and monitoring) a change to a keypath such as foo.bar will be invalid if the child bar can also be changed at the same time as foo.

To get around this we use the ractive.observe API method – this observes a particular keypath and is notified as soon as the value changes, either directly or indirectly (if an upstream or downstream keypath was changed). The syntax for this method is as follows:

```
ractive.observe(keypath, callback[, options])
ractive.observe(map[, options])
```

The method can take any one of the following arguments, which are summarized in Table 3-1:

Table 3-1. *Arguments for ractive.observe()*

Argument	Purpose
keypath	A string of one or more (space-delimited) keypaths to follow – we can use a * as a wildcard if desired.
callback	A function to call, with newValue, oldValue, and keypath as arguments.
map	We can instead call an object map of keypath-observer pairs, if several should be monitored at the same time.
options	Any one of several options that can be specified, such as [init] to initialize the observer, [strict] to determine if changes should be made or [context] to determine the context in which the observer should be called.
	A full list of the options available are listed at https://ractive.js.org/api/#ractiveobserve.

Let's put this into practice with an interactive demo using Codepen, to see how we can be notified as soon as any change is made to our Ractive code.

Observing Changes in Action

Observing changes in Ractive is easier than one might think – its similarity to the likes of jQuery means that it is a cinch to add in the basic event handler that we can use to notify us of any alterations to content. To prove this, let's take a look at an interactive demo I've set up in a Codepen, at https://codepen.io/alexlibby/pen/GmaevJ, and illustrated in Figure 3-9:

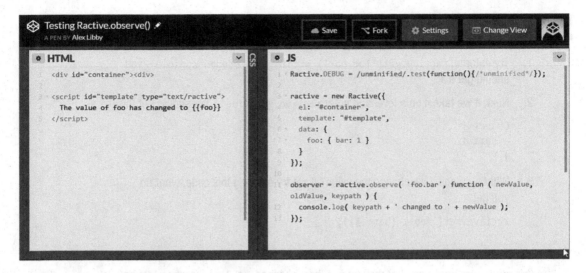

Figure 3-9. *Observing changes in Ractive*

The last three lines in the JS window are of most interest to us – this contains the code we need to use to observe changes. Let's start with the standard Ractive mustache in the HTML pane:

```
<div id="container"><div>

<script id="template" type="text/ractive">
  The value of foo has changed to {{foo}}
</script>
```

Switching to the JS window, we can see a basic Ractive instance that has been set up:

```
Ractive.DEBUG = /unminified/.test(function(){/*unminified*/});

ractive = new Ractive({
  el: "#container",
  template: "#template",
  data: {
    foo: { bar: 1 }
  }
});
```

...but it is these three lines that we need to use to observe for changes:

```
observer = ractive.observe( 'foo.bar', function ( newValue, oldValue, keypath ) {
  console.log( keypath + ' changed to ' + newValue );
});
```

Notice the similarity to jQuery? In our event handler, we specify the keypath to monitor (in this case foo.bar), followed by passing through the newValue, the oldValue and the keypath name. Let's try a few tests:

OBSERVING CHANGES IN RACTIVE

1. Try entering `ractive.get('foo.bar')` within the Codepen console – you should get a 1.

2. Next, if we take it up a level and enter `ractive.get('foo')`, we should get this:

   ```
   Object {
     bar: 1
   }
   ```

3. What happens if we change the value? If we try entering this code, what do you get?

   ```
   ractive.set('foo', {bar: 3});
   ```

At this point, we should see that the text `foo.bar changed to 3`, as shown in Figure 3-10:

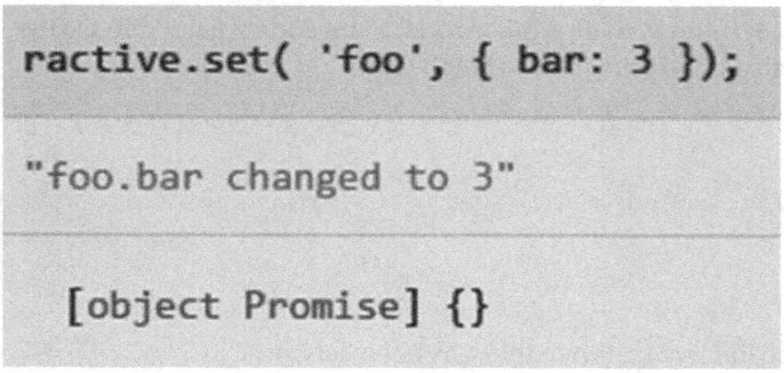

```
ractive.set( 'foo', { bar: 3 });

"foo.bar changed to 3"

[object Promise] {}
```

Figure 3-10. *Outcome of our observation*

Our observer has been triggered, and correctly displays the changed keypath name and new value. But what's the `[object Promise] {}` value below it? Perhaps it will become clearer if we look at the equivalent message in the DOM inspector, not Codepen's console:

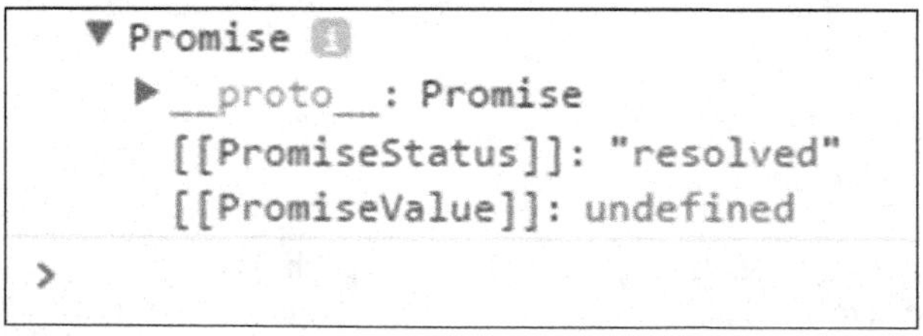

```
▼ Promise ▣
  ▶ __proto__: Promise
    [[PromiseStatus]]: "resolved"
    [[PromiseValue]]: undefined
>
```

Figure 3-11. *Outcome of our observation in raw Console format*

It's not something we've touched on yet, but many of the Ractive methods will return a Promise object. This means that we can tell if the request is still pending, if it has been satisfactorily resolved – or if things have gone pear-shaped and thrown an error! These promises can even be chained, so that a new promise may or may not take place, subject to the outcome of the previous one.

We can of course make use of these Promises elsewhere, using standard JavaScript-based libraries, such as jQuery, if desired. It may require the use of an Adaptor – we will cover this later in this chapter.

There will of course come a time when we no longer need to monitor the code – to complete the exercise, try entering `observer.cancel()` in the Codepen console window, then press Enter. It will show an undefined message (as confirmation that our observer has now been canceled). If you run step 3 from the previous exercise again, you should find that it will change the value, but we won't receive the same notification, as this has been canceled.

Observing Patterns

Observing changes in Ractive is straightforward when monitoring changes on simple data – but what about arrays? Frequently we may want to observe changes on data contained in an array, or which can't be bound to a single keypath. To get around this, we can use an asterisk in a pattern observer, to indicate whenever changes should be made at a particular point, or below this point.

Take for example this code, to list some of my favorite cities:

```
var ractive = new Ractive({
  el: myContainer,
  template: myTemplate,
  data: {
    cities: [
      {name: 'Copenhagen'},
      {name: 'Bruges'},
      {name: 'Vancouver'}
    ]
  }
});
```

If we transfer this to a Codepen, well have something akin to the demo available at `https://codepen.io/alexlibby/pen/qmzWRX`, and displayed in Figure 3-12:

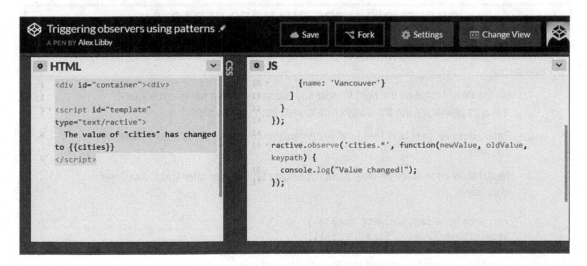

Figure 3-12. *Using pattern observers*

For clarity, let's explore the code in more detail – we have our standard container markup:

```
<div id="container"><div>
```

This is followed by our Ractive mustache and template:

```
<script id="template" type="text/ractive">
  The value of "cities" has changed to {{cities}}
</script>
```

The key to this demo is in the Ractive JavaScript we call next:

```
Ractive.DEBUG = /unminified/.test(function(){/*unminified*/});
var ractive = new Ractive({
  el: '#container',
  template: '#template',
  data: {
    cities: [
      {name: 'Copenhagen'},
      {name: 'Bruges' },
      {name: 'Vancouver'}
    ]
  }
});

ractive.observe('people.*', function(newValue, oldValue, keypath) {
  console.log("Value changed!");
});
```

Let's run a few tests:

OBSERVING MORE CHANGES IN RACTIVE

At the foot of the Codepen window, click on Console to display Codepen's console area, then follow these steps:

1. Hit the Clear button on the right to clear any messages within the console area – this isn't obligatory, but it's always nice to start from a clean slate.

2. Enter `ractive.get('cities');` at the console prompt, then press Enter – what do you get?

3. Next, follow code at the console prompt, pressing Shift+Enter after line 1, and Enter after line 2:

   ```
   var people = ractive.get('people');
   people.push({name: 'Strasbourg'});
   ```

4. This time around, try entering this line of code, and pressing Enter:

   ```
   ractive.set('cities.3', {name: 'Strasbourg'});
   ```

5. What happens when you enter this line of code and press Enter?

```
ractive.get('cities');
ractive.get('cities.3');
ractive.set('cities.1', {name: 'Freibourg'});
```

So – question is: do the results make sense? Bear with me on this – I know it sounds a little odd, as the answers are all on-screen! However, it's important to understand what's going on at this point:

In question 1, it's a simple case of getting the contents of the array set in our Ractive instance, and rendering it on screen; the result will be a listing of all three cities – don't forget: we're dealing with an array, so all of the values will be piped out to console, not just one!

In question 2, though, this bombed with an error – spot the deliberate mistake? The code is correct inasmuch as this is how you use the `.push()` method – the issue is that we're referring to an array that doesn't exist! If you modified the lines to use "cities" instead of "people," it will work as expected.

Our next question pushes a new value into the array – we now have four elements, not just three. At this point we're changing the contents of the cities array, so our observer is triggered; we can see the results of the newly updated array when entering the code shown in question 4.

In question 5 – we ask Ractive to return us the value of the array at position 1; as Ractive uses the same zero-base as JavaScript, this will return "Strasbourg" as the answer. We then replace the existing value of Bruges with Freibourg, by entering the `ractive.set` command in question 7, and a quick `ractive.get('cities')` will indeed confirm that the city name has been updated.

Okay – let's change focus slightly; until now, all of our examples have focused on triggering one action if a piece of data has changed. This isn't the limit of what `Ractive.observe()` can do; if needed, we can instigate a notification if any one of multiple triggers are fired.

At first glance this might sound a little crazy, but if we compare this to jQuery, it begins to make sense – there are occasions where we might have more than one way to trigger an observation. It's no different in Ractive; instead of setting three observers such as this:

```
ractive.observe('user.email ', updateServer);
ractive.observe('account.locked', updateServer);
ractive.observe('comments', updateServer);
```

...we can set one observe method, but apply all three triggers in the same statement:

```
ractive.observe('user.email account.locked comments', updateServer);
```

All we're doing is following the same principle used by jQuery – if all of the triggers point to the same notification process, then why write three lines of code, when we only need one?

While I leave that thought circulating in your mind, let's move on – it's time to get interactive! As Ractive is based on JavaScript, we can use it in conjunction with other libraries. What if we could get Ractive to talk to other libraries, instead of just using it in the same page?

Interacting with Other Libraries Using Adaptors

To adapt, or not adapt...that is the question...

To answer our question, one might be forgiven for thinking that it's not possible, or that we need to write lots of connecting code, just to make third-party libraries talk to Ractive. Yikes – the mere thought makes me shudder....

If truth be told, these answers are technically possible, but hardly the best way to solve this conundrum; instead, why not make use of adaptors? Leaving aside the poor attempt at misquoting Shakespeare at the start of this section, we can write an adaptor to effectively connect the libraries and get them talking to each other. If we were to do this, what benefit would we get? Well, there are two good reasons why this might help:

- We get a POJO, or Plain Old JavaScript Object – it's unfettered code that removes any custom formatting.

- Acts as a mirror for our data source, to capture and transfer changes from our third-party source to Ractive, and vice versa.

There are some good examples of adaptors available from the Ractive site; most notably, we have adaptors available for Backbone and adding Promise support directly, as Ractive objects. We'll work through the latter plugin in more detail a little later on in this chapter, but for now, let's explore the architecture of a standard adaptor in more detail.

Understanding the Architecture of an Adaptor

Ractive adaptors are not complicated – they act as a simple translation and sync layer between our data source and Ractive. Adaptors are designed to provide a POJO version of the data source to Ractive, then provide a mirror copy of that data through to Ractive.

There are a few key elements that should be present in any adaptor; let's take a look at the basic skeleton that makes up a typical adaptor, in more detail. We begin with a check to verify we're adapting the right type of object:

```
const myAdaptor = {
  filter: function ( object, keypath, ractive ) {
    // return `true` if a particular object is of the type we want to adapt.
  },
```

The filter function passes in the values shown in Table 3-2:

Table 3-2. *Values passed into filter function*

Property or function	Role it plays
object	The data source to adapt.
keypath	The keypath to object.
ractive	The Ractive instance that is currently using the adaptor.

Once we've determined that the adaptor should be applied, we need to set it up on our chosen object – the wrap function takes care of this role. It passes in the same values as before, along with prefixes to add the relevant keypath:

```
wrap: function ( ractive, object, keypath, prefixer ) {
  // Setup
```

At some point, we will need to remove it; the teardown function takes care of this, and cleans up any work that was done when the adaptor was set up:

```
return {
  teardown: function(){
    // Code executed on teardown.
  },
```

With the adaptor basics set up, it's time to call the methods that handle fetching and updating of data – the get method retrieves a plain JavaScript version of the adapted data:

```
get: function(){
  // Returns POJO version of your data backend.
},
```

We can then update the property against a specific keypath, using the set() method, with a new value:

```
set: function(property, value){
  // Data setter for POJO property keypaths.
},
```

Last, but by no means least, we have the reset method – this can be used to update the keypath, or tear down the adaptor:

```
    reset: function(value){ // Data setter for POJO keypath. }
  }
 }
};
```

Although setting up adaptors is very easy, it is worth bearing in mind that no two adaptors are likely to be the same – the final design means that it will be very specific to your requirements, and not one that can be reused without some change. There are a couple of other limitations we should we aware of, so let's cover these in more detail.

Exploring the Limitations of Adaptors

Adaptors are designed to be simple, to convert (or adapt) data to and from a back-end source to a Ractive instance. Their simplistic nature helps to keep our code performant and uncluttered, but there are a couple of considerations we should take into account when using them:

- Adaptors only adapt one level - An adaptor can only translate an object's immediate properties. If, for example, we have nested data in either the source or Ractive, it will not be updated, so it will need to be exposed as single items of data for an adaptor to work.

- No built-in infinite loop detection, for avoiding infinite loops – we may get a stack overflow error appear if we call ractive.set() on adapted data that fires a second ractive.set(), and so on. Ractive won't call the set() method if the data hasn't been changed. However we can't always easily tell if data has been changed in objects and arrays, so the method is called just in case the data might change, not because it has changed.

- Each adaptor will be different for each back-end data source – adaptors only provide the mechanism to talk, and listen, to the back-end data source. It won't apply any rules to dictate how this should happen, so an adaptor for an object will be different to an adaptor written to interact with a socket server.

Okay – enough of the theory: let's get practical! Over the new few pages we're going to create a simple adaptor to interface with a third-party plugin, which extracts the dominant color from an image. To get us started – let's take a look at an existing adaptor that is already available online, to see how we might create one later in this chapter.

Dissecting an Adaptor in the Wild

Adaptors are very easy to create, yet one of the downsides of using them is that they will be customized to your own requirements – this lack of clear reusability makes them less attractive to other developers. This said, they still serve a useful purpose if you don't want to have to write lots of code to manage conversion.

To see how simple they can be, we're going to dissect a copy of the Ractive-adaptors-Promise plugin by Lukas Werling, which is available from `http://lluchs.github.io/Ractive-adaptors-Promise/`. The full code listing is available at `https://github.com/lluchs/Ractive-adaptors-Promise/blob/master/src/Ractive-adaptors-Promise.js`; we'll focus on the part that is of most interest to us:

```
( typeof window !== 'undefined' ? window : this, function ( Ractive ) {

  'use strict';

  Ractive.adaptors.Promise = {
    filter: function ( object ) {
      // Detect "thenables" according to Promises/A+ §1.2.
      return object != null && typeof object.then === 'function';
    },
    wrap: function ( ractive, object, keypath, prefix ) {
      return new PromiseWrapper( ractive, object, keypath, prefix );
    }
};
```

This first block is where the magic happens – the first method within it verifies that the target is suitable for adapting, and the second takes care of the adaptation process. Lukas has separated out the code for the wrap function into its own distinct function; this may add a little confusion when reading the code for the first time. It however makes it easier to manage the code architecturally; as the wrap function is unlikely to change much, hiving it off makes the code simpler to manage as we can focus on the core part.

In this next block, the adaptor contains the PromiseWrapper object, which is called as a new instance in the preceding code.

```
function PromiseWrapper( ractive, object, keypath, prefix ) {
  var wrapper, setter;

  wrapper = this;
  setter = function ( result ) {
    // This wrapper might have been removed since.
    if ( !wrapper.removed )
      // Replace the wrapper with the actual result.
        ractive.set( keypath, result );
```

```
  };
  object.then( setter, setter );
}
```

The last part of the adaptor contains the methods we covered earlier in *Understanding the architecture of an adaptor* – it's worth noting that we're returning this as an object; this is slightly different to the standard architecture we talked about, but makes it easier to reference each method:

```
PromiseWrapper.prototype = {
  get: function () { return null; },
  set: function ( keypath, value ) {
    // No support for setting anything.
  },
  reset: function () { return false; },
  teardown: function () {
    // The Promises/A+ specification doesn't define a way to stop
    // "listening" to a Promise, so we just note the removal.
    this.removed = true;
  }
};
```

Now that we've explored a working plugin that is available in the wild, it's time – to create our own! For this next section, we're going to use a plugin to extract the prominent color from a photo, before adapting and merging the results into a Ractive instance.

Creating an Adaptor

One of the challenges faced by today's developer is that data will likely come from a variety of different sources, or need to be manipulated through use of a number of different plugins, to produce the desired result. A good example is an e-commerce website that sells hardware or electrical products; we might have a core database that stores the product details, but be supplemented by content from a different source, which contains safety or certification data.

This raises the natural question – how would we manage that data in a Ractive environment? The answer is by use of adaptors; we've touched on the basic architecture of such an adaptor, and covered an existing on in detail.

It's time for us to put this theory into practice, and create one for the first time. For our next demo, we'll use a JavaScript plugin to extract a dominant color from a photo, and render it on screen within a Ractive template. Figure 3-12 shows a completed screenshot of how such an example might look.

There are several plugins available on the Internet for this purpose – a good example is Vibrant.js by Jari Zwarts, which is available from http://jariz.github.io/vibrant.js/. This plugin was used to produce the screenshot shown in Figure 3-13 - the demo extracts a palette of five different colors from a photo, and renders the details of each on-screen.

Figure 3-13. *Extracting color values from a photo*

The colors produced range from a slightly desaturated red, through to the standard black, and finishes with a light grayish shade of orange. To really get the effect of what is possible, I would recommend viewing a Codepen that I've created, which shows this demo in action at `https://codepen.io/alexlibby/pen/bRGYay`.

Building the Demo

For our demo though, we're going to dial it back a bit, and use a simpler version – we'll use the Color Thief plugin by Lokesh Dhakar, available from `http://lokeshdhakar.com/projects/color-thief/`. It works in very much the same way as Vibrant.js – we can use it to get a color palette, or simply the dominant color. For our exercise, we will use the latter, along with the same photo; the finished article of what we'll create is displayed in Figure 3-14.

Figure 3-14. *Using Color Thief*

Before we get into creating our demo, there is one important point we should cover – we need to run this demo from within a web server; this can be a local web server such as Apache (`https://www.apache.org/`). If we try to run the demo from within the filesystem, then we're likely to see Canvas errors, such as the error shown in Figure 3-15:

```
⊗ Uncaught DOMException: Failed to execute 'getImageData' on
  'CanvasRenderingContext2D': The source width is 0.
```

Figure 3-15. *Canvas error*

My personal preference is to use WAMPServer, but if you have a personal preference, then please adjust the steps in the demo accordingly. We've touched on using Node.js and NPM when using Ractive, so if you want to use this route, then a good server to try is http-server, available from `https://www.npmjs.com/package/http-server`.

BUILDING OUR ADAPTOR

Okay – let's make a start; we'll work through setting up the demo. Don't worry about how it all works just yet – we will go through it in more detail afterward:

1. We'll break with tradition and create our demo from scratch – go ahead and create a new folder called `adaptor` in the `www` folder of our web server area.

2. In the file, add the following code, saving it as `adaptor.html` at the root of the `adaptor` folder:

```html
<!doctype html>
<html lang='en-GB'>
<head>
  <meta charset='utf-8'>
  <title>Beginning Ractive: Extacting Colors using Color Thief</title>
  <link rel='stylesheet' href='css/adaptor.css'>
</head>
<body>
  <div id="container"></div>

  <script id="template" type="text/ractive">
    <h3>Color Thief</h3>
    <p>Dominant color:</p>
    <p class="dominant" style="background-color: rgb({{dominant}})">
    RGB({{dominant}})</p>
    <img id="ctimage" src="img/demo-small.jpg">
  </script>

  <script src='js/ractive.min.js'></script>
  <script src='js/color-thief.min.js'></script>
  <script src='js/adaptor.js'></script>
</body>
</html>
```

3. We need to start adding our various script files – from the code download that accompanies this book, go ahead and extract the js folder that is with the adaptor folder. Save this within the adaptor subfolder we created at the start of this exercise.

4. Next up is the key to this exercise – our Ractive script! In a new file, go ahead and add the following code; we'll work through it section by section, beginning with setting a variable and initializing our adaptor:

```
var imgColor;
Ractive.adaptors.CTImg = {
```

5. The filter block checks to make sure that the adaptor is only applied to an image element:

```
filter: function ( object ) {
    // Detect if the data is an image element
    return object instanceof HTMLImageElement;
},
```

6. We set up the Color Thief plugin to work in the wrap function:

```
wrap: function ( ractive, object, keypath, prefixer ) {
    // Set up color thief for this piece of data because it's an image
    var colorThief = new ColorThief();
```

7. Once initialized, our adaptor returns a number of properties – teardown acts when the adaptor is destroyed:

```
    return {
teardown: function(){
    colorThief.destroy();
},
```

8. The get function takes our image and returns a value of type color as our replacement data:

```
get: function(){
    return colorThief.getColor(object);
},
```

9. We're not passing anything to Color Thief, so can leave the set function empty:

```
set: function(property, value){},
```

10. Finally if the return value from Color Thief changes, we need to update it in our Ractive instance:

```
        reset: function(value){
            // Always replace the data when the data is changed
            return false;
```

```
          }
        }
      }
    };
```

11. Save the file as `adaptor.js`, within the `js` subfolder of the adaptor folder we created back in step 1. With the adaptor set up, we can add it into our Ractive instance – go ahead and add this at the bottom of our script file, leaving 2–3 lines blank before it:

```
var ractive = new Ractive({
  target: '#container',
  template: '#template',
  adapt: [ 'CTImg' ],
  data: { dominant: null },
  onrender: function(){
    // set image on data. adaptor will capture it.
    this.set('dominant', this.find('#ctimage'))
  }
});
```

12. To finish, we need to add some CSS styling, an image, and a font – drop the following code into a new file, saving it as `adaptor.css` in a `css` subfolder within our project area:

```
@font-face { font-family: 'robotoregular'; src: url('../font/Roboto-Regular-
webfont.woff') format('woff'); font-weight: normal; font-style: normal; }
body { font-family: robotoregular, sans-serif; font-size: 0.875rem;
font-weight: 300; padding: 2rem; }
img {margin-left: 13.25rem; margin-top: -9.4rem; }
h3 { font-size: 2rem; font-weight: 100; margin-top: 0; }
#container { border: 0.0625rem solid #000; width: 36rem; border-radius: 0.4rem;
padding: 1rem; }
.dominant { width: 10.9375rem; padding: 0.3125rem; color: #000; border: 1px solid
#000; height: 0.9375rem; }
p.dominant { font-size: 1rem; line-height: 1rem; color: #fff; text-align: center; }
```

13. All that remains are an image and font – go ahead and extract a copy of the `img` and `font` folders from the code download that accompanies this book, then save both to the adaptor folder in our project area.

If all is well, when previewing the results, we should see our image displayed, along with the RGB value for the most dominant color within the image, as shown in Figure 3-16.

Figure 3-16. *The finished article*

Phew – it feels like we may have covered a lot, but if we break down our demo into several smaller parts, it isn't as hard as it looks! We will go through the detail shortly, but before we do so, we need to cover one last point about how we register and use our adaptor.

Registering and Using Our Adaptor

Creating our adaptor is only part of the story – before we can use it, we have to register it within our Ractive instance. Take another look at our adaptor code:

```
Ractive.adaptors.CTImg = { ... }
```

This is one way to register our adaptor – in this instance, we've registered it against the `Ractive.adaptors` static property, although ideally we should rewrite the first line to be more akin to this:

```
myAdaptors = { ... }
```

...and reference it using `Ractive.adaptors.myAdaptors = CTImg`, in place of what we have used in our demo. There are two other options that we can use to register adaptors; this depends on how we plan to use our adaptor:

- We can register it globally, via the `Ractive.adaptors` static property:

  ```
  Ractive.adaptors.myAdaptor = myAdaptor;
  ```

- We can register on a per component basis, via the component's `adaptors` initialization property:

  ```
  const MyComponent = Ractive.extend({
    adaptors: { myAdaptor }
  });
  ```

- In some instances, we may not want to make our adaptor available globally; we can instead register it on a per instance basis, via the instance's adaptors initialization property:

```
const ractive = new Ractive({
  adaptors: { myAdaptor }
});
```

Once our adaptor has been registered, we can now reference it in our Ractive instance – for this, we can make use of the adapt array or adaptors map: let's take a look at how they work in more detail.

Using Our Adaptor

With our adaptor registered, we can now use it within our Ractive instance – let's remind ourselves of the code we used in our demo:

```
var ractive = new Ractive({
  ...
  adapt: [ 'CTImg' ],
  ...
});
```

The CTImg refers to our adaptor – we use the adapt array to list all of the adaptors that need to be added to our instance, as summarized in Table 3-3:

Table 3-3. *Registering an adaptor*

Property	Description and usage
adapt (Array <string | Object>)	An array of adaptors to use. Values can either be names of registered adaptors or an adaptor definition. Format: `adapt: [ 'MyAdaptor', AdaptorDefinition ]`

adaptors
(Object <string | Object>)
	A map of adaptors where the key is the adaptor name and the value is an adaptor definition:
	
	`adaptors: { MyAdaptor: AdaptorDefinition }`
	
	We don't have to register an adaptor via adaptors if it is directly specified in the adaptor definition via adapt:
	
	`const Adaptor = { … };`
	`const instance = new Ractive({`
	`  adapt: [ AdaptorDefinition ]`
	`  // No need to use adaptors`
	`});`

Note though – if we registered adaptors in our instance using the adaptors initialization property, then there is no need to use adapt. Adaptors registered in this way are automatically used as if they had been set with adapt:

```
const instance = new Ractive({
  adaptors: { MyAdaptor: AdaptorDefinition } // No need to use adapt
});

const Component = Ractive.extend({
  adaptors: { MyAdaptor: AdaptorDefinition } // No need to use adapt
});

new Component({
  // No need to use adapt
});
```

Okay – let's move on: we've seen our adaptor at work with the Color Thief plugin, but I'll bet you have a dozen questions, right? Like – how does it work? What can I use with it? Isn't it overkill to use with a plugin like Color Thief? These are all good questions, so let's explore this and more in detail, to help understand how we can best use adaptors.

Exploring How the Adaptor Works

If we want to expand the art of the possible with Ractive, then one route we can take is to use adaptors – this simple tool can really increase what we can do with other plugins when working with this library. To understand how, it's important to come to grips with the architecture of a typical adaptor, as shown in Figure 3-17. We will do this using the context of the example adaptor we created earlier in this chapter:

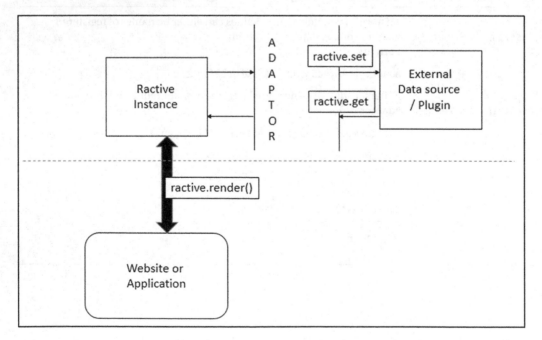

Figure 3-17. A schematic of a typical adaptor

We start with our web page – this provides the template for what should be shown on screen; there are no changes required to placeholders for our data.

The changes start to appear in our Ractive script file – our adaptor first filters out each element, to ensure that we apply the filter only when needed, that is, on an image, and not another element such as an <input> field. Within the wrap function, we set up a new instance of our plugin, then use the ractive.set() and ractive.get() methods to manage our data. This is the important part, as we don't always have to use both – this will depend on whether we're simply collecting data, or the data transfer is a two-way process.

In our instance, we don't use the ractive.set() method at all, as we're not providing information to Ractive; we just need to use ractive.get() to retrieve that information. But hold on, I hear you ask – how are we setting the desired image for Color Thief to work on? We handle that through setting object as a type HTMLImageElement. The trick here is in the use of the .onrender() method in our Ractive instance; we're not simply inserting static data into a mustache, but calculating which color value to return and render when calling the plugin. This method contains a function to find the image with the ID of ctimage, so it will only work on this image.

Now – don't get me wrong: creating an adaptor as a lightweight way of translating information from a plugin to Ractive, has its benefits. However, it may not always be the right solution: what if we need to write a good chunk of code to rework the values from a plugin, to fit into Ractive? Is using an adaptor sufficient, or should we use a component instead?

Creating Our Adaptor – an Epilogue

Over the course of the last few pages, we've worked through creating a simple adaptor that interfaces with the Color Thief plugin. At face value, it seems to work very well, but – there is one question that some of you may be asking: do we really need an adaptor, and if so, why?

Ordinarily we might not – there is nothing stopping us from using the Color Thief (or indeed Vibrant.js) plugin as it was intended; after all, as long as we can access our chosen element, then the plugin will work. However, there's a downside to this – what if the element doesn't exist, or isn't available at the time we use a plugin? How about trying to manipulate the data using Ractive at a later date?

There are a number of good reasons for wanting to use adaptors – let's take a look at a few:

- We don't have to write lots of extra code to manipulate how plugins work with Ractive – instead, we just take the resulting data and pass it into a Ractive keypath / reference;

- Plugins do not need to be adapted to work with Ractive, which makes upgrading them easier, and helps maintain separation of concerns;

- We can always manipulate the resulting data in Ractive at a later stage – to do so outside of Ractive might require lots of extra jQuery or JavaScript code, which makes it harder to manipulate, and increases page speed times;

- Components allow us to encapsulate existing plugins, and provide extra functionality – this will add extra weight to the page that may not be necessary;

- Ractive components can be hived off into a separate file for portability, but this means that we will be making more requests to the server, if our page is component heavy – adaptors are small and lightweight, and can sit in the same script file as our Ractive instance.

The key though to making the right choice will depend on a couple of factors – can an existing plugin produce the desired result, and how much would have to be adapted if the final result isn't quite what we want? If the plugin we're using already produces the right result, then all we need to do is to create an adaptor that provides the filter that passes content through to Ractive. If, however, the result requires a degree of work before we can use it, then we may prefer to create our own plugin, rather than add lots of extra code to manipulate that result. There is no right or wrong answer per se, but experience over time will soon give you an indication as to which is the right path to take!

Summary

A key concept when working with Ractive is managing data interaction - after all, without the glue between individual elements and what we see onscreen, we won't get very far! Let's take a moment to review what we've covered in this chapter.

We kicked off with a look at the basic principles of data-binding in Ractive, with particular focus on how we can manage data dependencies, be they direct or indirect. We also took a look at how computed properties can help simplify the calculation of our data.

Next up, we covered how we can be notified of any changes to our data, and use various API methods to perform tasks as soon as we have been notified of such changes. We also explored what might happen when we need to monitor for changes where we must use a wildcard type pattern to reference data.

We then rounded out the chapter with an extensive look at creating adaptors - this covered the basic format of such an adaptor, a look at one already in the wild, and the various steps to build, register, and use our adaptor. Last but by no means least, we explored how the adaptor worked, before covering off some final points on using adaptors.

Right - let's move on: we've covered the basic components of Ractive, explored how to create templates, and examined the various methods available to manage data. This is all good, but what happens when content is changed? This will spark some form of event, which we need to manage; that handling process will be the subject of the next chapter.

CHAPTER 4

■ ■ ■

Handling Events

We've created our templates and set up Ractive to manage our data, but hold on – what are we missing? How about responding to events that might be fired by elements on our page? Ractive, like other libraries, uses a publish / subscribe mechanism to manage events – indeed, you will see similarities to other libraries, such as jQuery. Over the course of this chapter, we'll dive in and take a look at how Ractive manages events, from using directives or event plugins, through to applying multiple events from a single handler.

Publishing and Subscribing to Events

A question – how many times have you written event handlers such as addEventListener('click', event), or $("input").on("click", handler)?

I'll bet the answer is a thousand times – Ractive, like many libraries, uses its own variant of the publish/subscribe mechanism to manage similar events. What makes it particularly attractive though is that Ractive-managed events are automatically unsubscribed and cleaned up at the point of teardown; this removes the need to do manual housekeeping. We have the added bonus that Ractive's code is very similar to that of jQuery, which makes learning very easy!

So – what does a typical Ractive event look like? Anyone who has spent time developing in jQuery will, of course, be familiar with the $("selector").on() mechanism; the same .on() and .off() event handlers are also available within Ractive. This is just a small part of what is available – Ractive events fall into five types: event API, lifecycle, DOM, custom, and component. All play their own individual role, although some will look very similar – this even includes their similarity to standard jQuery events!

This similarity in appearance to jQuery makes them easy to learn – we will in due course explore some of the theory behind how they operate, but there's no substitute for seeing things in action! With this in mind, let's turn our attention to building a simple demo that shows some basic events in operation.

Getting Acquainted with Events

For our next exercise, we're going to display the key code for any key pressed from the keyboard. It's a very simple demo, but perfect for showing off the basic type of event that is available in Ractive.

© Alex Libby 2017

A. Libby, *Beginning Ractive.js*, https://doi.org/10.1007/978-1-4842-3093-0_4

We'll build this one from scratch, so let's make a start:

SIMPLE EVENTS 1

1. We'll begin by creating a folder in our project area – call it simple events 1. Within this folder, create two new folders, called js and css.

2. In a new file, add the following code, saving it as simpleevents.html in the simple events 1 folder:

```html
<!doctype html>
<html lang='en-GB'>
<head>
  <meta charset='utf-8'>
  <title>Beginning Ractive: Getting Acquainted with Events</title>
  <link rel='stylesheet' href='css/simpleevents.css'>
</head>
<body>
  <h1>Creating Simple Events in Ractive</h1>
  <div id='container'></div>

  <script id="template" type="text/ractive">
    <p>Character code of key pressed:</p>
    <p><input value="{{keycode}}" on-keydown="@this.set('keycode', @event.
    keyCode), @event.preventDefault()"></p>
  </script>
  <script src='js/ractive.min.js'></script>
  <script src="js/simpleevents.js"></script>
</body>
</html>
```

3. This is just a start – to bring it to life, we need to add our Ractive script! In a second new file, add the following code – save it as simpleevents.js within the js subfolder we created in step 1:

```js
var ractive = new Ractive({
  template: '#template',
  el: '#container'
});
```

4. We need a copy of the Ractive library, so go ahead and extract a copy of ractive.min.js from the code download that accompanies this book, and put it in the js subfolder.

5. The last step is to add some simple styling – we won't win any awards anytime soon, but we can still make our demo look reasonable. For this, go ahead and add the following code to a new file, saving it as `simpleevents.css` within the `css` subfolder of our demo:

    ```
    @font-face { font-family: 'robotoregular'; src: url('../font/Roboto-Regular-
    webfont.woff') format('woff'); font-weight: normal; font-style: normal; }
    body { font-family: robotoregular, sans-serif; font-size: 0.875rem; padding:
    2rem; }
    #container { border: 1px solid #000; width: 30rem; clear: both; border-radius:
    0.4rem; padding: 1rem; }
    ```

If all is good, we should see something akin to the screenshot shown in Figure 4-1, when previewing the results in a browser:

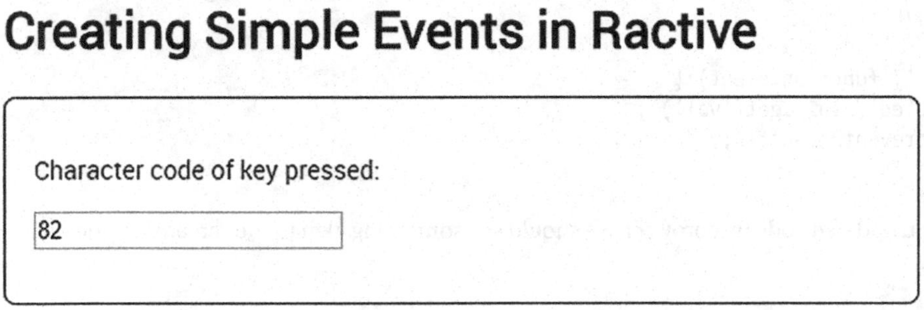

Creating Simple Events in Ractive

Character code of key pressed:

82

Figure 4-1. *Creating a simple event*

Try clicking inside the input field, then pressing any keys on your keyboard – the input field will show the two-digit code for that character. This simple demo is perfect to get started, but there is one small thing that isn't so good. Hopefully you will have noticed the inline JavaScript – doesn't look great having it there, right?

Amending Our Demo

Granted, it doesn't look great, having inline JavaScript in that line of code – at face value, it means we can't maintain separation of concerns; above all, it looks a messy if we have JavaScript peppering our HTML markup.

But hold on – it's not inline JavaScript. What, I hear you say – that is plain JavaScript, surely? In this instance – it's not JavaScript as such; the on-keydown method is a Ractive directive. Put simply, this tells Ractive to render this as a separate `.addEventLister()` method. In our case, the code would appear something akin to this:

```
input.addEventListener('keydown', function(event) {
  @this.set('keycode', @event.keyCode);
  @event.preventDefault();
});
```

It's worth noting though that you won't see any code rendered as such on the DOM or as inline JavaScript – this is to prevent polluting our markup with too much extraneous code.

In almost complete contrast, we can almost avoid the need to specify a function in some instances: if all we need to do was submit a form, then the following markup would accomplish this:

```
<div id='container'></div>

<script id="template" type="text/ractive">
  <form on-submit="submit">
    <input value="{{val}}">
  </form>
  <p>Text submitted: {{submitted}}</p>

  <p>Character code of key pressed:</p>
```

Go ahead and add the highlighted code to a copy of the simple event 1 demo, along with this markup into the js file within that project:

```
ractive.on('submit', function(event) {
  this.set('submitted', this.get('val'));
  event.original.preventDefault();
})
```

If we then run the updated code in a browser, we should see something akin to the screenshot shown in Figure 4-2:

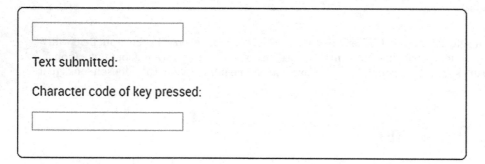

Creating Simple Events in Ractive

Text submitted:

Character code of key pressed:

Figure 4-2. *Updated events demo*

This time around, any text entered into the top <input> field will be rendered on screen when pressing Enter. Ractive takes care of the submission process automatically, as part of its two-way data binding that happens in the background.

To experience this in action, try running simpleevents2.html from the code download that accompanies this book.

At this stage, you may be wondering how this all works; I'll bet it feels like there should be more code involved, right?

Well, sorry to disappoint: this is as about as complex as it gets! Ractive was always designed to be simple and quick to use – granted, there are some additional features we can use (and will cover), but the core part of adding an event can be as simple as the one-liner in our demo.

Handling Different Event Types

Although technically the code is very straightforward, we should be aware of the different types of events that can be published within Ractive. In many cases, the syntax for each will be similar, but nevertheless there are five event types that can be generated:

- Event API events – published as a result of using the event APIs directly, such as `ractive.fire('someevent', 'Hello Ractive!')`.

- Lifecycle events published by an instance during each phase of its existence. This includes events such as `construct()`, `config()`, `update()`, or `teardown()`.

- Events published by the DOM, such as `<input onclick="...">`.

- Custom events, published by event plugins.

- Events, published by components, such as `<MyModal on-close="...">`.

Let's take a look at each event type in more detail, starting with publishing directly on a Ractive instance.

Publishing Directly

The simplest, and most direct, is to use the Event API directly on a Ractive instance – the syntax is very similar to that of jQuery. To see what I mean, let's rewrite the equivalent of that `ractive.fire ('someevent...')` example – if we had used jQuery, it would look like this: `$("element").trigger ('click', { greeting: "Hello, reader!" })`. Although the keywords used are clearly different, the format and syntax bear a close resemblance to jQuery. This makes it a cinch to create code that triggers event handlers, such as this example:

```
ractive.fire('welcome', 'Hello, reader!')
```

Other types of event sources will use event APIs to publish similar events at various points in their operation – let's take a look at the rest, in turn, beginning with lifecycling events.

Lifecycling Events

The second type of event will be apparent at different stages of the life of a Ractive instance – a range of different events (of type `function`) will be published at some point in the cycle, as indicated in Table 4-1:

Table 4-1. *Lifecycle events*

Name of event	A lifecycle event that is called when...
onconstruct	An instance is constructed but before any initialization option has been processed. Accepts the instance's initialization options as argument.
onconfig	An instance is constructed and all initialization options have been processed.
oninit	An instance is constructed and is ready to be rendered.
onrender	An instance is rendered but before transitions start.
oncomplete	An instance is rendered and all the transitions have completed.
onupdate	...`ractive.update()` is called.
oninsert	...`ractive.insert()` is called.
ondetach	...`ractive.detach()` is called. Note that `ractive.insert()` implicitly calls `ractive.detach()` if needed.
onunrender	... the instance is being de-rendered.
onteardown	.... the instance is being torn down.
ondestruct	...an instance is torn down and any associated transitions are complete.

An important point to keep in mind is that lifecycle event names are reserved, so they cannot be used as names for other events. We can also use the direct Event APIs to subscribe to lifecycle events, although there is a catch – the handler must be set prior to the event being published. This is all about timing: the safest option is to use an event's initialization options to ensure that each event is fired at an appropriate point.

Proxy Syntax

There are occasions when we might need to create event handlers to respond to events that don't yet exist. A great example is adding items to a shopping cart – after all, we can't update or remove something that doesn't exist in our cart, right?

To cater for this, Ractive makes available a proxy syntax that we can use, for this purpose. This inserts (or "proxies") events into our Ractive instance, from which event APIs handle each event:

```
Ractive({
  template: `
    <button on-click="buttonsubmit">Click to submit</button>
  `,
  oninit(){
    this.on('buttonsubmit', event => {
      console.log('button clicked')
    })
  }
})
```

In this instance, the `oninit()` lifecycle event is called as soon as our Ractive instance has been initialized and is ready to be rendered on-screen.

Expression Syntax

The third form of event is a little more complicated – how about combining the power of expressions with events?

This powerful combination opens up some real possibilities – instead of providing static values, we can get Ractive to calculate values based on expressions. These act in a similar fashion to inline scripts, with unfettered access to data, along with some additions and use of some special references, such as @this, @index, and @key.

The special references are listed in full at `https://ractive.js.org/api/#special-references`.

The expression syntax comes in two formats – a variation of the proxy syntax, and direct use of expressions. The first format accepts an array of values, where the first is the name of the event triggering the action, and the rest are arguments:

```
Ractive({
  el: 'body',
  template: `
    <button on-click="['buttonclicked', 'abc', 'xyz']">Click Me!</button>
  `,
  oninit(){
    this.on('buttonclicked', (event, msg, foo) => {
      console.log(msg + ' button clicked');
      console.log('This is the second value being passed: ' + foo);
    })
  }
})
```

This in some respects is akin to jQuery's event handler, where we might write something like this:

```
$("button").on('click', function(event, msg, foo) {
  console.log(msg + ' button clicked passing');
  console.log('This is the second value being passed: ' + foo);
});
```

Now we can see how similar Ractive is – the only real difference (apart from the syntax) being that we're embedding this function within a lifecycle event in our Ractive instance, and not on its own (as we might do with jQuery). In our Ractive example, we can simply make use of the values being passed, as shown in Figure 4-3:

```
                             Output

You're running Ractive 0.9.3 in debug mode - messages
application.

abc button clicked

This is the second value being passed: xyz
```

Figure 4-3. *Using the proxy form of expression syntax*

The second format is where things get interesting – we can use the power of expressions to work out dynamically what we're going to display! This opens up a host of possibilities for us: it might at first look intimidating, but it is worth bearing in mind that the functions we've included are very similar to ones we've already used. We're just putting them inline, and using the on- directive to tell Ractive to render these as addEventListener functions. Take a look at this example:

```
Ractive({
  el: 'body',
  data: { msg: '' },
  template: `
    <p>
      Value A: {{foo}}
      Value B: {{bar}}
    </p>
    <button on-click="@this.set('msg', 'Hello, World!')">Set message</button>
    <button on-click="@this.welcome(msg)">Print message</button>
    <button on-click="@this.fire('manualproxy', msg)">Print message via proxy</button>
    <button on-click="@this.set('foo', 1), @this.set('bar', 2)">Cccombo!!! </button>
  `,
  welcome(message){
    console.log(`${message}`);
  },
  oninit(){
    this.on('manualproxy', (event, message) => {
      console.log(`${message}`);
    });
  }
});
```

The @this reference points to our current instance of Ractive – in order, we're setting the typical "Hello, World!" message, before printing the message (either directly or via proxy), and finally setting two mustache references with one click.

Now – firing events may be great, but what if we need to know what triggered that event? Yes – there may be occasions where we need to know what type of event was responsible for effecting a change, or rendering output on screen. Thankfully we can do this really easily within Ractive – we can trap for a specific type of event, and take a course of action depending on what takes place. The downside is that we can't pass values to this function – this really is meant as a kind of signpost-only effect! Let's dive in and see what this means in reality for us.

Setting Event Context

If we construct a site or online application of some description, then it is a given that we will almost certainly (I would even say definitely) that we will trigger an event of some description. It goes without saying that it's not a case of if we trigger one, but when we trigger it!

On occasion, we may need to determine what triggered the event – getting this information is a cinch within Ractive. Any event handler that we create will always receive an event object as the first argument; we can use this to determine what type of event took place. Event objects within Ractive are a special instance of context objects, with some additional properties as appropriate.

You can see a list of context objects at `https://ractive.js.org/api/#context-object`.

The list of available properties is shown in Table 4-2:

Table 4-2. *A list of event context properties*

Property	Purpose
name	The name of the published event.
node	A reference to the DOM node publishing the event. Only available on DOM events.
event	A reference to the DOM event. Only available on DOM.
original	A reference to the DOM event. Only available on DOM.
component	A reference to the component that published the event. Only available on propagated events.

If we were to translate this into a working example, then it might look something like this:

```
Ractive({
  el: 'body',
  template: `
    <button on-click="buttonclicked">Click Me!</button><br>
    First name: <input on-click="buttonclicked" type="email" name="fname">
  `,
  oninit(){
    this.on('buttonclicked', event => {
      console.log(event.node.type); // submit
      if (event.node.type == "submit") {
        alert("The event type is submit");
      }
    });
  }
});
```

When run in a Codepen or using the Ractive playground, we might expect to see output such as that shown in Figure 4-4:

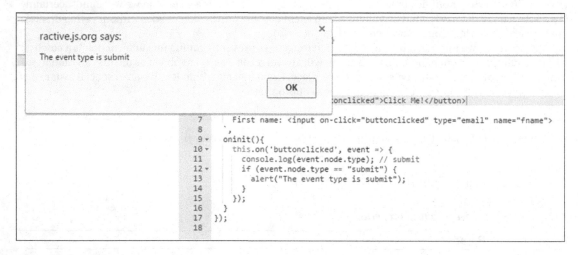

Figure 4-4. *Setting event context*

The key here is to treat the event as merely a means of working out which event fired – if we need to work out changes to values, or pass values to functions, then we can do this from within; we can't pass values to the `button-clicked` event handler.

Okay – time we moved on: let's explore something new. If we're in a position where we have a lot of events that are very similar that need to be triggered at some point, then a natural thing to do would be to write event handlers for each of them, right? It will work, but it's wasteful – why write multiple event handlers when we may only need to write one or two? Confused? Let me explain all – we can use wildcards to pattern match names in Ractive, so let's put them to good use and explore using them to handle events.

Using Wildcards in Events

A useful feature of events in Ractive is the ability to use pattern matching: this allows us to use a form of namespacing when creating events.

Namespacing, I hear you ask – what does that mean? Well, consider this: Let's say we have a dozen buttons on a page. The normal thing would be to write event handlers that catered for each button – but that is wasteful at several levels. If the buttons all perform very similar roles, then we will potentially be adding a fair amount of duplicate code, which adds unnecessary page weight and reduces our load times!

A better alternative is to use namespacing – we can add a tag to each event name; we can then write a single event handler that caters for multiple events. The net result is that we don't have to provide event handlers for every event we create; it may be sufficient to provide a couple, to achieve the same result. Not sure how this might work? I could explain, but there's no better substitute than seeing this in action, so let's set up a demo to see how this works.

Creating Namespaced Events

For this demo, we could use any number of different events – a good example though is the ubiquitous `.click()`, or at least the equivalent in Ractive! We'll set up a number of buttons in our template, then apply either one of two namespaced event handlers to each button.

NAMESPACE EVENTS

Let's get cracking:

1. We'll start by taking a copy of the `simple events 2` folder from a copy of the code download that accompanies this book, and save it as `namespace events` in our project area.

2. Within this new folder, go ahead and delete the `img` folder, then remove the `simpleevents2.js` file from the `js` subfolder in our new folder, and `simpleevents2.css` from the `css` folder.

3. Next, we need to update our markup – at the root of our new folder, delete the `simpleevents2.html` file. In a new file, add the following markup, saving it as `namespace.html`:

```html
<!doctype html>
<html lang='en-GB'>
<head>
  <meta charset='utf-8'>
  <title>Beginning Ractive: Creating Namespaced Events in Ractive</title>
  <link rel='stylesheet' href='css/namespace.css'>
</head>
<body>
  <h1>Creating Namespaced Events in Ractive</h1>

  <script src='js/ractive.min.js'></script>
  <script src="js/namespace.js"></script>
</body>
</html>
```

4. Okay – our markup is in place; we now need to make it work. For this, go ahead and add the following code to a new file, saving it as `namespace.js` inside the `js` subfolder:

```javascript
Ractive({
  el: 'body',
  append: true,
  template:
    '<div id = "container">' +
      '<button on-click="abc.bar">Click Me!</button>' +
      '<button on-click="abc.baz">Click Me!</button>' +
      '<button on-click="abc.bam">Click Me!</button>' +
      '<button on-click="abc.bar">Press Me!</button>' +
```

```
        '<button on-click="event.baz">Click Me!</button>' +
        '<button on-click="event.bam">Click Me!</button>' +
      '</div>',
    oninit(){
      this.on('*.bar', event => {
        window.alert('A bar event was published')
      })
      this.on('event.*', event => {
        console.log('An event button was clicked')
      })
    }
  })
```

At this point, our demo will work perfectly well as-is; to make it look a little more presentable though, let's add a little styling.

5. Add the following rules to a new file, saving it as `namespace.css` in our `css` subfolder:

```
@font-face { font-family: 'robotoregular'; src: url('../font/Roboto-Regular-
webfont.woff') format('woff'); font-weight: normal; font-style: normal; }

body { font-family: robotoregular, sans-serif; font-size: 0.875rem; padding:
2rem; }

button { margin-right: 0.625rem; }
h1 { margin-top: 6.25rem; }
```

Our demo is now ready to run – if we preview the results, we should see something akin to the screenshot in Figure 4-5:

Figure 4-5. *Viewing namespaced events*

Although this is a simple demo, it illustrates a key point when using events – we are not obliged to have to provide handlers that are tied to a specific event. Instead, we can create an event handler that can be triggered by multiple events, as long as the name matches the wildcard pattern being used. This is important to understand, so let's take a moment to explore what this means in practice.

Exploring What Happened

So – what did happen here? Well, in the main, we're using a standard Ractive on-click directive, but with a couple of differences.

The first change is in the directive itself:

```
'<button on-click="event.bam">Click Me!</button>' +
```

Notice the highlighted code in the above example? This is the **namespacing** – all we're doing is applying a shared tag to one or more click event handlers. Even though (as in our example), the two events didn't have an identical event handler applied to them, they still used the same one – the pattern set in the handler matches the names given, so the event can be fired:

```
this.on('event.*', event => {
  console.log('An event button was clicked')
})
```

Why is this important? It is all to do with duplication – or rather the ability to reduce or remove it! I know this example might be a little contrived, so bear with me on this:

Consider that for a moment, we have a simple calendar, where clicking on each day will produce a list of what happens each day. Now – we won't have anything on weekends, but we might have different things happen on each weekday.

Instead of providing different click handlers for each day, we could provide a namespaced handler for weekdays, one for Saturdays, and one for Sundays. Assuming that we have 30 days in a month (okay, I know some have 31, but it's just an example!) – we can already reduce the number of weekday click handlers from 20+ to one, Saturday handlers from four to 1, and the same for Sundays. A lot more efficient, I am sure you will agree!

Okay – let's change tack and sail on to look at another feature (groan – sorry: pun intended!) in Ractive – event propagation. There may be times when we have a number of child elements inside a parent element, and that we need to assign click handlers to both. By default, most event handlers assigned to inner elements will bubble up to their parent elements; in this instance, click handlers applied to the inner elements will also fire the parent element. This isn't always desirable – we can manage this by blocking it; before we do so, let's take a look at how event propagation works within Ractive.

Managing Event Propagation

Event propagation is not a new concept – it, or rather event bubbling as it should be termed in this instance – has been around for some years. It was designed to allow for those instances where we might trigger a click, but have multiple event handlers respond. In a nutshell, the innermost event is triggered first (such as a link in a table), but this will bubble up to each containing element and trigger this at the same time until such time as it can no longer trigger an event or it reaches the top.

Why is this important? Well, there may be occasions where we create events that have to act on inner elements, but that the event handler bubbles up to parent elements and leads to undesirable effects. In an ideal world, we should create events that only act on specific elements, but there are occasions when we may have to limit propagation. Event propagation is so prone to causing issues, that Philip Walton wrote a detailed article on the pitfalls of blocking it, and why it is better to leave events to run as intended.

You can see Philip's article on the CSS-Tricks website at `https://css-tricks.com/dangers-stopping-event-propagation/`.

Leaving aside the pitfalls, there may be occasions when we have to control propagation – in Ractive, propagation falls into one of two categories: DOM and Component. We'll cover component propagation later in Chapter 6, but for now, let's explore how we can control propagation at a DOM level in more detail.

Building Our Demo

For this demo, we're going to completely change how we run it – up until now, we've either built our exercises using a text editor, or in a Codepen. These have worked well, but in each instance we've had to add in links for the Ractive library, CSS, etc – it's a pain when you do this multiple times, and that it isn't always necessary! Instead, we're going to use an online playground that has been set up for quick tests such as this – it's available at `http://ractive.js.org/playground`.

If you prefer to use more traditional playgrounds, this demo is available at `https://codepen.io/alexlibby/pen/MoJERM` (with event propagation not set), and at `https://codepen.io/alexlibby/pen/GErmwO` (with event propagation set).

MANAGING EVENT PROPAGATION

Let's take a look:

1. Fire up a new browser session, and head over to `https://ractive.js.org/playground`.

2. Click on the cog symbol, then scroll down to the External Scripts section, and set the Ractive.js entry to Latest.

3. Click on the Script tab to the right, and paste in the following:

```
Ractive({
  el: 'body',
  template: `
    <div on-click="ancestorbuttonclick">
      <button on-click="descendantbuttonclick">Click Me!</button>
    </div>
  `,
  oninit(){
    this.on('ancestorbuttonclick', event => {
      console.log('This will not run');
    });
    this.on('descendantbuttonclick', event => {
      console.log('This will run');
      return false;
    });
  }
});
```

4. Hit the green right arrow to the top right of the playground window, then click on the `Output` tab about halfway down the screen.

5. You will see a `Click Me!` button — try clicking on it a few times.

6. Go ahead and click on the Console tab to the right – you will see the results of this clicking action there; it will only show the descendantbuttonclick handler having been fired (as illustrated in Figure 4-6):

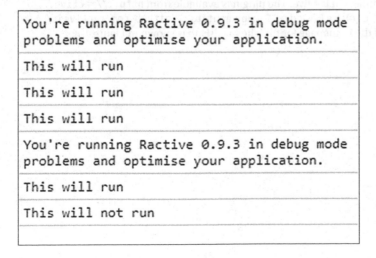

> Output
>
> You're running Ractive 0.9.3 in debug mode - problems and optimise your application.
>
> This will run
>
> This will run
>
> This will run

Figure 4-6. Output of a propagated event

7. Try removing the return false; statement at line 14, then the green right arrow, before clicking the same Click Me! button again a few times – what do you get?

8. Press Ctrl + Z to reinstate line 14 – running the demo again and clicking on the green arrow should confirm that we only see one statement in the console window.

In answer to step 6, we should see that both event handlers fired – Ractive will automatically bubble up to the parent handler, unless we set return false; within the child event handler. We can see the evidence in the screenshot shown in Figure 4-7:

> You're running Ractive 0.9.3 in debug mode problems and optimise your application.
>
> This will run
>
> This will run
>
> This will run
>
> You're running Ractive 0.9.3 in debug mode problems and optimise your application.
>
> This will run
>
> This will not run

Figure 4-7. Output of not setting event propagation

If return false; has been set in an event handler (which isn't recommended), this will stop propagation. Ractive will automatically check to see if the event is a DOM event; if it is, then event. stopPropagation() and event.preventDefault() will be called automatically, so that our event handler does not bubble up and cause unexpected results elsewhere in our code.

■ **Tip** If you want to clear the console window in the Ractive playground at any time, then hit the Ø symbol to the far right.

Okay – let's move on: it's time to take things up a notch! So far, we've explored how to use events within Ractive, but what about creating custom events? Many events can be catered for with the standard handlers available in Ractive, but there may be occasions when creating a new one might be more useful. It's straightforward to create one, so let's begin by dissecting one already available in the wild, before we create own plugin.

Dissecting an Event Plugin

When working with Ractive for the first time, it's easy to get swallowed by the wide array of event options available for configuring each instance, or which are triggered within a Ractive-enabled page.

However, there will come a time when we outgrow what Ractive can offer as part of core, or we find we're creating the same event code time and again – code that would be better served as a plugin! There are a number of event type plugins already available; the most complete list so far is available on the Ractive documentation site at https://ractive.js.org/integrations/#plugins/, although it is worth searching with Google to see if others are available that have yet to be listed on the site.

So – what does a plugin look like? Well, there is a standard format we can follow to create such a plugin – we can either use the plugin template option available from https://github.com/ractivejs/plugin-template, or code it by hand – we'll explore this in more detail, a little later on this chapter. For now, let's take a look at one available in the wild to understand how Ractive plugins work.

There are several examples we can use, but a nice simple one is ractive-events-keys – this was created by Rich Harris, one of the developers of Ractive. The plugin is available from https://ractive. js.org/ractive-events-keys/, with the source hosted on GitHub at https://github.com/ractivejs/ ractive-events-keys. A screenshot of the homepage for this site in GitHub is shown in Figure 4-8:

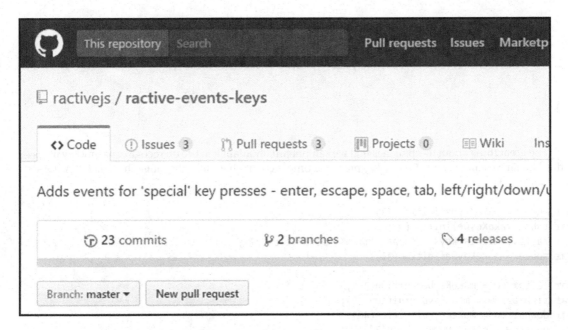

Figure 4-8. *The ractive-events-keys plugin on GitHub*

Head over to main source for the plugin, at https://github.com/ractivejs/ractive-events-keys/ blob/master/src/ractive-events-keys.js; there, you will see the core functionality of this plugin. The plugin is a couple of years old, but the principle is still valid.

Now that we've been introduced, let's explore the code block by block, so we can see how it works in more detail. We begin with the makeKeyDefinition function, which takes a number as an argument; this number will relate to the key being pressed at the point the function is called. Within this function we have the keydownHandler event handler; this gets the key code for the button just pressed:

```
function makeKeyDefinition(code) {
  return function (node, fire) {
    function keydownHandler(event) {
      var which = event.which || event.keyCode;

      if (which === code) {
        event.preventDefault();
        fire({
          node: node,
          original: event
        });
      }
    }
  }
}
```

If this button matches the assigned key variables, we cancel the normal action and instead fire off details of which event has been triggered and matched by the plugin.

This function is triggered by the node.addEventListener event handler, when the event handler attached to the passed node is triggered by a keypress. When we're done with the plugin, we simply call the teardown function to remove the event handler:

```
    node.addEventListener('keydown', keydownHandler, false);
    return {
      teardown: function teardown() {
        node.removeEventListener('keydown', keydownHandler, false);
      }
    };
  };
}
```

The great thing about this plugin is that we can potentially adapt it to fire on recognizing any key press – it does mean we can only trap for one key press at a time though! That aside, the plugin has the following set as default:

```
var enter = makeKeyDefinition(13);
var tab = makeKeyDefinition(9);
var ractive_events_keys__escape = makeKeyDefinition(27);
var space = makeKeyDefinition(32);

var leftarrow = makeKeyDefinition(37);
var rightarrow = makeKeyDefinition(39);
var downarrow = makeKeyDefinition(40);
var uparrow = makeKeyDefinition(38);

exports.enter = enter;
exports.tab = tab;
exports.escape = ractive_events_keys__escape;
exports.space = space;
exports.leftarrow = leftarrow;
exports.rightarrow = rightarrow;
exports.downarrow = downarrow;
exports.uparrow = uparrow;
```

We could easily create our own plugin that removes keys we don't need to trap for, and replace them with our own definitions. Irrespective of which keys we want to trap for, we could run our plugin using a configuration instance such as this one:

```
var ractive = new Ractive({
  el: 'body',
  template: myTemplate,
  events: { escape: keys.escape, space: keys.space, ... }
});
```

Hopefully this will begin to make a little more sense shortly – we're going to use this plugin as a basis for our own version. We don't need to trap for all of these key presses, so instead, we're going to replace them with a different set, but still make use of the existing functionality. Let's dive in and make a start with creating our first Ractive plugin.

Creating Custom Events

Ractive already comes with a good selection of events, but there are occasions where existing options are not sufficient, and that we would be better served by creating our own plugin. Why? Well, as one of my friends used to say, here's a starter for ten:

Imagine you find yourself reusing the same event code throughout multiple projects. We could copy and paste, but this isn't an efficient use of our time. Instead, why not encapsulate the functionality as a plugin? This can then be distributed on sites such as GitHub or NPM, as long as it is suitable to be shared!

Exploring the Plugin Architecture

To really understand how event plugins work, it's worth spending a few minutes exploring a basic template that we can use for any event plugin:

```
const myEvent = function(node, fire){
  // Setup code
  return {
    teardown: function(){
      // Cleanup code
    }
  };
}
```

In a nutshell, all we are creating is a simple function that can set up our event on a DOM element. We have to provide two arguments - node and fire – as part of initializing the plugin. Once the plugin is initialized, it returns an object, which includes a teardown property we can use to clean up the plugin when we've finished using it.

Within the plugin, we have a number of properties available for use, as shown in Table 4-3:

Table 4-3. *Properties available for writing custom event plugins*

Name of property	Purpose
node	This is the element to which the event is being applied. This must be passed as a minimum when creating custom event plugins.
fire	This function must be called when the event is fired – this takes a single argument, which is the event object received by the handlers. In addition to the node property that we must pass, an original property should also be passed. This references the native DOM event object supplied by the native handler, if available.
teardown	This function is called once the element is torn down. This allows the event to clean up after itself.

The event object can be augmented with additional properties – the values for these will depend on the data context the node is operating in, as shown in Table 4-4.

Table 4-4. *Additional properties for custom event plugins*

Name of property	Purpose
context	A reference to the data context that surrounds the node.
keypath	A string that leads to the current data context.
index	A number that references the index number of the data, should the data context be in an array.

With this all in mind – let's make a start on writing our plugin! We'll begin with writing the core functionality, then follow this up with a few comments on how to register our plugin within Ractive, and a demo to showcase its use.

Writing Our Plugin

Our version is based on the original ractive-events-keys plugin, originally created by Rich Harris several years ago. The format will be largely the same, but our version adds a registration section, reduces the key bindings to just trapping for spaces, and renames a few functions.

CUSTOM PLUGIN

We'll start with setting up our plugin:

1. First, go ahead and create a new folder within our project area – call this custom plugin. Within this, add a folder marked js, one marked css and a third marked font. The last three folders will be used later for our demo.

2. In a new document, add the following code – this resembles our plugin. We'll go through it section by section, beginning with the registration module to ensure we have a valid browser window and Ractive instance:

```
(function ( global, factory ) {

  'use strict';

  if ( global.Ractive ) {
    factory( global.Ractive );
  } else {
    throw new Error( 'Could not find Ractive! It must be loaded before the
    Ractive-events-space plugin' );
  }
}
  ( typeof window !== 'undefined' ? window : this, function ( Ractive ) {
    'use strict';
```

3. We then initialize the `onSpace` function – If the event is triggered, we determine which key was pressed; assuming it matches the defined keys (at the end of the plugin), we cancel the default action for that key. This allows us to operate whatever has been defined as the function in our Ractive instance:

```
function onSpace(node, fire) {
  function defineKeyAction(event) {
    var which = event.which || event.keyCode;

    if (which === 32) {
      event.preventDefault();

      fire({ node: node, original: event });
    }
  }
}
```

4. The final steps are to bind a listener for our event, which is fired as soon as the key is pressed, but not released:

```
node.addEventListener( 'keydown', defineKeyAction, false)
window.addEventListener( 'keydown', defineKeyAction, false)
```

5. We then assign a teardown function – this cleans up the plugin, at the point we have finished using it:

```
return {
  teardown: function () {
    node.removeEventListener( 'keydown', defineKeyAction, false );
    window.removeEventListener( 'keydown', defineKeyAction, false );
  }
}; }
```

6. This is the most important part – we have to bind this custom event to Ractive's event namespace, so that it recognizes it. We can then define our action within the Ractive instance, as an `on-*` directive:

```
Ractive.events.space = onSpace;});
```

7. Save the file as `ractive-events-space.js` within the `js` subfolder we created at the beginning of this demo.

Our plugin is now created! It's time to put it to good use, but before we do so, we need to touch on how plugins should be registered within the Ractive space. The observant of you will spot that we've already done it within this plugin; it's important to know that we can choose from any one of three different methods, depending on how we plan to use our plugin.

Registering Custom Events

Even thoguh we've created our plugin, a key part of using it is to register it within our Ractive instance. This may sound complicated, but in fact is much easier than you think!

There are three ways to register plugins - which route you use will depend on how you intend to use the plugin:

- We can do it globally, via the `Ractive.events` static property:

  ```
  Ractive.events.myEvent = myEvent;
  ```

- We can register it as part of any component we create, using the component's events initialization property:

  ```
  const MyComponent = Ractive.extend({
    events: { myEvent }
  });
  ```

- A third option is to register it on a per instance basis, through the instance's events initialization property:

  ```
  const ractive = new Ractive({
    events: { myEvent }
  });
  ```

If we take a look at our plugin in closer detail, we can see that it was registered globally; this means that we don't have to register it within our Ractive instance, as it is already assigned to the `Ractive.events` registry. If we do decide to register our plugin globally, then for any methods that we need to use externally, we should export event names as required for our projects.

Okay - let's move on: it is time to make use of our plugin, to see if it really works. Don't worry - I am sure that like other developers, you get that sense of trepidation when previewing your work for the first time. I certainly do, so without further ado, let's get on and set up a demo to use our new plugin.

Making Use of Our Custom Event

At this stage, our plugin has been created and registered - we can now make use of it! There is nothing special to this: you will see that we're using principles that we've already covered in earlier chapters.

To show it off, let's create a simple demo that traps for presses of the space bar, and fires a message to console if one is detected:

USING OUR CUSTOM PLUGIN

1. We'll start by setting up our markup – in a new file, go ahead and add the following code, saving it as `custom.html` at the root of the custom plugin folder we created in the previous exercise:

```
<!doctype html>
<html lang='en-GB'>
<head>
  <meta charset='utf-8'>
  <title>Beginning Ractive: Trapping for Custom Events</title>
  <link rel='stylesheet' href='css/custom.css'>
</head>
<body>
  <script src='js/ractive.min.js'></script>
  <script src='js/ractive-events-keys.js'></script>
  <script src="js/custom.js"></script>
</body>
</html>
```

2. We need to bring it to life by adding our plugin, so in a new file, add the following code —save this as `custom.js` in the `js` subfolder we created in step 1 of the previous exercise:

```
Ractive({
  el: 'body',
  template: `
    <h1>Trapping for Custom Events</h1>
    <input on-space='console.log("Space bar just pressed")'>
  `
});
```

3. We're almost there – our demo won't look great without at least some basic styling, so go ahead and add the following rules to a new file, saving it as `custom.css` in the `css` subfolder of the custom plugin folder:

```
@font-face { font-family: 'robotoregular'; src: url('../font/Roboto-Regular-webfont.woff') format('woff'); font-weight: normal; font-style: normal; }
body { font-family: robotoregular, sans-serif; font-size: 0.875rem; padding: 2rem; }
button { margin-right: 0.625rem; }
h1 { margin-top: 3.25rem; }
input { width: 14.375rem; }
```

We're there - if we try to run our demo in a browser, we should see something akin to the screenshot in Figure 4-9, where the space bar has been pressed a few times:

Trapping for Custom Events

gbsdnfmnm

| ⌖ ⬚ | Elements | Console | Sources | Network | Performance |

| ⊘ | top ▼ | Filter | | Info ▼ |

▶ `Ractive.js 0.9.0-edge in debug mode, more...`

⑧ `Space bar just pressed`

>

Figure 4-9. *Using our custom plugin*

Although this plugin is a relatively straightforward one, there are a few important points that are worth exploring in more detail:

- We could have chosen any character to trap, as the method is the same for each character or key - as long as it has a valid HTML character available, then we can add that to the key bindings at the foot of the plugin.

- Our plugin was registered globally, so it would work on any Ractive instance - this isn't necessarily the best way to achieve this, although it is tempting! When adding in plugins (be they events, adaptors, or something else), it is important to consider how your plugin will be used, and to register it using the most appropriate method. For example, if we make use of the plugin in a component, but **not outside of that plugin, then it would be more efficient to register the plugin within the component, and not globally.**

- Most of the code used will follow the same format throughout - the key elements of our code are between lines 15 to 29, and the two lines at 33 and 34. The rest can be be left as-is, which will give you a good starting point for future plugin development.

That aside - have a try at adding in a new letter! It's easy to do - we only need to add in a single line to assign that letter to the event handler. Start with searching online to confirm what the letter's HTML code should be - there are plenty of online resources for this; a good starting point is to try the reference list available form Toptal.com, which is at `https://www.toptal.com/designers/htmlarrows/letters/`. Once you have the code, it should be a cinch to add that assignment in - a clue: it's a one liner, and only needs to be added in one place...

Summary

We've reached the end of the chapter on handling events - it has certainly been an eventful ride, if you pardon the pun! Let's take a moment to review what we've covered in this chapter.

We kicked off with a look at how events operate within Ractive, which we followed with a simple demo to get acquainted with writing events in code. We then amended this demo to include an extra event type.

Next up, we covered the different event types, such as lifecycle or proxy types, before learning about setting the event context and using a form of pattern matching in creating events. We then moved onto explore event namespacing and propagation, before beginning to create our own plugin.

We then took a look at dissecting an event plugin already available in the wild, to understand how it works and learn about the architecture of a standard event plugin, before creating and using our own version of the plugin. We then rounded out the chapter with a look at some important points about the use of custom plugins, such as considering how best to register them in our Ractive projects.

Now that we have a basic site, to which we can apply our own styling and handle basic events - what's next? Well, it's time to get animated: after all, what is a site in today's modern Internet, without some form of visual movement? A non-starter, I fear...

Summary

CHAPTER 5

■ ■ ■

Animating Content

At this stage we'll have a site that works and which allows us to interact with back-end data. Trouble is, it's likely to look a little…well, static, right? We can easily add sparkle with animation – do it right, and it will look great; done without care and it will look terrible! We can do some of this with CSS: to take it further though, we will need to resort to using JavaScript. Fortunately Ractive has its own way of managing animation; we'll explore the various methods we can use throughout the course of this chapter.

Making Content Move

Take a look at a random selection of 100 sites, and I bet the odds are good that most of them will contain elements that move.

It does not matter which, or how frequently, but the key is that content is dynamic – after all, one can soon lose interest if a site is static! Animating content has long been a double-edged sort in web development; it should never be the focus of any message, but provide that extra decoration to help reinforce the core of that message. If done well, then animation can give a site a real edge over others; done badly, and it will bomb faster than a lead weight in water!

Within Ractive, content can be animated, or transitioned - in many cases, people might consider both to be one and the same thing, but there is a clear difference. Transitioning content requires a trigger to run, whereas animations can be run either with or without a trigger. We'll explore this difference over the course of this chapter – to get us started, let's take a look at transitioning content within Ractive.

Creating Transitions with Ractive

So – how does one create a transition within Ractive? It's really easy – all transitions are added through the use of external plugins. A basic transition will look something like this:

```
<div>
  <button on-click="['show', 2]" fade-in>Click me!</button>
</div>
```

Simple, huh? This is Ractive to a T (so to speak) – it was designed with simplicity in mind. In this instance, we're using the common fade-in property, but we can equally use any property, as long as there is a plugin available for it, and it has been registered into our Ractive instance. To see what it looks like in action, let's knock up a quick demo in the Ractive playground.

© Alex Libby 2017

A. Libby, *Beginning Ractive.js*, https://doi.org/10.1007/978-1-4842-3093-0_5

```
CREATING A BASIC TRANSITION
```

1. Go ahead and browse to `https://ractive.js.org/playground` - in the HTML window, add the following code:

    ```
    <h1>Creating Simple Transitions in Ractive</h1>
    <div id='container'></div>
    <script id="template" type="text/ractive">
      <div slide-in>Click me!</div>
    </script>
    <script src="https://cdn.jsdelivr.net/npm/ractive-transitions-slide"></script>
    ```

2. Click on the Script tab next, then add this:

    ```
    var ractive = new Ractive({
      template: '#template',
      el: '#container'
    });
    ```

3. We'll provide a little styling to make it resemble something of a button, so go ahead and drop these rules into the CSS tab:

    ```
    #target { text-align: center; }
    div.slide { font-size: 2.5em; background-color: #999; color: #fff;
    border-radius: 0.4em; border: none; cursor: pointer; width: 25rem; height:
    5.2rem; line-height: 5.2rem; padding-left: 0.5rem; text-align: center; }
    ```

4. Before we run our demo, we need to set our code to use Ractive – click on the cog symbol, and change the Ractive.js entry to `Latest`.

5. At this point, go ahead and preview the results – it won't be anything outrageous, but it will show a simple button that slides into view, using the `ractive-transitions-slide` plugin, as shown in Figure 5-1:

Creating Simple Transitions in Ractive

Figure 5-1. *A div sliding into view*

The great thing about using Ractive is that we're not using JavaScript to render this code – as in modern browsers; it uses CSS transitions, but will fall back to timer-based animations in older browsers.

A version of this demo is available in the code download, within the `simple transition` folder.

We can see evidence in Figure 5-2 of the CSS animations used from within the console - to do this, we can set a breakpoint on the <div> (more on this in a moment), to see the CSS transition code we've used:

```
▼<div id="container">
    <div class= slide  style= height: 83.1875px; border-top-width: 0px; border-bottom-
    width: 0px; padding-top: 0px; padding-bottom: 0px; margin-top: 0px; margin-bottom:
    0px; overflow-y: hidden; transition-property: height, border-top-width, border-
    bottom-width, padding-top, padding-bottom, margin-top, margin-bottom; transition-
    timing-function: ease-in-out; transition-duration: 0.3s;  A sliding div /div   == $0
    </div>
```

Figure 5-2. *Example CSS styling used in animation*

To achieve this, using Chrome, go ahead and follow these steps:

ENABLING A BREAKPOINT

1. Press F12, or right-click on the div in our demo, and select Inspect.

2. Switch to the Elements tab.

3. Right-click on the <div id="container"> element, and select Break on... | attribute modifications.

4. Repeat step 3, but this time select node removal from the context menu.

5. Repeat step 3 again, and this time select subtree modifications from the menu.

6. Refresh your browser window – it will then run through the demo and pause at the breakpoint, at which point the applied styles will be visible in the Elements window.

Exploring the Theory Behind Transitions

Cast your mind back to the beginning of this chapter, where we saw this simple transition code:

```
<button on-click="['show', 2]" fade-in>Click me!</button>
```

At face value, one might be forgiven for thinking that this looks very easy – the highlighted words are all that is required to add a basic fly effect to our button. Granted, we might not want to fly in a button, but the same principle applies, irrespective of the element we're using.

The trouble is, if you look at the source code for many plugins, it's likely you will see something different – you may see code akin to <div intro="fly">. This is indeed valid code, so why the confusion?

The answer to this question is that transitions have gone through some dramatic changes in syntax – the intro keyword dates from an older version of Ractive, but the current standard now favors this approach:

```
<div myFly-in>Intro-only</div>
<div myFly-out>Outro-only</div>
<div myFly-in-out>Intro and outro</div>
```

It's worth noting that this format is **not** compatible with newer versions of Ractive – indeed, this format was deprecated on or around 0.8, and has since been removed from use.

This aside, any transition we create (or use) in Ractive can be controlled by the t transition helper; we can also see what transition effects are registered by entering ractive.transitions at a console prompt in the browser.

In this example, we reference our plugin by name (or name given when registering it), followed by either -in, -out, or the shorthand -in-out. The latter tag simply represents whether the effect is to be applied on entry, exit, or both. We can control this from within the plugin itself, through the use of the t.isIntro, method; if a check for this doesn't return true, then it is assumed to be an effect that should be applied on an existing transition.

We will cover this and more, later in the book, in the section *Exploring the Transition API*.

For now, let's move on – many of the effects we use in Ractive are based around CSS; this makes them more lightweight, yet just as performant (if not better!). We are limited by the classic effect such as easeIn or easeOut, so let's take a moment to consider how we can use them in Ractive.

Adding Easing Effects

The sharp-eyed among you may notice that in the background, Ractive uses transition-timing-function to provide an easing effect. We're not limited to using typical easings such as linear, easeIn, easeOut, and easeInOut, but can add a little spice in the form of cubic-bezier-based animations such as the custom example shown in Figure 5-3:

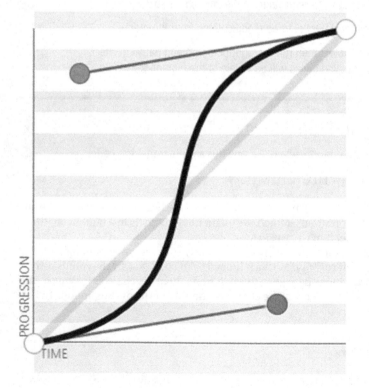

Figure 5-3. *An example easing based on cubic-bezier values (Source:* http://cubic-bezier.com*)*

This was taken from the cubic-bezier.com site – it's a great site for playing around with different easing values; we can then incorporate them into a Ractive transition. Take, for example, the above easing – which you can see at http://cubic-bezier.com/#.78,.13,.15,.86 – and let's turn that into an animation:

```
<div class="slide" slide-in="{delay:500, duration: 1000, easing: 'cubic-bezier(0.78, 0.135,
0.15, 0.86)'}">A sliding div</div>
```

See how easy that was? The proof is in the pudding – to really see how easy, head back to the exercise at the beginning of this section. Go ahead and try modifying the click hander line, as indicated:

```
<div class="slide" slide-in="{delay:500, duration: 1000, easing: 'cubic-bezier(0.78, 0.135,
0.15, 0.86)'}">A sliding div</div>
```

Now run the code – this time around you will see a completely different effect! Granted, the cubic-bezier values we've used are arbitrary, and probably ones we would never use in a real-case scenario. But – the principle is still the same: we can use the site to create our easing, then simply replace the values in the cubic-bezier(...) code with our new easing. As long as we keep the numbers comma-separated, then the easing will work. We can see a screenshot of how this code would look in an example, in Figure 5-4 (taken using the Ractive playground, but a similar result will show in the stand-alone demo too):

```
▼ <div id="container">
    <div class="slide" style>A sliding div</div>
  </div>
▼ <script id="template" type="text/ractive">
              <div class="slide" slide-in="{delay:500, duration: 1000, easing:
    'cubic-bezier(0.785, 0.135, 0.15, 0.86)'}">A sliding div</div>

  </script>
```

Figure 5-4. Cubic-bezier values in action

If, however, you want to use standard easings, then these work just as well – head over to http://www.easings.net for a whole host of examples; you will find some will also give cubic-bezier equivalents as a bonus! There is a small but critical problem though – there will be occasions where we may want to apply multiple transitions to an element. If we take a theoretical (but realistic) example such as this:

```
<button slide-in-out on-click='["show", 2]'> Click me!</button>
```

...there may be occasions when if we run the code, it looks terrible! The reason for this? The downside of chaining animations together means that subsequent animations often kick in before the previous one has had time to complete. If we find this is the case, then we can take advantage of a useful feature in Ractive – using promises.

Chaining Promises in Ractive

If you spend any time developing animated content, then at some point you will come across a need to run multiple animations in sequence. It doesn't matter how many you chain, or how long or how short this animation will be, there will always be one question on our minds: is the timing right?

If we get the timing right, then the animation will work well; get it wrong, and it will crash and burn faster than a lead ball in a tank full of water! (Okay – something of a dodgy analogy there, but hopefully you get the idea.) To prevent this from happening, we can make use of promises to fire the next animation only when Ractive has completed the previous animation. In terms of code, it will look like this:

```
ractive.on({
  show: function ( event, which ) {
    ractive.set( 'visible', null ).then( function () {
      ractive.set( 'visible', which );
    });
  }
});
```

The key to this is that we're not firing off the animations at this point; instead we're displaying or hiding an element in order. As the animation is tied to that element, it will automatically fire when the element is rendered onscreen. It's easier to see this in action, so without further ado, let's put together a two-part demo - before we get into the detail of true chaining, we'll take a look at a simpler format first.

Chaining Multiple Transitions with Ractive

The simplest form of chaining transitions in Ractive is to apply multiple effects to a desired element, such as this typical example:

```
<button slide-in slide-out="{ duration: 5000 }">Click me!</button>
```

Assuming we've specified an appropriate plugin to use (as many transitions require this), our example specifies two transitions – slide in and slide out. In many cases, this will work fine for simple transition effects, but there is a risk that transitions might collide, as we're not controlling when they fire (the duration is for how long, and might start before the end of the previous transition). If we need to step things up a notch, then using Promises will help provide better control.

To understand what this means in practice, let's work through a simple exercise that shows a button transitioning across the screen. This exercise will be in two parts - there is a reason for this, which will become clear at the end of the exercise.

For now, let's make a start with part 1 of our demo.

CHAINING MULTIPLE TRANSITIONS

1. We'll start by setting up our folder structure – go ahead and create a subfolder within our project area, called basic chaining 1.

2. Inside that folder, add two new folders – one each called js and css.

3. From a copy of the code download that accompanies this book, go ahead and extract a copy of the font folder from one of the previous exercises; save this in the basic chaining 1 folder.

4. From the code download, extract copies of ractive.min.js and ractive.min.js.map from a previous exercise, and place these inside the js folder we created in step 2.

5. We also need some styling, so go ahead and extract a copy of basicchaining.css from the code download that accompanies this book, and drop it into the css folder.

6. We need to add the ractive-transitions-fly plugin we're going to use for this demo, so go ahead and extract a copy from the code download that accompanies this book, and store it in the `js` subfolder.

This plugin is a version I've updated to work with Ractive 0.9.3.

---

7. Our demo won't work without a Ractive instance, so let's fix that by adding the following code into a new file, saving it as `basicchaining.js` into the `js` subfolder:

```
var ractive = new Ractive({
  template: '#template',
  el: '#container',
  data: { shown: true }
});

setTimeout(function() {
    ractive.toggle('shown');
}, 2000);
```

8. Last but by no means least – we need our markup! For this, go ahead and add the following code to a new file at the root of our `basic chaining 1` folder:

```
<!doctype html>
<html>
<head>
  <meta charset='utf-8'>
  <title>Beginning Ractive: Getting Acquainted with Transitions</title>
  <link rel="stylesheet" type="text/css" href="css/basicchaining.css">
</head>
<body>
  <div id="container"></div>

  <script id="template" type="text/ractive">
    {{#if shown}}
      <div on-click="console.log('You\'ve clicked this button!')"
      fly-in-out="{ duration: 500 }">
        this will fly in and out of view
      </div>
    {{/if}}
  </script>

  <script src="js/ractive.min.js"></script>
  <script src="js/transitions-fly.js">
</body>
</html>
```

9. Save this as `basicchaining.html` – if all is well, we should see the following when previewing the results in a browser window, as indicated in Figure 5-5:

Creating Simple Chained Transitions in Ractive

Figure 5-5. *Running our demo*

To really see this demo working, we should open our console log to view the results of clicking the button – inside, we will see the screenshot shown in Figure 5-6:

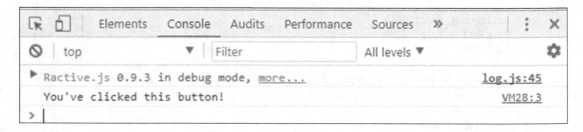

Figure 5-6. *Screenshot of console log*

Now – anyone spot something odd? Chances are you may not, but if you look carefully at the highlighted code below:

```
<button on-click="console.log('You\'ve clicked this button!')"
fly-in-out="{ duration: 500 }">Click me!</button>
```

You might begin to think that something doesn't quite seem right, does it? You would be absolutely right – that highlighted code is Ractive's way of handling effects, but only when the *-in and *-out are the same. In a sense we are chaining multiple transitions together, although as we are using the same effect in both directions, Ractive allows us to use a shorthand method to implement this in our code.

Moving on – at the start of this section, I mentioned our exercise would be in two parts: let me reveal why. There are two ways to chain animations within Ractive.

The first, that we've just covered, works fine for simple chaining. The downside of chaining events is that if we're not careful, some events may fire before others have completed – not a good place to be! Thankfully we can fix that by taking advantage of a key concept in Ractive: creating and using Promises. Let's explore what this means in more detail, with the second part of our demo.

Making a Promise

Interesting title, that...perhaps that's something I should do more often...

Yes – leaving aside the terrible pun in the title of this section (oh – and before you ask: yes, it was indeed intended!), promises play a key role in Ractive. They are great for executing tasks in the right order; this helps to maintain the right effect, as we can be sure that the next task will only start once the previous one has been completed.

To understand the benefit of using Promises, it's worth seeing them in action – to do this, we can take a copy of previous demo, and modify the Ractive instance.

MAKING A PROMISE

Let's make a start:

1. Take a copy of the basic chaining 1 folder, and save it as basic chaining 2.

2. Inside the new version of basicchaining.html, go ahead and replace the script template with this code:

```
<script id="template" type="text/ractive">
  {{#if visible === 1 }}
    <button on-click="['show', 2]" fly-in-out="{ duration: 5000 }">Click me!</
    button>
  {{elseif visible === 2 }}
    <button on-click="['show', 3]" slide-in="{ duration: 5000 }" fade-out>And
    me!</button>
  {{/if}}
</script>
```

Insert the two highlighted lines (below), after the call to ractive.min.js:

```
<script src='js/ractive.min.js'></script>
<script src="https://cdn.jsdelivr.net/npm/ractive-transitions-fade"></script>
<script src="https://cdn.jsdelivr.net/npm/ractive-transitions-slide"></script>
<script src="https://cdn.jsdelivr.net/npm/ractive-transitions-fly"></script>
```

3. Look for basichaining.js within the js subfolder – replace the contents of the file with this new code:

```
var ractive = new Ractive({
  template: '#template',
  el: '#container',
  data: { visible: 1  }
});

ractive.on( 'show', function ( ctx, which ) {
  this.set( 'visible', null ).then( function () {
    ractive.set( 'visible', which );
  });
});
```

4. Save both the script file and the main markup file. If we run the demo in a browser, we'll see the button slide in, as indicated in Figure 5-7. This time though, if we click on the button, it will progress through a series of set transitions; these will not try to crash into each other when running the demo:

Creating Chained Transitions using Promises in Ractive

Figure 5-7. *Chaining transitions using Promises*

Perfect – transitions in our demo won't collide with each other! This is just a small part of what we can achieve when working with transitions though; how about creating our own plugins, for example? We'll take a look at doing so a little later on, but for now, let's deep dive into the API in more detail, so we can get acquainted with some of the commands we'll want to use when creating our plugin.

Comparing with CSS

Before we explore the API though, some of you may be starting to ask a question – surely the use of JavaScript isn't the best way to animate an object, right?

It's a good question, and one that has been asked many times before – the simple answer is that it depends on your requirements. I know this might sound like a cop-out, but there is a good reason for this: CSS-based animations are improving all of the time, but have yet to reach the same level of ability that JavaScript has mastered. Let me explain this further.

With JavaScript, we have the ability to produce complex animations that can be controlled as needed – CSS animations will only run once, unless you hover over an element that has had an animation applied to it. It's important to note that we could use JavaScript to animate CSS-based animations, but this is a different beast; in our example here, we're referring to animating content using either CSS or JavaScript, but not a mixture of both.

Why is this important for Ractive? The answer lies in its use of requestAnimationFrame, which makes each animation (or transition) very efficient.

The reason for this is that we would typically set a regular interval when running an animation – this is prone to not being honored if system resources are low, and continual use induces an element of "layout thrashing" (where the page is constantly being reflowed before we can see any update.

This is not good for your code, browser, or the user's PC – making use of requestAnimationFrame takes the guesswork out of animating content, as it calls the next function to update the screen when it wants to repaint, where hardware and the browser are ready to make the update. Furthermore, we can slow down any animation not visible on screen – after all, why run something when people can't view it? The overall effect is that the frames per second count will be lower, which won't hammer resources so much, and therefore reduce the power used in the user's PC.

If you're interested in the differences between animating using CSS and JavaScript, then this article on the Google Developers Network is a good starting point: `https://developers.google.com/web/fundamentals/design-and-ui/animations/css-vs-javascript`

Okay – let's move on: it's time to dive into the API as promised, so we can start to create some plugins for use within Ractive.

Exploring the Transition API

Until now, we've touched on how transitions can be added through the use of plugins – this helps to keep the core part of Ractive light, while also allowing us to be selective about which plugins we want to use.

For some though, the mere mention of having to learn an API to create such a plugin might be enough to put them off – in reality, it's simpler than it might at first seem. There are only a handful of methods we need to worry about when using the API the key to making them work is the t or transition helper object, which relates to the transition we're manipulating in our code. Let's first get acquainted with some of these API methods available for use, as shown in Table 5-1:

Table 5-1. *API methods for creating transitions*

Property	Purpose
t.animateStyle()	Animate CSS properties to a certain value.
t.complete()	This signals to Ractive that the animation is complete.
t.getStyle()	Retrieves a CSS property value from t.node.
t.setStyle()	Sets a CSS property on t.node to a value.
t.isIntro / t.isOutro	Determines which direction the transition is being rendered; this allows transition direction to be changed depending on direction.
t.name	The name of the transition.
t.node	The node that's entering or leaving the DOM.
t.processParams()	Builds a map of parameters whose values are taken from the provided arguments. When used with a single number or string argument, serves as a shorthand for creating a map with a duration property.

A full listing of the API methods can be found in the Appendix, or at `https://ractive.js.org/api/` `#transition-object`.

Now that we've been acquainted with the API methods available for creating transition plugins, let's use these to create a transition plugin; we'll start with a look at the framework we can use to assemble our plugin.

Creating Transition Plugins

So – we've talked about creating a plugin, but what is involved? Well, I'll confess – the name plugin is probably a misnomer; transition plugins are just functions that are called to animate a specific element. Let's take a look at the basic framework of such a plugin:

```
const myTransition = function ( t[, ...args]] ) {
  // Manipulate the DOM.
  // Call t.complete() when completed.
};
```

Looks pretty simple, right? There are a couple of key parts to this function:

- t is a transition helper object that aids in the implementation of the transition.

- [args] is an array of arguments passed in via the transition directive.

The important thing to note though is that transitions work asynchronously; we must call t.complete() when the transition has finished, and that any styling applied to the transition itself will automatically be removed once the transition effect has been completed. With this in mind, let's move on and take a look at creating our plugin – our next stage is to explore the makeup of an existing one, so we can get a feel for how our plugin might look.

Exploring a Plugin in the Wild

So far, we've become acquainted with some of the transition plugins available for use in Ractive, and we have met some of the API methods available for creating such plugins. It is time though, to really get creative and build our own!

Before we get down and dirty with a text editor, it's worth exploring the makeup of an existing plugin – in many cases (at least for simple ones), the format will be very similar to other plugins. For this, I've picked the classic fade effect; this was created by the original developer for Ractive – Rich Harris, back in 2013. Let's take a look at the code in more detail, beginning with the self-registration function:

```
(function (global, factory) {
  typeof exports === 'object' && typeof module !== 'undefined' ? module.exports = factory() :
  typeof define === 'function' && define.amd ? define(factory) :
  global.Ractive.transitions.fade = factory();
}(this, function () { 'use strict';
```

This method is common on a number of Ractive plugins; it allows the plugin to be self-registered within the global Ractive instance, so any Ractive instance can use it.

Next up, we begin to set some default values for our plugin – note the use of linear as our easing type; we'll explore more of this at the end of this section:

```
var DEFAULTS = {
  delay: 0,
  duration: 300,
  easing: 'linear'
};
```

The real meat of our plugin comes in the form of the fade function; into it we pass the t transition helper, with params that take care of any arguments we need to pass into the function. We then make use of t.processParams to build a map of parameters from the arguments; this is effectively stringing together all of the settings needed to operate our transition:

```
function fade(t, params) {
  var targetOpacity;
  params = t.processParams(params, DEFAULTS);
```

We then work out which direction our effect will render; we then get the current state of the opacity value from our CSS for this element, before setting the appropriate opacity value (based on direction):

```
if (t.isIntro) {
  targetOpacity = t.getStyle('opacity');
  t.setStyle('opacity', 0);
} else {
  targetOpacity = 0;
}
```

The last stage is the most important of all – it's time to render that transition! We use `t.animateStyle` to effect the change (using the parameters we've assembled), before calling `t.complete` to signify that the animation is completed, and returning the final state of the fade function to our code:

```
  t.animateStyle('opacity', targetOpacity, params).then(t.complete);
  }
  return fade;
}));
```

Now – the sharp-eyed among you will say I did promise to return to the easing value used in this plugin. There is a reason for this – remember the demo we ran back in *Making a Promise*, from earlier in this chapter? This is a graphical representation of what our effect looks like – we can see in Figure 5-8 that the linear effect is very consistent:

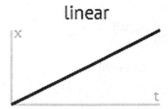

Figure 5-8. *Graphical representation of fade action (source: easings.net)*

I've taken a screenshot of the fade values that show when running the demo; these are displayed in Figure 5-9:

```
Filter

element.style {
  ☑ opacity: 0;
  ☑ transition-property: opacity;
  ☑ transition-timing-function: ▨linear;
  ☑ transition-duration: 2s;
}
```

Figure 5-9. *CSS animation settings for fade plugin*

Our effect looked a little...well...plain, right? There is nothing wrong with this effect; indeed, there may be occasions when we have to use it.

UPDATING OUR TRANSITION

However, I'm all for pushing out and trying different things – as a basic change, try this, using a copy of the code from the `basic chaining 2` exercise from earlier in this chapter:

1. Browse to easings.net first – this is a great site for showcasing different easing effects. Go ahead and pick an effect (for this one, I'll use `easeInOutSine` as an example).

2. Click on the graphic for your chosen effect, then scroll down to the CSS section. You will see the transition effect:

    ```
    div {
      -webkit-transition: all 600ms cubic-bezier(0.445, 0.05, 0.55, 0.95);
      transition:         all 600ms cubic-bezier(0.445, 0.05, 0.55, 0.95);
    }
    ```

    Granted, the site's CSS is a little outdated, but it's the cubic-bezier value that is of interest to us – make a note of this value.

3. Next, add the following code into a new file called `ractive-transitions-newfade.js`, and save it in the same `js` subfolder.

4. Open it up in a text editor, and look for the `easing: 'linear'` value. Replace it with the value highlighted from step 2.

5. Look for any instance of the word `fade`, and replace it with `newfade` – they should be on or around lines 4, 13, and 27.

6. Go ahead and save the file – try rerunning the demo now. What do you get?

If we use that break trick we covered earlier (where we pause playback on attribute changes), we'll see something akin to the screenshot in Figure 5-10 for our newfade plugin:

```
element.style {
  opacity: 0;
  transition-property: opacity;
  transition-timing-function:
      cubic-bezier(0.445, 0.05, 0.55, 0.95);
  transition-duration: 0.3s;
}
```

Figure 5-10. *Our updated easing for newfade.js*

This is all we need to do to update the plugin – as long as it is a fade effect, we can then use any number of fade easing effects. It's a nice simple change that can add a little extra sparkle to our Ractive-based projects – I'm a great believer in keeping things simple where possible!

Okay – let's move on and step things up a bit: it's time we wrote our own plugin! We'll use a similar structure as before, but this time edit the code so that it makes better sense for our plugin. The reason for this may not be immediately apparent, but it will all become clear once we develop our plugin.

Creating Our Own Plugin

When researching content for this section of the book, I was initially tempted to create a plugin that used a transition effect. However, this has already been done before – why not do something different? With that in mind, our next exercise will be based on creating a plugin that operates a transform effect instead. This might at first sound complicated, but in reality it is a lot simpler than one might imagine.

We don't need to use JavaScript to work out some complicated function that performs our transition – we can simply make use of CSS styling to produce our effect, as shown in Figure 5-11:

Creating and using a Rotate plugin in Ractive

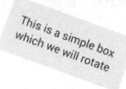

Figure 5-11. *Our rotate plugin, using CSS*

This uses a standard transform() property, which we apply to the <div> element shown in the screenshot – let's make a start on replicating this effect.

CREATING A ROTATE PLUGIN

1. Take a copy of the basic chaining 2 folder we set up from a previous exercise, and save it as ractive-transitions-rotate within our project area.

2. Delete the contents of the css folder — we will replace the styling later in this exercise.

3. In the js subfolder, go ahead and delete the three transitions plugins (fade, fly, and slide), and the basicchaining.js file; we should be left with ractive.min.js and ractive.min.js.map.

4. At the root of our ractive-transitions-rotate folder, add the following to a new file, saving it as simplerotate.html:

```
<!doctype html>
<html lang='en-GB'>
<head>
  <meta charset='utf-8'>
  <title>Beginning Ractive: Creating Custom Transition Plugins</title>
  <link rel='stylesheet' href='css/simplerotate.css'>
</head>
```

```
<body>
  <h1>Creating and using a Rotate plugin in Ractive</h1>

  <div id='container'></div>

  <script id="template" type="text/ractive">
    <div id="box" rotate-in>This is a simple box which we will rotate</div>
  </script>

  <script src='js/ractive.min.js'></script>
  <script src="js/ractive-transitions-rotate.js"></script>
  <script src="js/simplerotate.js"></script>
</body>
</html>
```

5. This provides the basic markup – to make it all work, we need to add our Ractive
    instance. Add the following code to a new file, saving it as `simplerotate.js` in the
    js subfolder:

```
'use strict';

Ractive.transitions.rotate = function rotate(t, params) {

  var DEFAULTS = {
    transform: 'rotate(20deg)'
  };

  params = t.processParams(params, DEFAULTS);

  t.setStyle('transform', params.transform);

  t.complete;
}
```

6. We're almost there – it looks a little plain without some styling! Fortunately we can
    fix that by adding these rules to a new file:

```
@font-face { font-family: 'robotoregular'; src: url('../font/Roboto-Regular-
webfont.woff') format('woff'); font-weight: normal; font-style: normal; }

body { font-family: robotoregular, sans-serif; font-size: 0.875rem; padding:
2rem; }

#box { background-color: #eee; color: #000; width: 8rem; padding: 1rem; margin-
top: 2rem; margin-left: 3rem; }
```

7. Save the file as `simplerotate.css` into the `css` subfolder – if all is well, we should
    see our box rotate, as shown in Figure 5-11 at the start of this exercise.

Although this is a simple plugin, our demo exposes some key points around creating effects-based plugins in Ractive – the first of which is the process for registering plugins of this type. Don't worry: it's very easy, and works in the same way as we've already covered elsewhere in this book. Before we go into exploring how our demo works, let's pause for a moment and cover the different methods we can use to register our plugin.

Registering Transitions

If we take a look at the first few lines of our code, we'll see this bunch of lines:

```
(function (global, factory) {
  typeof exports === 'object' && typeof module !== 'undefined' ? module.exports = factory() :
  typeof define === 'function' && define.amd ? define(factory) :
  global.Ractive.transitions.rotate = factory();
}(this, function () { 'use strict';
```

This ugly block of code is a self-registering module – it checks to ensure the module returns an object when exported doesn't return undefined (i.e., exists), and works out if we're using this as an AMD module. In short, it sets up the module for use within Ractive. When using any plugin within Ractive, we must register it for use within our instance; we can do this globally, as we've done in this instance.

However, this isn't always necessary, or ideal – there may be times when you need to limit the availability of a plugin to a specific instance. Fortunately there are several ways to achieve this – you will note the similarities with earlier plugins that we've used:

- We can do it globally, via the `Ractive.transitions` static property:

  ```
  Ractive.transitions.myTransition = myTransition;
  ```

- If we're designing for a component, we can do it via the component's `transitions` initialization property:

  ```
  const MyComponent = Ractive.extend({
    transitions: { myTransition }
  });
  ```

- If we need it in a specific Ractive instance, then we can do it via the instance's `transitions` initialization property.

  ```
  const ractive = new Ractive({
    transitions: { myTransition }
  });
  ```

At this point it's worth noting that our use of the global registration method is purely for convenience; we could have chosen either this or the last method, which would have worked equally as well. Although our plugin uses a transform, the same principle applies; it's not uncommon to see transitions used at the same time as transforms, so registering our plugin in the `Ractive.transitions` space should be an acceptable compromise.

Okay – let's change tack: we covered some key points throughout the course of this exercise; it's worth taking time out to explore some of these in more detail.

Exploring What Happened

Our demo was designed to be very simple, but nonetheless it contains some key points for creating plugins within Ractive. Let's take a look at them in turn, beginning with our markup.

If we take a look through our code, we can see our markup contains the highlighted keyword:

```
<script id="template" type="text/ractive">
  <div id="box" rotate-in>This is a simple box which we will rotate</div>
</script>
```

This is our keyword to activate our plugin – any transition effect can be added using *-in, *-out, or *-in-out directives. In summary, these control the direction of our effect – a good example is fading; our effect might fade in from an opacity of 0 to 1 (fade-in), fade out to nothing (fade-out), or do both (fade-in-out). In our case, we want the plugin to rotate the box div automatically, when we load the page – as we've specified the *-in attribute, this is sufficient to trigger the plugin to perform its action. If, for example, we had specified rotate-out, or even rotate-in-out, then this would have been enough to rotate the div from an angled to horizontal position, or perform both actions in sequence.

Let's switch to our plugin code, which looks like this:

```
'use strict';

Ractive.transitions.rotate = function rotate(t, params) {

  var DEFAULTS = {
    transform: 'rotate(20deg)'
  };

  params = t.processParams(params, DEFAULTS);

  t.setStyle('transform', params.transform);

  t.complete;
```

We kick off our plugin by setting our default values – in our instance we only have one, but if we had been creating a true transitions plugin, this is where we would set default values for settings such as transition-delay, transition-duration, and transition-timing-function.

Next up, we set up our function – into it we pass t as a transition helper object, along with the default values; we then use t.processParams to build a map of parameters that is taken from the arguments we pass into the plugin. We then use t.setStyle to apply these values; we call t.complete() to signify that the plugin has completed and control can be returned back to our Ractive instance. To prove it adds the desired effect, we can see the addition of transform: rotate(20deg) in our code, as shown in Figure 5-12:

```
element.style {
    transform: rotate(20deg);
}

#box {
    background-color: ☐#eee;
    color: ■#000;
```

Figure 5-12. *The effects of running our rotate plugin*

There is something we should be aware of though – our example doesn't use promises at this point. This is deliberate: t.setStyle is perfect for applying a single attribute; anything else would be overkill. It doesn't return a Promise though, hence why we've not used them here. If we need to have a Promise returned, then t.animateStyle() should be used instead.

That aside, there is one important question we should answer though – why use Ractive, when we might be able to simply apply the transform using plain CSS? Well, the answer is simple: control, and support for older browsers. It allows us to tie in control for the element being manipulated by Ractive; we can also make use of CSS-based styles or automatically fall back to timer-based animations for older browsers.

At this point, I'm going to throw a curveball into the mix...and say that we can improve on our plugin! I'll bet you'll be asking how; the improvement we can make is in simplifying our code even further. It makes an assumption that we'll be registering our plugin globally – as long as this suits your needs, then this is something we can live with. Let's take a look at how our code might look:

```
'use strict';

Ractive.transitions.rotate = function rotate(t, params) {
  var DEFAULTS = {
    transform: 'rotate(20deg)'
  };
  params = t.processParams(params, DEFAULTS);
  t.setStyle('transform', params.transform);
  t.complete;
}
```

This time around, we've made some changes to our code, to bring it more in-line with the current plugin architecture used in Ractive; this also makes it easier to learn how to develop plugins. We've moved our default values inside the main function, and assign that function directly to the Ractive.transitions global object.

You can include a self-registering module if desired, although my research indicates that many plugin authors began to remove this part – potentially due to issues with how it registered, or to provide better control.

For those of you who like to really deep dive into code – try entering ractive.transitions into a console session, and pressing Enter. You will initially see Object{} returned (in Figure 5-13); try expanding it, to see the full details for our plugin:

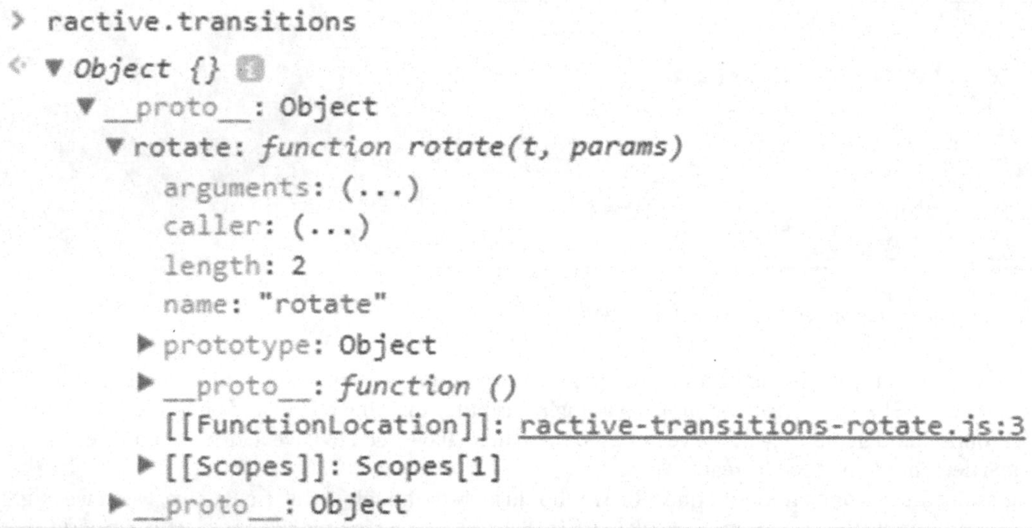

```
>  ractive.transitions
<  ▼ Object {} ⊡
     ▼ __proto__: Object
       ▼ rotate: function rotate(t, params)
           arguments: (...)
           caller: (...)
           length: 2
           name: "rotate"
         ▶ prototype: Object
         ▶ __proto__: function ()
           [[FunctionLocation]]: ractive-transitions-rotate.js:3
         ▶ [[Scopes]]: Scopes[1]
       ▶ __proto__: Object
```

Figure 5-13. Our rotate plugin, as seen from console

Right – onwards we go: no rest for the wicked, as I like to say! We've covered a fair amount on transitions, creating plugins, and exploring how they work, but what about the flip side of the coin? Okay, granted, it should be a three-sided coin (transitions, transforms, and animations). Either way, the one side we've not touched on yet is how we can use animations within Ractive, so let's turn our attention to exploring this in more detail.

Creating and Using Animation

If you've spent any time developing with jQuery, then you will have a good head start in the world of Ractive animation.

A sweeping statement to make, but if you look carefully at the animate code we're about to create, you will notice that the two are very similar! This is intentional – Ractive was designed to be simple to use, and this similarity to jQuery and JavaScript makes it easier to learn. With this in mind, let's take a look at a typical `Ractive.animate` statement:

`ractive.animate('panel', 200, { duration: 3000 });` To break this down, the above statement uses the following elements:

- `'panel'` – the keypath or property we're animating.

- `200` – the value we're animating to (in this case, position on screen).

- `duration`: this is how long the animation should take to complete.

- optionally, we can in an easing value (which we will cover in more detail later in this chapter).

To really get a feel for how easy it is to use `ractive.animate()`, there is nothing better than to see it in action – with this mind, let's create a simple demo. For this, we'll animate a `<div>` element across the page: it will look something like the screenshot in Figure 5-14, although technology is such that we can't see the motion in print!

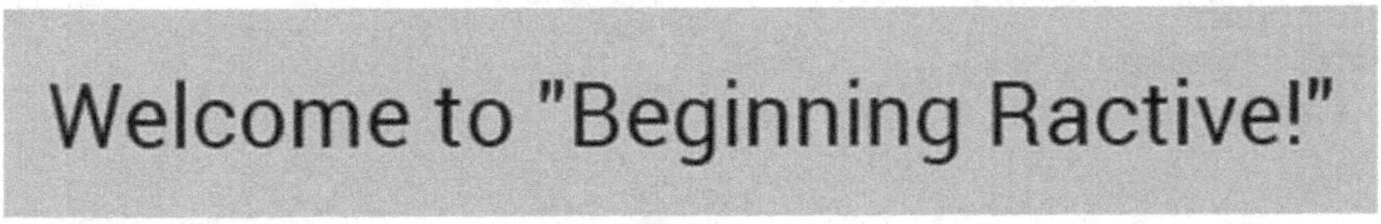

Welcome to "Beginning Ractive!"

Figure 5-14. *A simple animation example*

CREATING A SIMPLE ANIMATION

This is a simple exercise to put together, so without further ado, let's get cracking:

1. We'll start by taking a copy of the `ractive-transitions-rotate` folder, and saving it as `simple animation` within our project area.

2. Next, delete the contents of the `css` folder and the `simplerotate.html` markup file at the root of this folder.

3. From the `js` subfolder, remove all except the `ractive.min.*` files.

4. Next, let's add our markup – save the following code to a new file marked `simpleanimation.html`, at the root of the simple animation folder:

```html
<!doctype html>
<html lang='en-GB'>
<head>
  <meta charset='utf-8'>
  <title>Beginning Ractive: Getting Acquainted with Animation</title>
  <link rel='stylesheet' href='css/simpleanimation.css'>
</head>
<body>
  <div id='container'></div>
  <script id="template" type="text/ractive">
    <span id="sprite" style="left: {{left}}px">
      Welcome to "Beginning Ractive!"
    </span>
  </script>
  <script src='js/ractive.min.js'></script>
  <script src='js/simpleanimation.js'></script>
</body>
</html>
```

5. This provides the basic markup – to make it all work, we need to add our Ractive instance. Add the following code to a new file, saving it as `simplerotate.js` in the js subfolder:

```
var Ractive = new Ractive({
  el: '#container',
  template: '#template',
  data: { left: 0 }
});

Ractive.animate('left', 400, {
  duration: 2000,
  step: function(t, v) { console.log('step', t, v); },
  complete: function(t, v) { console.log('complete', t, v); }
});
```

6. We're almost there – it looks a little plain without some styling! Fortunately we can fix that by adding these rules to a new file:

```
@font-face { font-family: 'robotoregular'; src: url('../font/Roboto-Regular-
webfont.woff') format('woff'); font-weight: normal; font-style: normal; }

body { font-family: robotoregular, sans-serif; padding: 2rem; }

#sprite { background-color: #ccc; color: #000; font-size: 2rem; padding: 1rem;
width 10rem; position: relative; }
```

7. Save the file as simpleanimation.css into the css subfolder – if all is well, we should see our box slide from left to right, as shown in Figure 5-14 on the previous page.

Okay – this is a simple demo that shows how `animate()` works, but the example is a little theoretical! Let's step things up a notch and create something a little more practical – how about animating a temperature gauge? This should be easy enough to do, so let's dive in and take a look.

Displaying Average Temperatures for Copenhagen

If someone asked me what my favorite city was, then around the middle of 2016, I would have had to say Vancouver. However, a week's vacation to Copenhagen changed all that – there were lots of things that made it a superb vacation, but if pushed, I would have to say the exceptional service I had when eating out in the evenings played a big part!

Anyway – I digress; let's get back on track: for this next demo, we're going to use the average temperatures shown in Table 5-2 for Copenhagen, and turn them into a simple temperature chart.

Table 5-2. Average temperatures for Copenhagen

Month	Average High Temperature
January	37
February	36
March	41
April	49
May	60
June	66
July	69
August	69
September	61
October	53
November	44
December	39

Source: tripsavvy.com

The use of temperatures is a good way to show off animating simple elements, with each bar going from 0 to the desired temperature for the month.

BUILDING A TEMPERATURE CHART

Let's make a start on building up our demo:

1. We'll start by taking a copy of the `simple animation` folder and saving it as `animation demo` within our project area.

2. Next, delete the contents of the `css` folder and the `simplerotate.html` markup file at the root of this folder.

3. From the `js` subfolder, remove all except the `ractive.min.*` files.

4. Next, let's add our markup – save the following code to a new file marked `temperatures.html`, at the root of the `simple animation` folder:

```
<!doctype html>
<html lang='en-GB'>
<head>
  <meta charset='utf-8'>
  <title>Beginning Ractive: Getting Acquainted with Animation</title>
  <link rel='stylesheet' href='css/temperatures.css'>
</head>
<body>
  <h1>Average High Temperatures</h1>
```

```
<div id='container'></div>

<script id="template" type="text/ractive">
Location: {{cities.name}}

<div class='temperatures'>
  <!-- the chart -->
    <div class='bar-chart'>
      <!-- 12 sections, one for each month -->
      {{#each cities.months: i}}
        <div class='bar-group'>
          <!-- average high temperature -->
          <div class='bar-outer high {{ (high >= 0) ? "positive" :
          "negative" }}' style='height: {{ scale(high) }}px;'>
          <div class='bar-inner'></div>
          <span class="temp">{{ cities.months[i].high|0 }}°F</span>
      </div>
    <!-- month label -->
    <span class='month-label'>{{ monthNames[i] }}</span>
  </div>
{{/each}}
 </div>
</div>
 </script>
 <script src='js/ractive.min.js'></script>
 <script src='js/temperatures.js'></script>
</body>
</html>
```

5. With our markup in place, let's now add the Ractive script required to make it all
    work – go ahead and add the following to a new file, saving it as `temperatures.js`
    in our js subfolder:

```
var updatedData = {
  "name": "Copenhagen, Denmark",
  "months": [ { "high": 37 }, { "high": 36 }, { "high": 41 }, { "high": 49 },
  { "high": 60 }, { "high": 66 }, { "high": 69 }, { "high": 69 },
  { "high": 61 }, { "high": 53 }, { "high": 44 }, { "high": 39 } ]
}
var ractive = new Ractive({
  template: '#template',
  el: '#container',
  data: {
    monthNames: [ 'J', 'F', 'M', 'A', 'M', 'J', 'J', 'A', 'S', 'O', 'N', 'D' ],
    cities: {
      "name": "Copenhagen, Denmark",
```

```
      "months": [ { "high": 0 }, { "high": 0 }, { "high": 0 }, { "high": 0 },
        { "high": 0 }, { "high": 0 }, { "high": 0 }, { "high": 0 }, { "high": 0 },
        { "high": 0 }, { "high": 0 }, { "high": 0 } ]
      },
      scale: function ( val ) {
        return 3 * Math.abs( val );
      }
    }
});
ractive.animate( 'cities', updatedData, { duration: 500} );
```

6. We're almost there – the demo will look a mess without some styling, so let's fix that by adding the following to a new style sheet file, saving it as temperatures.css in the css subfolder:

```
@font-face { font-family: 'robotoregular'; src: url('../font/Roboto-Regular-webfont.woff') format('woff'); font-weight: normal; font-style: normal; }

body { font-family: robotoregular, sans-serif; font-size: 0.875rem; padding: 2rem; height: 100%; padding: 1em; margin: 0; box-sizing: border-box; }

.bar-chart { position: relative; width: 100%;    height: 100%; padding: 0 0 3em 0; box-sizing: border-box; }
.bar-chart span { position: absolute; width: 100%; left: -2px; font-size: 1.2rem; line-height: 0; z-index: 6; }
.bar-group { position: relative; height: 100%; float: left; text-align: center; padding: 0.5rem; width: 2.333333%; }
.bar-outer { position: absolute; width: 100%; padding: 0 1px; box-sizing: border-box; bottom: 20%; }
.positive .bar-inner { border-radius: 2px 2px 0 0; border: 1px solid #333; bottom: 0; position: relative; width: 45px; height: 100%; background-color: #c4c4c4; }

.temperatures { position: relative; width: 100%; height: 100%; padding: 15rem 0 0 0; }
.temp { font-size: 0.9rem; margin-top: -1.8rem; top: 0.8em; font-weight: bold;}
.month-label { bottom: -1em; font-size: 0.6rem; }
```

7. Make sure all files have been saved and closed – if all is well, we should something akin to the screenshot shown in Figure 5-15:

Average High Temperatures

Location: Copenhagen, Denmark

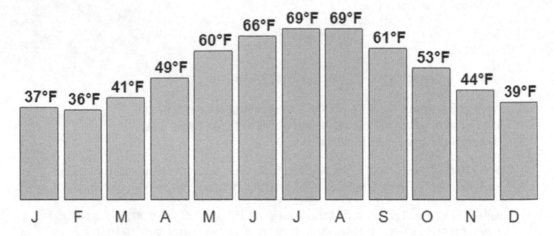

Figure 5-15. *Average temperatures for Copenhagen*

This is a perfect way to try out new animation styles – this includes easings, which we will cover a little later in this chapter. There are a number of key points we should explore, so let's take some time out to review what we've covered in our demo in more detail.

Understanding How Our Demo Works

Our temperature chart is an interesting demo – at face value, its purpose is simple enough; delve into the code and we see some useful concepts:

We start with a simple keypath reference – we replace {{cities.name}} with Copenhagen, Denmark, which is rendered onscreen. When it comes to rendering each of the bars, we could do each individually, but this isn't an efficient use of our time or resources. Instead, we're using the #each statement to work through the array of cities.months, to set the appropriate value for each bar. This is then topped off with the numerical value displayed at the head of the bar.

Where things get really interesting though is in the Ractive instance itself – we use this excerpt to scale up each bar:

...style='height: {{ scale(high) }}px;'>

This ties directly to the scale function that is in our Ractive instance – for this to work, we take the absolute value of each number, then multiply this by 3 to arrive at the visual height of the bar. To get there, we use ractive.animate, running our animation over a period of 500ms:

```
ractive.animate( 'cities', updatedData, { duration: 500 });
```

This takes the cities reference, and uses the updatedData array as the destination values:

```
var updatedData = {
  "name": "Copenhagen, Denmark",
  "months": [ { "high": 37 }, { "high": 36 }, { "high": 41 }, { "high": 49 },
  { "high": 60 }, { "high": 66 }, { "high": 69 }, { "high": 69 }, { "high": 61 },
  { "high": 53 }, { "high": 44 }, { "high": 39 } ]
}
```

It's worth noting that we had to specify the months reference twice in our code – the first instance contains the upper extreme values, and the second instance will be set to 0 as our starting point.

In this example, our animation is a fairly standard arrangement – it is a little plain! We can add visual interest with the use of external plugins; there are some great examples available on the Web that we can download and use in our applications. It's important to use a modicum of care, as animations done badly will make people lose interest faster than a lead balloon being dropped; do it right, and we can really add some sparkle to our pages...

Working with External Plugins

Throughout the course of the last few pages, we've explored different types of animation (be it transforms, transitioning content, or pure animation). We've used a number of different plugins – it's important to note that Ractive doesn't contain this functionality as part of core by default; whatever we choose to do will require the use of a plugin of some description.

There are a handful of plugins listed on the main Ractive site – you can see the details below, or at `https://ractive.js.org/integrations/`. The plugins listed were created by Rich Harris, one of the developers for Ractive:

- Ractive-transitions-fade, available from `https://ractive.js.org/ractive-transitions-fade`.

- Ractive-transitions-fly, downloadable from `http://ractivejs.github.io/ractive-transitions-fly`.

- The Slide effect plugin is available from `https://ractive.js.org/ractive-transitions-slide/`.

- For a typewriter effect, take a look at ractive-transitions-typewriter, available from `https://ractive.js.org/ractive-transitions-typewriter`.

The list also includes a user-contributed plugin called Scale by Ayman Mackouly; this can be downloaded from `https://github.com/1N50MN14/Ractive-transitions-scale`. It's worth having a good look on Google, as many plugins are not listed on the main Ractive site; three examples I found are:

- If you've ever created animations, then you may have come across the Animate.css library - we can easily make use of in Ractive, with this binding: `https://www.npmjs.com/package/ractive-animatecss`.

- If you've spent any time with animation, then there's a good chance you will have heard of Velocity, by Julian Shapiro – there's a plugin which makes use of his library: `http://cfenzo.github.io/ractive-transitions-velocity/`

- For a more interesting effect, try this one: `https://www.npmjs.com/package/ractive-transitions-slidehorizontal`

Hopefully there's something there to get you started, and whet your appetite! Let's move on and revisit a subject we've touched on briefly earlier: notice how we included some cubic-bezier values as easing effects? The great thing about Ractive is that it includes a simple method to harness the power of easings within each instance – time to ease ourselves in, so to speak...!

Easing Content on Pages

Groan – that's a terrible pun! Okay – hands up, I've done better....

Leaving aside terrible puns, take a look back at *"Creating Transitions with Ractive"* from earlier in this chapter – remember this?

```
slide-in='{delay:500, easing: "cubic-bezier(.97,.84,.36,.13)"}
```

Here we've touched on the use of easings, using the cubic-bezier functions – this added a little extra flair to the slide-in transition. This is great, but is still a little limiting though; what if we really wanted to mix things up and take things much further?

Ractive already has four easings built in to the library – linear (the default), easeIn, easeOut, and easeInOut. However, we can add more, using the Ractive.easing object, and if needed, apply them using the easing map in our Ractive instance. Let's take a look at a few examples:

```
return -1 * Math.pow(4,-8*pos) * Math.sin((pos*6-1)*(2*Math.PI)/2) + 1;
```

Don't worry – I'm not going to ask you something stupid like "Recognize this...?"! That, though, is the elastic function, taken from the excellent GitHub resource owned by Dan Rogers, at https://github.com/danro/easing-js. It's a cinch though to turn it into something that can be used within Ractive – all we need to do is encompass this in a function, and assign it as the elastic property within the Ractive.easing object:

```
Ractive.easing.elastic = function ( x ) {
  return -1 * Math.pow(4,-8*x) * Math.sin((x*6-1)*(2*Math.PI)/2) + 1;
};
```

This will work perfectly well if our project only used the elastic easing within one Ractive instance – a more appropriate use would be something akin to this:

```
const myElastic = function ( x ) {
  // Calculation
  return -1 * Math.pow(4,-8*x) * Math.sin((x*6-1)*(2*Math.PI)/2) + 1;
};
```

We simply pass in a value x between 0 and 1, which represents progress along a timeline; this will return a numeric y value that represents its progression along the timeline. At this point, our plugin is created, but not registered for use within Ractive – the process is similar to registering other plugins, so let's take a moment to explore this in more detail.

As a test – take a look at `https://github.com/danro/easing-js/blob/master/easing.js`; this contains a host of different easings. How would you convert these for use in Ractive?

Registering an Easing

To register an easing plugin is a cinch – there are three ways in which we can register them, which will depend on where our easing plugin is meant to be used:

- We can register the plugin globally using the `Ractive.easing` property:

  ```
  Ractive.easing.myEasing = myEasing;
  ```

- If we're using it within a plugin, then registration takes place within the component's easing initialization property:

  ```
  const MyComponent = Ractive.extend({
      easing: { myEasing }
  });
  ```

- If we don't need to register our easing plugin in every instance (and that this will often be the case), then we can register it through the instance's easing initialization property:

  ```
  const ractive = new Ractive({
      easing: { myEasing }
  });
  ```

Assuming our plugin is now registered, we're free to use it in our projects – let's take a look at how to do this, in more detail.

Using Our Easing Plugin

This is probably the easiest part of the process - adding our easing effect is as simple as specifying it in our ractive.animate statement, thus:

```
ractive.animate('foo.bar', 1, { easing: 'myEasing' });
```

To prove this, let's revisit the last demo, where we set up an average temperature chart for Copenhagen. To add our easing, just follow these steps:

ADDING AN EASING VALUE

1. Look for the ractive.animate statement in our script, and amend as highlighted:

    ```
    ractive.animate('cities', updatedData, { duration: 500, easing: 'myElastic'});
    ```

2. We also need to add it to our Ractive configuration, so go ahead and add the extra line as indicated:

    ```
    template: '#template',
    el: '#container',
    easing: { myElastic },
    data: {
    ```

3. Save the file – if we preview it again, we should see a different effect applied to our temperature bars.

There you have it – a simple change, but as long as we are careful about the type of effect we add, it will give our pages that little bit of extra sparkle!

Summary

Creating a website or online application without some form of animated content is almost a big no-no - it's important to strike the right balance between providing that extra edge and not overdoing the intended effect! Over the course of this chapter, we've covered a lot of material on the ups and downs of animating or transitioning content, so let's pause for a moment to review what we've learned.

We kicked off with a look at creating a simple transition effect, before exploring the drawbacks of animating content without some form of control, and how to apply that direction with the use of Promises. Next up we moved on to look at the transition API methods available within Ractive, before learning how to create and register our own plugin for use within Ractive.

We then moved on to explore animation, with a brief look at creating a simple animation, before applying the principle to a more complicate temperature chart demo. We then covered how this worked, before exploring some of the other third-party plugins we can use to animate or transition content in Ractive.

Then we rounded out the chapter with a look at creating easing effects - we discovered how similar these are to standard JavaScript easing methods, and that it doesn't take a lot of effort to adapt them for use within Ractive.

Phew - that was definitely one animated journey, if you pardon the play on words there! The journey doesn't stop though: we've started to cover a number of principles around creating plugins. There is still plenty more to explore, which we will revisit in Chapter 7, but for now, let's turn our attention to creating components for reuse within Ractive.

CHAPTER 6

■ ■ ■

Creating Components

Although Ractive has a healthy API, there will be times when we want to encapsulate functionality into a reusable component – after all, why rewrite code when we've already written something from a previous project that might work?

Making use of capabilities within Ractive, we can create all manner of components for future use – throughout the course of this chapter, we'll take a look at how we can encapsulate code into a reusable component, and explore how we can make them available for others to use.

Initializing Our Component

If you spend any time working with front-end libraries or frameworks, you cannot fail but to come across components. These are just reusable blocks of code that encapsulate templates, styling, behavior - and of course data!

This concept of using components is nothing new – indeed, Ractive uses them in much the same way as other libraries such as Bootstrap. Making a component is not difficult, but a useful skill to master – it is worth spending time learning how to create components, as it will help save time during the development process.

If we strip back a typical component, we'll find it's made up of three elements – these are data, styling, and a template. At their most basic level, all we need to provide is a template, thus:

```
var HelloWorld = Ractive.extend({
  template: '<h1>Hello world!</h1>'
});

var ractive = new HelloWorld({
  el: 'body'
});
```

Of course this is a little plain – let's ramp it up, with the addition of a styling option and data:

```
// A subclass of Ractive
const MyComponent = Ractive.extend({
  template: `
    <div class="my-component">
      <span class="message">{{ message }}</span>
    </div>
```

```
  `,
  css: `
    .message { color: #c4c4c4 }
  `,
  data: { message: 'Hello World' }
});
```

Any component we create will inherit from Ractive – it means we can interact with it, just as we would a Ractive object. When we register it for use within a Ractive instance, we can simply call the component's name without specifying a default template, and it will know what needs to be rendered on screen.

■ **Note** It is possible to use components within a component; all components are individual Ractive instances, so they can be treated in the same way as if we were using a normal Ractive instance.

Some of you may ask though – given the pressures of development, what is the benefit of creating components? Surely this adds to the burden of producing code, particularly if we're running against time? They are good questions, so let's take a moment to reflect on them in more detail.

Why Create Components?

A question – anyone remember the time when you added styling to the <head> of your code, and tucked away all of your scripting into <script> blocks at the end of the page ... sounds familiar, doesn't it?

This practice has served developers well for many years, but at a cost – it increases what many term as cognitive load. A phrase developed by the psychologist John Sweller in the late 1980s, this refers to how much mental effort needs to be used in working memory.

What does this mean for us? I am sure you like to work on the basis of keeping your style sheets in one area, HTML markup files in another (typically at the root?), and other assets in similarly arranged folders. There is nothing wrong with this, except for one thing – it's based on a misunderstanding of separation of concerns: we take it too literally! What we should really do is keep everything together that is required for one part of the site – in this case a component.

Ractive helps enormously with this: instead of splitting files into separate locations, we must keep all files required for a component in the same location. This might seem odd at face value (and indeed somewhat intuitive), but it helps to reduce the burden on anyone who uses your component! Ultimately it might seem like extra work, but this can be tempered by how often we may reproduce the same code. If it is more than just a few times, then it's worth considering putting the relevant core parts of this code into a component for future reuse.

Leaving aside the reasons for why we would create components for a moment, it's worth noting that we have two options open to us, when it comes to the build process. The first, and easiest, option is to simply write each component as a script block into a JavaScript file; this is fine for smaller sites, but not scalable for larger entities.

The second option is to use a component loader – we can instead store components as plain HTML markup files, and use it to load in each component as needed. There are plenty of loaders available for use, such as ractive-load (plain JavaScript), or ractive-component-loader, for Webpack. The beauty about using this method is that we can do away with the extraneous code required to convert our files into components; our files will be just plain markup, which makes it simpler to code!

If you would like to learn more about using loaders, then please browse at `https://github.com/ractivejs/component-spec#hello-world-again` for more details.

Okay – let's move on: up until now, we've included our markup, data, and styling in each example as part of each Ractive instance. This works sufficiently well, but has its limitations; it's time we worked to remedy some of these limitations by exploring the process for creating components in more detail.

Working Through a Simple Example

Over the last two decades, I must have lost count of the number of times I've clicked on a checkbox somewhere on a website – I think I had a bookmark list that hit a little over 12,000 links at one point, so it's fair to say I've clicked on a few over the years!

The one thing I've noted though is that dozens of websites don't bother to style checkboxes – in many cases, there probably isn't a desire, was too problematic, or it's the age-old excuse that "it never featured in our designs…". Fortunately with CSS3 and Ractive, this is less of an issue – CSS3 removed many of the browser quirks required when styling checkboxes in general; we can then incorporate these styles into a Ractive component with little difficulty. This keeps the code self-contained, and is perfect for those instances where we might use a whole bunch of checkboxes, but we don't want to have to worry too much about styling them!

A small point – our component will be styled for IE9+ and recent versions of other browsers such as Chrome and Firefox; this is in line with current support levels for Ractive in the browser.

To get an idea of what we're going to create, Figure 6-1 shows a screenshot of a styled checkbox that has already been ticked:

Creating a Checkbox Component

☑ This is a title

Figure 6-1. *Our checkbox component*

Let's make a start on building our component:

BUILDING A CHECKBOX COMPONENT

1. We'll start by creating some markup we can use to test our component – create a folder in our project area called `checkbox`, then add the following to a new file, saving it as `checkbox.html` at the root of our folder:

```
<!doctype html>
<html lang='en-GB'>
<head>
  <meta charset='utf-8'>
  <title>Beginning Ractive: Creating Components</title>
  <link rel='stylesheet' href='css/checkbox.css'>
</head>
<body>
  <h1>Creating a Checkbox Component</h1>
  <div id='container'></div>

  <script src='js/ractive.min.js'></script>
  <script src='js/checkbox.js'></script>
</body>
</html>
```

2. Next, we need to assemble some media files – for this, go ahead and copy the `img` and `font` folders from the `checkbox component` folder in the code download that accompanies this book; save the folders in our `checkbox` subfolder.

3. We need the Ractive library files, so go ahead and create a new folder called `js` in the `checkbox` subfolder, then copy across copies of `ractive.min.js` and `ractive.min.js.map` into this folder.

4. We also need to create a `css` folder in our checkbox folder – go ahead and do that now.

5. Now comes the interesting part – the magic that makes our checkbox happen! In a new file, go ahead and add the following code; we start with the component itself:

```
var Checkbox = Ractive.extend({
  isolated: true,
  template: '<input type="checkbox" id="c1" name="cc" /><label for="c1"><span>
</span>{{title}}</label>',
  data: {
    checked: false
  },
```

```
  css: `
    input[type="checkbox"] { display: none; }
    input[type="checkbox"] + label span {
      display: inline-block; width: 1.1875rem; height: 1.1875rem;  margin:
      -0.125rem 0.625rem 0 0; vertical-align: middle; background: url(./img/
      check_radio.png) left top no-repeat; cursor: pointer; }
    input[type="checkbox"]:checked + label span {
      background: url(./img/check_radio.png) -1.1875rem top no-repeat;
    }
  `
});
```

6. Leave a line in that file, then add the following Ractive instance:

```
var checkbox = new Checkbox({
  el: '#container',
  data: {
    title: 'This is a title',
    active: true
  }
});
```

7. Save the file as `checkbox.js` in the `js` subfolder of our `checkbox` folder.

8. Our basic functionality is in place along with some styling for our checkbox – we still need to make some tweaks, to ensure our demo looks presentable! Go ahead and add the following rules to a new file, saving it as `checkbox.css` within the `css` folder we created back in step 4:

```
@font-face { font-family: 'robotoregular'; src: url('../font/Roboto-Regular-
webfont.woff') format('woff'); font-weight: normal; font-style: normal; }
body { font-family: robotoregular, sans-serif; position: relative; height: 100%;
padding: 2.5rem 30%; margin: 0; }

#container { font-size: 1.2rem; font-weight: bold; color: #40464b; letter-
spacing: 0.0625rem; }

h1 { width: 480px; }
```

At this point, we can preview the results in a browser – if all is well, we should see a styled checkbox appear on screen, as shown at the start of our exercise.

Perfect – we have a component on the page; we can begin to use this in our projects. The thing is, how does it all work? Creating components exposes an interesting concept, so let's take a look at this in more detail.

Exploring How Our Component Works

Anyone who knows me personally will know that I am what IT technicians might call a "bonnet lifter" – this innocuous-sounding phrase describes anyone who likes to peek at how things work: it can frequently spell trouble for overworked IT techies!

If we lift under the bonnet of this demo, taking a peek at the compiled code will show our inline CSS, an extract of which is shown in Figure 6-2:

```
▼ <style type="text/css">
    /* Ractive.js component styles */

    /* {a8fab02d-b548-e860-cccd-8c7e68f302b1} */

        input[type="checkbox"] {
          display: none;
        }

        input[type="checkbox"] + label span {
          display: inline-block;
```

Figure 6-2. *Viewing our compiled style sheet*

What does that long string of letters and numbers represent? Well, a look further down will show a reference to the same string of characters:

In this instance, we're using the `data-ractive-css` tag to specify which CSS styling to use – the long string indicated in Figure 6-3 will match up with that shown in Figure 6-2. It's simply a marker for Ractive to indicate which styles should be used in our component.

```
  <h1>Creating a Checkbox Component</h1>
▼ <div id="container">
  ▼ <input data-ractive-css="{a8fab02d-b548-e860-cccd-8c7e68f302b1}" type="checkbox" id="c1"
  name="cc" value="on">
      #shadow-root (user-agent)
    </input>
  ▶ <label data-ractive-css="{a8fab02d-b548-e860-cccd-8c7e68f302b1}" for="c1">…</label>
  </div>
```

Figure 6-3. *Linking the style sheet to our markup*

A word of caution – simply adding `another` `<input type="checkbox">` won't be enough – it won't render on screen. To see a (work in progress) example of how you might begin to add a second instance, take a look at checkbox-multple.js in the code download that accompanies this book. It will need further development, so it shouldn't be used in the production environment just yet though!

The real magic though takes place in managing data – Ractive takes care of updating the right fields automatically for us, so let's dive in and take a look.

Managing Data Binding

Cast your mind back to Chapter 2, *Creating Templates*, where we explored one of Ractive's strengths – binding data. Remember how we talked about how data can easily be updated, and that Ractive takes care of dependencies automatically for us?

The same applies to components – Ractive is able to manage data automatically for us, using any one of the following three principles:

- **data mapping** – applying data from a Ractive instance to a component;

- **data context** – maintaining data separation where appropriate;

- **isolation** – preventing unintended updates to ancestor data.

Let's take a look at each in turn, starting with data mapping.

Mapping Our Data

A key strength of Ractive is its ability to update data on the fly very quickly – this might either be via the console as part of a test, or at some point within our code. If we take our checkbox component demo as an example and preview the results, we should see the same familiar text we had from before, shown in Figure 6-4:

Creating a Checkbox Component

■ This is a title

Figure 6-4. Our checkbox component, before updating the text

MINI EXERCISE – CHANGING THE TEXT OF OUR CHECKBOX

To prove how easy it is to update the text, let's run through a couple of examples:

1. Open a new console session in your browser, by pressing F12 or Ctrl + Shift + I.

2. At the prompt in the Console tab, enter the following code, and press Enter:

```
ractive.findComponent("checkbox").set("title", "Changing title...")
```

3. Notice how the text value of our checkbox now says "Changing title..."?

If we preview the results after making the change outlined in step 2, we can see the updated text value shown in Figure 6-5:

Figure 6-5. *Our updated checkbox*

It's worth noting that in every instance, a Promise is returned, with a status of "resolved" – we can see this shown in Figure 6-6:

```
[R  [      Elements    Console    Audits    Performance    Sources    »           ⋮  ✕

⊘  | top                    ▼ |  Filter                     All levels ▼                ⚙

▶ Ractive.js 0.9.3 in debug mode, more...                      log.js:45
> ractive.findComponent("checkbox").set("title", "Changing title...")
◁ ▶ Promise {[[PromiseStatus]]: "resolved", [[PromiseValue]]: undefined}
> |
```

Figure 6-6. *Return value of our text change*

It is worth noting that we can't use the standard `ractive.set()` command to update keypath values within a component – if we try to, then it will return a Promise on completion, but the content on screen will not be updated.

Maintaining Data Context

An important feature within Ractive components is maintaining a separate data context – this is to ensure we don't pollute data held in the enclosing instance. However, if there is an explicit mapping in place, then data held in both the component and its parent instance will be updated.

What does this mean for us? In practice, it means we can initiate multiple instances of a component, safe in the knowledge that data will not accidentally leak into other instances. Of course, it still means that we can update the wrong instance, but we only have ourselves to blame! Leaving that aside, let's take a moment to explore how this works in action.

MAINTAINING DATA CONTEXT

For this next exercise, we'll use Codepen to make the changes:

1. We'll start by browsing to `https://codepen.io`, then click on Create | New Pen.

2. In the JS pane, go ahead and add the following code:

```
Ractive.components.MySelector = Ractive.extend({
  data: {
    shades: '',
    option: ''
  }
})

var ractive = Ractive({
  el: "#container",
  template: `
    <MySelector shades='{{colors}}' option='1' />
  `,
  data: {
    name: 'Colors',
    colors: ['red', 'yellow', 'black']
  }
})
```

3. We need to configure our Codepen to use Ractive, so click on Settings | JavaScript.
    Add this link in under the Add External JavaScript option, then hit Close:

    `https://cdn.jsdelivr.net/npm/ractive`

4. At the bottom of the screen, look for Console and click it – we will be making use of
    Codepen's console feature throughout this demo.

This demo is best seen in a vertical split view, so go ahead and click on Change View, then pick the left-hand
option under Editor Layout. To make it even easier, the HTML and CSS views can be minimized, as they are not
required for this demo.

---

5. In the Console tab, which should be on the right, go ahead and add the following
    lines of code, then press Enter – what do you get back?

    ```
    const widget = ractive.findComponent('MySelector')
    widget.get()
    ```

6. Now try entering `ractive.get()` at the console command line – what is returned
    this time?

7. Let's alter the values shown – this time, try running `ractive.set('colors.1', 'green')` at the command prompt.

8. What happens if you repeat step 6 – what values does it return?

9. If we now re-run step 7, does it return the same values as before?

An interesting set of results, right? I'll bet that some of the results aren't quite what you expect, so let's take a moment to explore them in more detail. For question 1, we should return the following answer:

```
Object {
  option: 1,
  shades: ["red", "yellow", "black"]
}
```

At first glance you might not have expected anything to be returned for shades, but take another look at the code; you should find that shades is mapped through to {{colors}}, so will return the values we've seen in this example. In question 2, we simply return the values already specified in our Ractive instance:

```
Object {
  colors: ["red", "yellow", "black"],
  name: "Colors"
}
```

In question 3, this is where things start to get interesting – we updated the `colors.1` value; this will change the yellow value to green (based on index order). However, as colors is mapped through to shades, any modifications on one side will affect the other: in this instance running the same `.get()` commands for both ractive and widget will return the same results for both, leaving the other values untouched.

Isolating Content

So far, we've talked about Ractive's ability to maintain data separation as part of creating a component – by default, data is kept isolated unless there is a specific mapping between the component and its ancestor. If we take this block of code as an example, it won't render anything on screen:

```
Ractive.components.ChildComp = Ractive.extend({
  template: 'Message returned: {{ message }}'
})

const instance = Ractive({
  el: 'body',
  template: '<ChildComp />',
  data: {
    message: 'ChildComp will not know anything about this message'
  }
})
```

In this instance, ChildComp won't print anything, as although the message is referenced in the component, it isn't defined. To overcome this, we can set the `isolated` property to `false` – by default this is set to true, so it is blocking access to the message keypath within the parent instance.

Rendering Content in Context

At this point, we have a working checkbox component – it renders onscreen using a dark, moody color scheme, and we can customize the text assigned to it. Seems pretty standard – is there anything else we need to add to it?

Well, what if we did need to add something? A good example might be additional text – if we had to do this by default for several checkboxes, then it seems sensible to add it in as part of the component. Fortunately this is easy to achieve – Ractive provides the {{yield}} method, which we can use to override what is passed from the parent to be displayed within the component; for convenience, a {{content}} method also exists, but this is for internal use within a component only.

For more details on using the {{yield}} method, please browse to `https://ractive.js.org/api/#yield` – more details are available for the {{content}} method at `https://ractive.js.org/api/#content`.

For our next example, we'll make use of {{yield}} as we'll be passing content through from the parent instance to our component. We will need to make changes to our component and how it is called from Ractive.

MAKING USE OF YIELD

Let's make a start:

1. We'll start by editing the component itself – go ahead and open up a copy of `checkbox.js` from earlier, then modify this line as highlighted:

```
</label><br>{{yield disclaimer}}',
```

2. Our method for initializing the component within Ractive also changes – comment out the existing block beginning with `var checkbox = new Checkbox..` (around line 29), and add the following code underneath it, leaving a line in between:

```
var ractive = new Ractive({
  el: '#container',
  template: `
    <checkbox title="This is a test">
      {{#partial disclaimer}}<div class="disclaimer">This is a test disclaimer -
      click <a on-click="@.disclaim(), false" href="#">here for details</a>.
      </div>{{/partial}}
    </checkbox>
  `,
  components: {
    checkbox: Checkbox
  },
  data: {
    title: 'This is a title',
    active: true
  }
});
```

149

3. Save the file, then preview the results – if all is well, we should see an updated checkbox appear, this time with our fake disclaimer text, as shown in Figure 6-7:

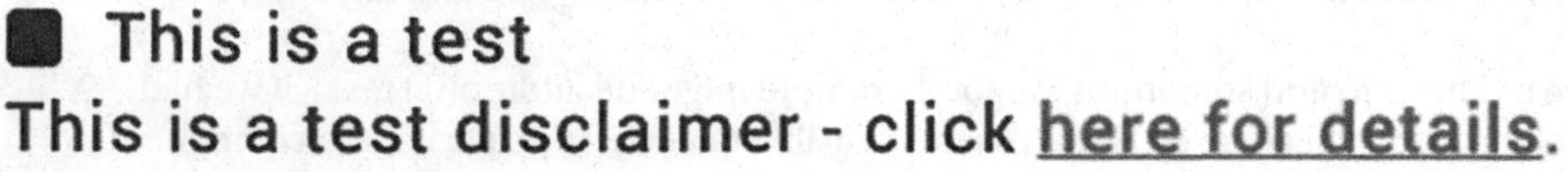

■ **This is a test**
This is a test disclaimer - click here for details.

Figure 6-7. Using {{yield}} in a component

The magic to making this work is in two places – to pass our content over, we make use of a {{partial}}. This has the name disclaimer against it; we match this with the reference within our Ractive instance's template. Anything within the {{partial}} tags that are located within our <checkbox> object will be rendered on screen, within our component.

Registering and Using Our Component

Over the course of the last few pages, we've explored how to create a simple checkbox component – as with many plugins within Ractive, we need to register our component for use within any project. This is an essential step, otherwise it isn't visible to Ractive; fortunately there are three ways to register our component, depending on our needs:

- We can do it globally, via the Ractive.components static property – perfect if we're using multiple instances of Ractive, and don't want to register multiple times:

```
// Available to all instances of Ractive.
Ractive.components.MyComponent = Ractive.extend({ ... });
```

- We can do it on a per component basis, via the component's components initialization property:

```
// Only available for instances of AnotherComponent.
const AnotherComponent = Ractive.extend({
  components: { MyComponent }
});
```

- We may prefer to limit registration to individual instances as needed, using the instance's components initialization property:

```
// Only available to this specific instance.
  const ractive = new Ractive({
  components: { MyComponent }
});
```

When it comes to using the component though – we have two options we can use: we can mount it directly on an element, or we can reference it in our Ractive application. Mounting it on an element takes the form of initating a new instance of our component as an object:

```
var checkbox = new Checkbox({
  el: '#container',
  data: {
    title: 'This is a title',
    active: true
  }
})
```

Notice how similar this is to a standard Ractive instance? This is intentional – when we specify a Ractive component using this method, we treat initialization as if we were initializing a new Ractive instance. It also means that we can do things such as registering a new instance of a component with the same properties, but with a new name:

```
Ractive.components.secondCheckbox = checkbox;
```

If we were to run the checkbox demo in a browser, then executed this command, we would see the results shown in Figure 6-8:

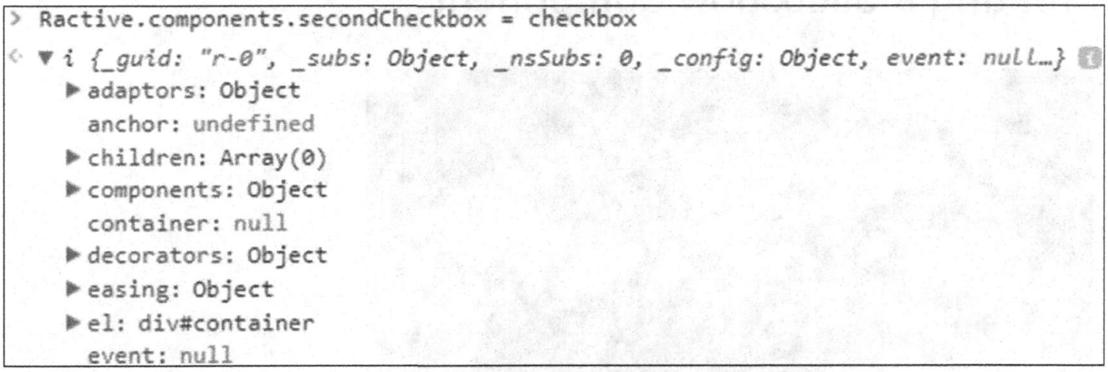

```
> Ractive.components.secondCheckbox = checkbox
< ▼ i {_guid: "r-0", _subs: Object, _nsSubs: 0, _config: Object, event: null…}
      ▶ adaptors: Object
        anchor: undefined
      ▶ children: Array(0)
      ▶ components: Object
        container: null
      ▶ decorators: Object
      ▶ easing: Object
      ▶ el: div#container
        event: null
```

Figure 6-8. Setting a new instance of a component

However, we may prefer to mount a component against our Ractive application for general use; we can either register it globally (using the example of our checkbox from earlier):

```
Ractive.components.checkbox = Checkbox;
```

...or specify it as part of the Ractive configuration, this time specifying the slideshow component:

```
var ractive = new Ractive({
    ...
  components: {
    slideshow: Slideshow
  },
    ...
});
```

Which method we use will of course depend on our requirements – there is clearly no need to register it globally, if we're only going to make limited use of a component, for example!

Okay – let's move on: we've constructed a simple component in the form of a checkbox; it's perfectly useful, but a trifle limiting! Let's take things up a notch, and look at building something a little more in-depth: how about a slideshow? I'm sure you will make use of one at some point, so let's dive in and see what is required to construct such a component using Ractive.

Taking It to the Next Level

A question – how many times have you visited a site, only to see the ubiquitous slider effect being displayed, in all its glory? I'll bet the answer will range from "a fair few" to "too many – I've lost count" – sound like a familiar story? If done well, a slider can impart the proverbial thousand words (too badly misquote that phrase); done badly....well, let's just not go there...

For our next project, you've probably guessed the theme by now; we're going to build a slider! These are not difficult to build; the magic is really in making sure our images are up to scratch, with only minimal code required to implement the sliding effect.

However, the key thing here is that this example is based on the one given in the original documentation for Ractive; this is also partially an exercise in taking an existing idea, and letting it evolve into something new. To give you an idea of how our slideshow component will look, a screenshot of it is shown in Figure 6-9:

Figure 6-9. *Our completed slider effect*

For this exercise, I will be using images from the Pixabay library, hosted at `https://pixabay.com`. I've chosen images of cameras, as this is one of my many interests; if you want to use something else, then please make sure you pick the right size – the size I used was 640px by 426px; for different sizes, please adjust the CSS styling accordingly.

CREATING A SLIDESHOW COMPONENT

Okay – without further ado, let's make a start on developing our slideshow component:

1. We'll start by creating a new folder in our project area – give it the name slideshow.

2. Next up, go ahead and copy the img, css and font folders from the code download that accompanies this book – drop all three into the slideshow folder; we'll be making use of both shortly.

3. We will also need to add some scripting, so go ahead and add a new folder called js into the new area.

4. It's time to start adding some code – we'll make a start with the HTML markup that will form the basis for our demo. Go ahead and add the following code into a new file at the root of the slideshow folder, saving it as slideshow.html:

```
<!doctype html>
<html lang='en-GB'>
<head>
  <meta charset='utf-8'>
  <title>Beginning Ractive: Creating Components</title>
  <link rel='stylesheet' href='css/slideshow.css'>
</head>
<body>
  <h1>Creating a Slideshow Component</h1>

  <div id=container'></div>

  <script id="slideshow" type="text/ractive">
    <div class='slideshow'>
      <div class='main'>
        <a class='prev' on-click="goto(current - 1)"><span>&lsaquo;</span></a>
        {{#if images[current]}}
          <div class='main-image' style='background-image:
          url("{{images[current].src}}");'></div>
        {{/if}}
        <a class='next' on-click="goto(current + 1)"><span>&rsaquo;</span></a>
        <span class="caption">{{images[current].caption}}</span>
      </div>
    </div>
  </script>
  <script src='js/ractive.min.js'></script>
  <script src='js/slideshow.js'></script>
</body>
</html>
```

5. We next need to add copies of the Ractive library files – for this, extract copies of ractive.min.js and ractive.min.js.map into the js subfolder.

6. It's time to now add in our main script, which is where the magic happens; for this, add the following code to a new file. We'll go through it section by section, starting with defining some variables:

```
var images = [
  { src: './img/camera1.jpg', caption: 'Proin eget pretium neque pellentesque
  malesuada vestibulum aliquam' },
  { src: './img/camera2.jpg', caption: 'Phasellus et dolor a nunc dignissim' },
  { src: './img/camera3.jpg', caption: 'Mauris nunc ante ultrices ut' },
  { src: './img/camera4.jpg', caption: 'Lorem ipsum dolor sit amet consectetur' },
  { src: './img/camera5.jpg', caption: 'Aenean congue mauris rhoncus aliquet
  massa ante' },
  { src: './img/camera6.jpg', caption: 'Nunc in sapien non ipsum ultricies
  egestas' }
];
```

■ **Note** The odd looking text is from the Lipsum text generator, available at `http://www.lipsum.com/` – please feel free to adjust to suit.

7. Next up comes the main component – here we're setting a standard template, then using the `goto` function to control the carousel motion for switching in each image:

```
var Slideshow = Ractive.extend({
  template: '#slideshow',
  goto: function ( index ) {
    var images = this.get( 'images' );
    // handle wrap around
    var num = ( index + images.length ) % images.length;
    this.set( 'current', num );
  },
  data: function () { return { current: 0 } }
});
```

8. Last, but by no means least, we add in the Ractive instance that initializes a new instance of our slideshow component, complete with images:

```
var slideshow = new Slideshow({
  target: '#container',
  data: {
    images: images
  }
});
```

9. Save this file as `slideshow.js` into the `js` subfolder.

At this point, if all is well, we should be able to see our slideshow appear when previewing the results in a browser. It won't be perfect at this stage, but could easily be used as a basis for something more complex, in future projects. There are however a few useful pointers we should examine, so let's take a moment to review the code in more detail.

Understanding How It All Worked

Although the code may at first appear a little complex, in reality it's not that difficult to understand; it uses principles we've already touched on earlier in this book. To make it easier to understand, let's have a look at the two key files in more detail, namely, slideshow.html and slideshow.js. We'll start with the markup first:

```
<script id="slideshow" type="text/ractive">
  <div class='slideshow'>
    <div class='main'>
      <a class='prev' on-click="goto(current - 1)"><span>&lsaquo;</span></a>
      {{#if images[current]}}
        <div class='main-image' style='background-image: url("{{images[current].
        src}}");'></div>
      {{/if}}
      <a class='next' on-click="goto(current + 1)"><span>&rsaquo;</span></a>
      <span class="caption">{{images[current].caption}}</span>
    </div>
  </div>
</script>
```

Switching to the markup (as shown in step 4), we see the the now familiar container, in the form of <div id="container"></div> - we can of course use any name we choose, but it helps to be consistent in the naming approach you use, so you can reuse code at a later date.

Below the container <div> this is the <script> tags that form our slideshow component – we nest a few <divs> to help with layout; inside this we have next and previous links that call the appropriate function in our Ractive instance, using an on-click directive. The real magic here is the {{#if}}…{{/if}} statement; this checks for the presence of images in the images array (from within our component). If they are present, it will render each in turn on screen. We then top this off with a <span> that simply renders the caption for the chosen image on screen, directly from the array.

Moving on, let's now focus our attention on our component – here's a recap of our component code:

```
var Slideshow = Ractive.extend({
  template: '#slideshow',
  goto: function ( index ) {
    var images = this.get( 'images' );
    // handle wrap around
    var num = ( index + images.length ) % images.length;
    this.set( 'current', num );
  },
  data: function () { return { current: 0 } }
});
```

By now, some of this will be familiar – we're using Ractive.extend to create our new component, which will use the #slideshow template. We've added a goto function that gets the images element on the page, then calculates the index of the next item to scroll to, and assigns this to num. Our data function is present simply to ensure that image 0 is the first one that is displayed on screen, when the component is initialized.

To round it off, we have a Ractive instance initialized based on our new slideshow component – it's worth noting that even though it is a component, it will as if they are just another Ractive instance. Inside this instance, we specify our target container as #target, and assign the images array as the source for our data within this component.

Yay – we have a working component! The key to this is keeping it simple – in many cases, we can build our components using standard HTML markup and CSS, with only a smattering of JavaScript-based functionality required. This is the principle that other developers have used to great effect by producing components; many are available for download from places such as Google or the NPM directory. To help get you started, I've picked out a few examples for you to try out in your projects – let's take a look at them in more detail.

Using Pre-Built Components

The beauty about using Ractive to create components is that we're not limited in what we can design. Each component is made up of nothing more than standard JavaScript, CSS and HTML markup, with only minimal additional code required to encapsulate it into a component!

This makes it easy to construct components for reuse – it's worth taking a look online, as others have already produced components for this purpose. There are several good places to look, although Google and NPMJS (https://www.npmjs.com/) are my personal favorites. A quick search online as part of researching for this book has thrown up a few possibilities that might be worth exploring:

- **Ractive-Require**: a component loader for Ractive, available from https://github.com/CodeCorico/ractive-require.

- **Bootstrap:** fancy making use of Bootstrap's CSS? Try this component out, available from https://github.com/skyrpex/ractive-components-bootstrap-modal.

- **Select**: A <select> replacement component for Ractive, downloadable from https://github.com/jondum/ractive-select.

- **Stepper**: if you need to customize input[type="number"], this isn't easy; instead try using this component, available from https://github.com/jondum/ractive-stepper.

- **Splitter:** this splits Ractive files; it's available from https://github.com/engagespark/racsplit.

- **Datepicker**: need to present a date? Try ractive-datepicker, available from https://github.com/jondum/ractive-datepicker.

In most cases, using them should be very straightforward – many will simply require linking in (as we did for the transition / animation plugins, back in Chapter 5), then we can register them using the components property, thus:

```
components: {
  stepper: require('ractive-stepper')
},
```

There is a downside to using plugins from other authors though – not all component authors are good about keeping their projects up to date! In some cases, though, if the component is relatively straightforward, it may only need minor tweaks to get it working; perhaps this is a good opportunity to update it and release it as a new version?

Taking Care of Events

At some point in development, we will need to respond to events of some description – this might be when we open or close a modal dialog box, for example.

We've already covered event handling within the DOM or of lifecycle events in detail, back in *Chapter 4, Handling Events*; the great thing about Ractive is that many of the events that can be used in the DOM, can also be used within components with little change. Let's refresh our memory with a simple example:

```
Ractive({
  template: `
    <button type="button" on-click="['clickedArray', 'Hello, World!']">Push me!</button>
  `,
  oninit(){
    this.on('clickedArray', (event, msg) => { console.log(msg); })
  }
});
```

Although event handlers can take different forms (such as proxied events, or responding to simple functions), the most common usage is likely to be the ubiquitous on-click handler! For this, we're using the on-* directive; this maps through to the `clickedArray` event handler in our Ractive instance.

Managing Event Propagation in Components

Where things get a little more interesting is if we need to use event propagation – the same principles apply as to using it in the DOM. The only real difference is that when it comes to reference a propagated event, we must use namespacing – these events are normally namespaced with the publishing component's name as a prefix.

To understand what this means in practice, let's take a look at an example – go ahead and browse to `https://codepen.io/alexlibby/pen/BdavoR`. I've set this up as a Codepen-based example this time, so we can get the full effects of using console without any other messages appearing. Here's the code reproduced from the demo:

```
Ractive.DEBUG = false;

const Child = Ractive.extend({
  template: '<span></span>',
  oncomplete(){
    this.fire('childevt');
  }
});

const Parent = Ractive.extend({ components: { Child }, template: '<Child />'});

const instance = Ractive({ target: "body", components: { Parent }, template: '<Parent />'
});

instance.on('Child.childevt', function(){
  console.log('Hello World!');
});
```

This looks pretty straightforward, right? The starting point is the `const instance = Ractive` line; here we're specifying our main Ractive instance, whilst at the same time registering our `Parent` component. Our `Parent` component in turn registers an instance of a `Child` component.

When our Ractive instance is initialized, this automatically initializes the `Child` component; this inserts `"Hello World!"` to the Codepen console area, as indicated in Figure 6-10:

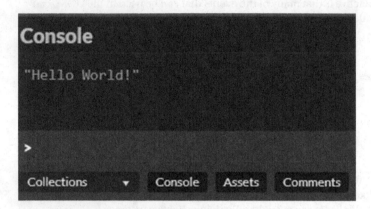

Figure 6-10. *Event propagation at play*

The observant of you may also notice the presence of the `cm-string` class in the above screenshot; don't worry, this is coming from Codepen, and not our demo!

Stopping Event Propagation

There may be occasions though when we don't want events propagating – a typical example might be to control click handlers for elements that are nested; after all, we don't want a whole series of events firing one after another!

Fortunately this is easy to set up – the simplest option is to add a return false; into the event handler; try adding the following lines of code into the Parent component, immediately after `template: '<Child />'`:

```
onrender: function() {
 this.on('Child.childevt', function(){ return false; });
}
```

This has the effect of calling both `event.stopPropagation()` and `event.preventDefault()`, provided the event we're stopping is a DOM event. An alternative method is to assign an event handler using the `on-*` directive – the danger though is that if this replacement event is not stopped, then this will continue to propagate too!

For some more in-depth examples of stopping propagation within components, please refer to the main documentation at `https://ractive.js.org/concepts/#stopping-propagation`.

Okay – let's change tack: we're almost at the end of this chapter; how about we try out something completely different? So far, we've worked on the basis of creating our own component, but what if we wanted to use an existing component library such as jQuery UI? This is easy enough to do, so let's dive in and take a look.

Working with Third-Party Libraries

There are hundreds of third-party JavaScript libraries available for use on the Web – many are regularly updated, with too many slowly gathering dust as their lead developer has moved onto other projects.

One library that is still very much in use is the well-known jQuery UI component project; this popular library has been around late 2007 and is used on over 193,000 of the top 1 million websites worldwide (according to the libscore.com website). To prove we can integrate the two within a project, we'll use it to implement a jQuery UI datepicker that can be controlled from within a standard Ractive instance. To prove it's possible, Figure 6-11 shows a screenshot of what to expect as our prototype:

Figure 6-11. *Ractive and jQuery UI working together*

For our next exercise, we're going to use a slightly different approach and treat it as something of a proof of concept – it's still perfectly valid, but would need further development before using it on a production machine. Go ahead and take a copy of the jqueryui component folder from within the code download that accompanies this book. Save it to our project area, then run the jqueryui.html file at the root of this folder.

What may surprise you though is that if you were expecting lots of additional, complex code, then I am sorry to disappoint – it doesn't need a great deal! I should qualify this though – our code is very basic, and definitely needs filling out with more functionality:

```
var datepickcmp = Ractive.extend({
  el: 'container',
  template: '#template',
  data: {
    label : "Date"
  },
  onrender: function ( options ) {
    $( "#datepicker" ).datepicker();
  }
});

var datepick = new datepickcmp();
```

The key to making it this happen is within the onrender function, where we initiate our datepicker instance – we use a label keypath/reference, but this is simply to add a label to our input box, as shown in Figure 6-11.

All of our functionality is encased in a datepickcomp component; we can then initialize it in the same way as any standard Ractive component. It does mean that with a little care and planning, we're not obliged to have to create our own components – we can always try writing wrappers for existing third-party libraries, such as jQuery UI!

Summary

One of Ractive's key strengths has been its lightweight approach to implementing functionality - we use nothing more than plain HTML, CSS, and JavaScript, which makes for a very easy learning experience! The same can be said for building components; over the course of this chapter we've explored how easy it to create components, so let's take a moment to consider what we've covered in this chapter.

We kicked off by introducing the steps needed to initialize a basic component - we discussed the reasons why it is beneficial to take that extra time and create components to help with saving time and effort at a later date. We then moved onto building a simple checkbox component, exploring how to set it up and provide default styling in our projects.

Next up came a look at data binding - we discussed how Ractive automatically manages updates to both text on screen, and within each data context created for each component. With our component created, we then moved onto understanding how to register and use it in within our projects.

We then took things up a notch by creating our own slideshow component - we saw how it used similar techniques, but this time adding event handlers and incorporating ancillary media. We then moved onto look at using pre-built components, as an alternative to using our own, before stepping aside to cover the theory behind managing events and event propagation. We then rounded out the chapter by exploring a proof of concept that proves we can easily create Ractive components that use third-party libraries such as jQuery.

Phew - we've certainly covered a lot of ground in a short space! But never fear - our journey does not stop here: we still have more plugins to create, such as decorators, and getting to grips with automating our build process. There's plenty more to come, so let's continue with a look at building more plugins in the next chapter of our journey.

CHAPTER 7

■ ■ ■

Building Plugins

So far, we've created our site with Ractive, set up methods for manipulating data, and taken care of handling events – all good so far, right?

Well, we can do more – in the previous chapter we explored creating reusable components for projects. Let's take this theme of reusability a step further, by creating plugins for reuse in our projects! Over the course of this chapter we'll explore some of the other plugin types that are available for Ractive, and learn how easy it is to create them in our projects.

The Plugin Types So Far

For many years, it was common practice to try to include everything in a core file – this made developing easy as everything was in one place, but this was at the cost of lugging around a large core file! With the emphasis on speed being our number one priority, this approach of storing functionality in a single file won't work, so a different approach is needed.

One of the core tenets of Ractive is speed – to this end, it has moved to encompassing functionality within separate plugins. While this can increase the number of requests to the server (not ideal, although we can mitigate by bundling multiple plugins into one file), it does mean that we focus on what we need, and can discard the rest. We've already seen this approach in use back as far as Chapter 3, *Binding Data*, where we created a plugin to adapt content generated by the Color Thief plugin used in one of the demos. We then touched on creating event plugins in Chapter 4, *Handling Events*; we continued this into Chapter 5, with a look at creating transition and easing plugins.

What else is available, I hear you ask? Well, there are three other types we can use, and which we have yet to cover:

- **Decorators** – a simple means to add behavior to, or augment, a node.

- **Interpolators** – these plugins transition from one object or array or value, to another, such as from one color to another (using color names).

- **Partials** – snippets of code that can be reused within templates or as part of larger partials.

We can of course always use existing plugins created by other authors, and made available online. This will work for a while, but become too limiting; after all, not every plugin we come across will suit our needs exactly! There will come a time when it is beneficial to create our own plugin, so without further ado, let's continue with that theme and kick off with a look at creating decorator plugins.

© Alex Libby 2017
A. Libby, *Beginning Ractive.js*, https://doi.org/10.1007/978-1-4842-3093-0_7

Working with Decorators

Cast your mind back to Chapter 3, *Binding Data*, where we covered how to create an adaptor plugin that interfaced with the excellent Color Thief plugin, created by Lokesh Dhakar?

In some respects, decorators can be seen to complement adaptors – the latter are perfect for translating data from an external source into something that Ractive can consume; decorators are designed to add behavior to, or augment, a node at the point of rendering it. They really come into their own when used with external libraries such as jQuery UI (which we touched on briefly at the end of the previous chapter), or Bootstrap (which we will come onto in Chapter 8, *Working with Other Libraries*).

To really see how decorators operate, we need to see them in action – over the course of the next few pages, we will create our own version of that ubiquitous UI tool, the tooltip, as a plugin; let's first take a look at the basic skeleton of a decorator plugin.

Writing Our First Decorator Plugin

As is often the case with plugins, we can make them as simple or as complicated as we like – I'm a keen advocate of the 1:1 ratio, where our plugin shouldn't do more than one thing. Clearly this isn't going to be possible in every instance, but we should equally not try to overcomplicate our design!

A perfect example of where decorators can be used to great effect, are within tooltips; Figure 7-1 shows a screenshot of such an example, which we will create shortly in our next exercise:

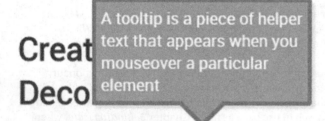

Figure 7-1. *Our tooltip decorator*

Before we dive into coding, it's important to understand the basics of how these operate. At a very basic level, a decorator plugin contains two functions; the `teardown` function must be present, but the `update` one is optional and can be omitted if it is surplus to requirements:

```
const myDecorator = function(node[, ...args]) {
  // Setup code
  return {
    teardown: function(){
      // Cleanup code
    },
    update: function([...args]){
      // Update code
    }
  };
};
```

Decorators are called on if Ractive detects that they are to be used; they pass a node argument into the decorator, which is a reference to the element where the decorator should be applied. Arguments may also be provided if needed – if these are updated, then this has the effect of calling the teardown function first; this has the effect of setting up the decorator again on the target element.

Okay – let's move on: time to put some of this theory into practice! For our next demo, we're going to create a tooltip plugin that uses CSS instead of images to provide styling. Our demo will be spread over several pages, so without further ado, let's make a start with coding our plugin.

BUILDING OUR DECORATOR

1. We'll begin by creating a folder in our project area; save this folder as tooltip.

2. Within this folder, go ahead and create two folders – save one with the name css, and the other with the name js.

3. From a copy of the code download that accompanies this book, go ahead and extract a copy of the font folder from a previous project, and save it into the tooltip folder.

4. We also need our two ractive files – go ahead and extract copies of ractive.min.js and ractive.min.js.map from a previous project, and save these into the js subfolder.

5. We're now at a stage where we can start to code! Open up a new document, then add the following code, which we'll go through step by step:

```
var tooltipDecorator = function ( node, content ) {
    var tooltip, handlers, eventName;
```

6. Next add the start function – this takes care of handling the mouseover event:

```
var start = function ( event ) {
    tooltip = document.createElement( tooltipDecorator.elementName );
    tooltip.className = tooltipDecorator.className;
    tooltip.textContent = content;
    node.parentNode.insertBefore( tooltip, node );
},
```

7. Once our mouseover event has been fired, we need to keep track of the mouse position – we'll do that with a move function:

```
move = function ( event ) {
    tooltip.style.left = event.clientX + tooltipDecorator.offsetX + 'px';
    tooltip.style.top = ( event.clientY - tooltip.clientHeight + tooltipDecorator.
    offsetY ) + 'px';
},
```

8. At some point we will exit the tooltip area; the `leave` function will take care of removing the tooltip until the next time we enter the tooltip area:

```
leave = function () {
  tooltip.parentNode.removeChild( tooltip );
}
```

9. We need to add code that assigns each of these functions to the relevant mouse event, so go ahead and add this object:

```
// Assign functions to event handlers
handlers = {
  mouseover: start,
  mousemove: move,
  mouseleave: leave
};
```

10. This penultimate `for...` event takes care of firing the appropriate handler for the event that is triggered:

```
// add event handlers to the node
for ( eventName in handlers ) {
  if ( handlers.hasOwnProperty( eventName ) ) {
    node.addEventListener( eventName, handlers[ eventName ], false );
  }
}
```

11. To tie it all together, we must end our plugin with a `teardown` function – this removes each of the event listeners prior to tearing down our plugin:

```
return {
  teardown: function () {
    for ( eventName in handlers ) {
      if ( handlers.hasOwnProperty( eventName )) {
        node.removeEventListener( eventName, handlers[ eventName ], false );
      }
    }
  }
};
```

12. Phew – we're all most there we just need to add some final default values to make our plugin work:

```
tooltipDecorator.className = 'ractive-tooltip';
tooltipDecorator.element = 'p';
tooltipDecorator.offsetX = -100;
tooltipDecorator.offsetY = -40;
```

13. Go ahead and save the file as `tooltip.js` within the `js` subfolder. We now need to add some styling, so let's move onto the second part of our exercise.

Styling Our Plugin

We now have the basics of our plugin in place, but it will look awful without some form of styling – we could take the old school approach of using background images, but this isn't necessary.

We can instead use a pure-CSS approach; with the help of the *CSSArrowPlease!* website (http://www. cssarrowplease.com/), it's easy enough to set up some suitable styles. The trick to making it all work is to use pseudo-selectors; it might not work for older browsers that don't support them, but this is a small price to pay as it really only affects IE8 or older browsers.

ADDING STYLING TO OUR DECORATOR

That aside, let's get styling:

1. Go ahead and create a new file, then add the following styles, saving the file as
   tooltip.css in the css subfolder:

   ```
   @font-face { font-family: 'robotoregular'; src: url('../font/Roboto-Regular-
   webfont.woff') format('woff'); font-weight: normal; font-style: normal; }

   body { font-family: robotoregular, sans-serif; position: relative; height: 100%;
   padding: 3rem 30%; margin: 0; font-size: 1rem; color: #353535; }
   ```

2. The trick to making our tooltip plugin work lies in the following styles – the
   .ractive-tooltip covers some general styles:

   ```
   .ractive-tooltip {
     position: fixed;
     display: block;
     width: 12.5rem;
     padding: 0.3rem;
     background: #a9a9a9;
     border: 0.25rem solid #838383;
     box-shadow: 0.1875rem 0.1875rem 0.1875rem rgba(0, 0, 0, 0.1);
     border-radius: 0.1875rem;
     color: #ffffff;
   }
   ```

3. ...while the :before and :after styles take care of the arrow on our callout
   modal:

   ```
   .ractive-tooltip:after, .ractive-tooltip:before {
     top: 100%;
     left: 50%;
     border: solid transparent;
     content: " ";
     height: 0;
     width: 0;
     position: absolute;
     pointer-events: none;
   }
   ```

165

```
.ractive-tooltip:after { border-color: rgba(169, 169, 169, 0); border-top-color:
#a9a9a9; border-width: 1.25rem; margin-left: -1.25rem; }

.ractive-tooltip:before { border-color: rgba(131, 131, 131, 0); border-top-color:
#838383; border-width: 1.625rem; margin-left: -1.625rem; }
```

4. At this point go ahead and save the file.

We now have all of the components in place to make our tooltip work – let's continue with our demo, with a look at how we register our decorator plugin in more detail.

Registering and Using Our Decorator

Registering a decorator plugin is very easy – the process follows the same principles as used for other plugins, inasmuch as there are three ways to register a decorator:

- We can register it globally, via the Ractive.decorators static property:

  ```
  Ractive.decorators.myDecorator = myDecorator;
  ```

- If we want to register on a per component basis, we can do so, using the component's decorators initialization property:

  ```
  const MyComponent = Ractive.extend({
    decorators: { myDecorator }
  });
  ```

- We may prefer to register it as needed for each instance – we can do this using the instance's decorators initialization property:

  ```
  const ractive = new Ractive({
    decorators: { myDecorator }
  });
  ```

Which method you use will really be dictated by each project's requirements – I personally find that a good rule of thumb is to register globally, if out of all of the instances used in your project, most of them require the decorator to be used in some capacity.

If however you only need it in a couple of instances, then I would recommend registering individually; this applies equally to whether you use the plugin within a component, or within a Ractive instance. Note – there is no hard and fast rule; it's all about being sensible with our choices!

REGISTERING OUR DECORATOR

With this in mind, let's add the code we need to register our decorator:

1. Go ahead and open up `tooltip.js`, if it isn't already open – miss a line, then add the following code:

```
tooltipDecorator.className = 'ractive-tooltip';
tooltipDecorator.element = 'p';
tooltipDecorator.offsetX = -100;
tooltipDecorator.offsetY = -40;

Ractive.decorators.tooltip = tooltipDecorator;

ractive = new Ractive({
  el: 'container',
  template: '#tpl'
});
```

2. Save the file – to use our decorator, we need to provide an environment; for this, go ahead and add the following code to a new file, saving it as `tooltip.html` at the root of our tooltip folder:

```
<!doctype html>
<html>
<head>
  <meta charset='utf-8'>
  <title>Beginning Ractive: Creating Decorators</title>
  <link rel='stylesheet' href='css/tooltip.css'>
</head>
<body>
  <h1>Creating a Tooltip Decorator</h1>
  <div id='container'></div>

  <script id='tpl' type='text/ractive'>
    <p>This text contains <span as-tooltip="'A tooltip is a piece of helper text
    that appears when you mouseover a particular element'">tooltips</span>.</p>
  </script>

  <script src='js/ractive.min.js'></script>
  <script src='js/tooltip.js'></script>
</body>
</html>
```

3. Save the file – if all is well, we should see the tooltip appear when hovering over the word tooltip in our demo.

Yes – we finally reached the end of what is now our working demo! It may seem like we've covered a lot of code, but in reality the principles we've covered are very straightforward. Let's take a moment to reflect on what we've covered in more detail.

Exploring What Happened

Although our demo looked complicated, the bulk of it is used to either create and assign event handlers to node elements, or remove them as appropriate; we add some additional styling, where making use of CSS pseudo-selectors means that we avoid the need for additional media.

If we take a look at the code from our plugin in more detail, there are three parts that are of particular interest to us. The first is in how we define the element used to create our tooltip, set a CSS class, and define the content within:

```
tooltip = document.createElement( tooltipDecorator.elementName );
tooltip.className = tooltipDecorator.className;
tooltip.textContent = content;
```

A little further down, we set the move function – this is assigned to the mouseover event. This works out where to set the tooltip, based on the current mouse position plus any assigned offset value:

```
move = function ( event ) {
  tooltip.style.left = event.clientX + tooltipDecorator.offsetX + 'px';
  tooltip.style.top = ( event.clientY - tooltip.clientHeight + tooltipDecorator.offsetY ) +
  'px';
},
```

Of course this function by itself won't make sense; it will come alive once we define the various values needed for the move function:

```
tooltipDecorator.className = 'ractive-tooltip';
tooltipDecorator.element = 'p';
tooltipDecorator.offsetX = -100;
tooltipDecorator.offsetY = -40;
```

These values have to be set before we assign our decorator plugin to the Ractive.decorators property:

```
Ractive.decorators.tooltip = tooltipDecorator;
```

We can see the results of our assigned decorator plugin, if we enter Ractive.decorators at the console, as shown in Figure 7-2:

```
> Ractive.decorators
  ▼ Object {tooltip: function} ℹ
     ▼ tooltip: function ( node, content )
          className: "ractive-tooltip"
          element: "p"
          offsetX: -100
          offsetY: -40
          arguments: null
          caller: null
          length: 2
          name: "tooltipDecorator"
        ▶ prototype: Object
        ▶ __proto__: function ()
          [[FunctionLocation]]: tooltip.js:1
        ▶ [[Scopes]]: Scopes[1]
     ▶ __proto__: Object
>
```

Figure 7-2. *Viewing our decorator via console*

At this stage, there is one question we should ask ourselves – are we able to release our plugin for others to use, and hopefully help with maintaining or improving it? Granted, there will be occasions where releasing it won't be possible if we're working on a solution for internal company use. However if there isn't any issue in releasing our plugin, then it opens up a whole host of questions that need answering...

Making It Available for Others

One of the first questions we need to ask is ironically not where we want to host our plugin, but how we create it! This may seem a little nonsensical given we've just worked our way through creating one, but there is a way to automate much of the initial steps in creating any plugin we author. This opens up a real can of worms (proverbially speaking) – we will go through this in more detail shortly, but for now let's concentrate on how we can use Grunt to cover some of the grunt work for us.

Plugins also exist for vanilla NPM (https://www.npmjs.com/package/ractive); there are versions also available for Gulp, although these are either now out of date, or no longer maintained.

Using the Plugin Template for Grunt

For most projects, we can easily use a text editor to create a Ractive-based plugin – the exact type doesn't matter; they are just JavaScript files, which can be created in any application. However, for some, there may be a need to ensure consistency across all plugins developed; this includes both the initial framework, and checking any code added for consistency.

This simply isn't efficent - for this we need a task runner! Fortunately there is a Grunt-based plugin that can help with automating the initial creation; it's available for download from https://github .com/ractivejs/plugin-template. At this point though, it's important to note that this approach won't suit everyone; it requires a reasonable amount of prior knowledge of Grunt, Node.js, and ultimately using Git. If this isn't for you, please skip forward to the section *Creating Interpolator Plugins* later on in the chapter.

For those of you who would like to investigate the possibility of using Grunt, we'll go through the major steps required as part of the next exercise. For the sake of brevity, I will only go through each task at a high level; I would recommend searching on Google for specifics on how to install the relevant packages for your environment, if you do not already have them installed.

There are a few steps involved, so let's make a start – for each example, I've assumed we're using our `Ractive` project folder as a basis for completing this exercise. There are a few dependencies required to make it work – some are optional, depending on your circumstances, whilst others are required:

- A working installation of Node.js and NPM is required – for the purposes of installing, the default settings will work fine.

- You will also need a working installation of Git for the command line in your environment; a good search online will bring up details of how to achieve this.

- If you're able to publish your results online, then a GitHub account will be needed - this can be free or chargeable, depending on whether you can release your efforts with an open source license or a proprietary one.

SETTING UP PLUGIN TEMPLATE WITH GRUNT

Assuming our dependencies are installed and operational, let's make a start:

1. The first step is to create a new repositoryon GitHub, similar to my example shown in Figure 7-3, for a fictitious `ractive-transition-shake` plugin:

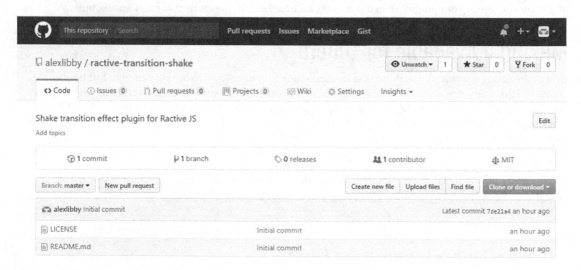

Figure 7-3. *An example GitHub site*

2. Next up we need to install Grunt as our task runner using Node.js — we would do this using the following commands; both are required to allow the Ractive template to work correctly:

```
$ npm install -g grunt-cli    # the taskrunner itself
$ npm install -g grunt-init   # the project scaffolding module
```

3. This can also be done as one line - $ npm install -g grunt-cli grunt-init, for those of you already familiar with NPM. We can see the results of a successful installation in Figure 7-4:

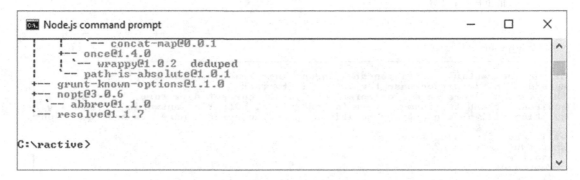

Figure 7-4. Installing Grunt and dependencies

4. With Grunt installed, the next step will be to clone the Ractive plugin template locally using Git; this is used by grunt-init to create our plugin file. The command to do it will appear similar to that shown in Figure 7-5, where the base_template folder will be a subfolder within our ractive project folder:

```
C:\ractive>git clone https://github.com/ractivejs/plugin-template /base_template

Cloning into '/base_template'...
remote: Counting objects: 566, done.
remote: Total 566 (delta 0), reused 0 (delta 0), pack-reused 566
Receiving objects: 100% (566/566), 621.91 KiB | 730.00 KiB/s, done.
Resolving deltas: 100% (119/119), done.
Checking connectivity... done.

C:\ractive>_
```

Figure 7-5. Cloning the grunt-ractive template project

For convenience, the URL to use is `https://github.com/ractivejs/plugin-template` /base_template, where /base_template is the destination folder on our PC.

5. Before we can create our template, we need to create a folder to store our new plugin in – in our example, go ahead and create a folder called `ractive-transition-shake` in our Ractive project folder, then change our working directory to this folder.

6. We can now create our plugin – for this, run the `grunt-init` command as shown in in Figure 7-6:

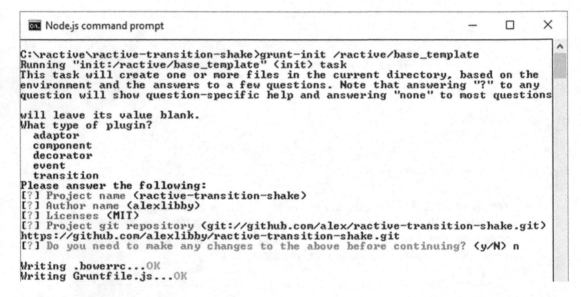

Figure 7-6. *Choosing our options for our plugin*

7. The next task we have to complete is to run `grunt-init`, which must be run from within the plugin folder – this is used to create our plugin template, based on the answers we give.

8.   Once we've made our choices, Grunt will go away and provision our template; the screenshot shown in Figure 7-7 shows a successful provision of our plugin template:

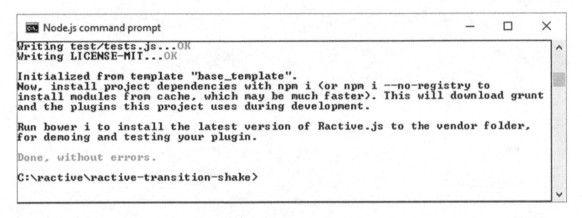

Figure 7-7. *Confirmation that our template has been created*

9.   We're almost there – just a couple more tasks to do! Up next, we will need to update any dependencies used within our project, by entering npm i at the Node.js command prompt:

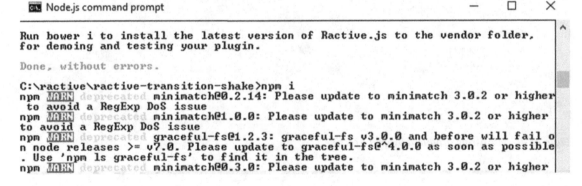

Figure 7-8. *Updating final dependencies*

10. Once completed we can open up the contents of our newly created folder: the contents of which will look similar to the extract shown in Figure 7-9:

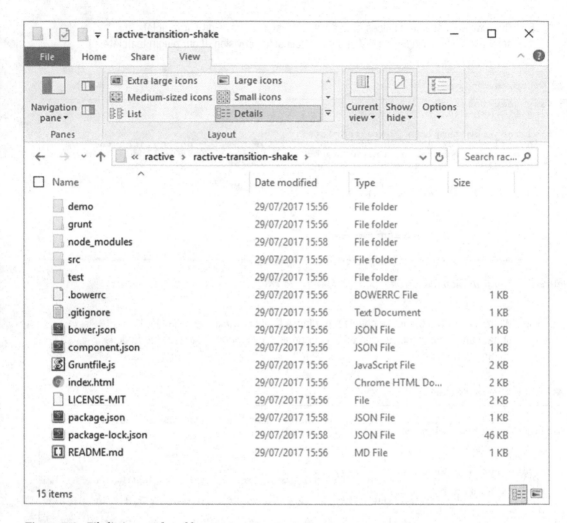

Figure 7-9. *File listing produced by grunt-ractive*

At this point our plugin template is provisioned, ready for us to start developing into something more complex. There are a couple of points to bear in mind though, as part of development:

- If we take another look at Figure 7-8, it's possible to see some errors displayed; the plugin-template facility hasn't been updated since 2015, so some of the dependencies will be out of date. This isn't likely to be too much of an issue though, as the basic provision of our template is a means to an end; if we're using NPM, then dependencies should be updated as part of the process.

- It is likely you will also see two warnings displayed, which relate to two missing sections; this is something we can easily fix! To do this, open up the `package.json` file we've will have created, and add the following sections as indicated, adjusting to suit:

```
"author": {
        "name": "alexlibby"
},
"repository": {
  "type": "git",
  "url": "https://github.com/alexlibby/ractive-transition-shake.git"
},
{ "license": "ISC" } { "license": "ISC" }
```

This is not the only Node.js based plugin that is available for use with Ractive – if our preference is to concentrate on compiling components from HTML markup files, then we can try the `grunt-ractive` plugin by Khaled Ahmed, available from `https://www.npmjs.com/package/grunt-ractive`. There are a handful of other projects listed in the NPM plugin directory at `https://www.npmjs.org`; many are a few years old, and may not work with current versions of Ractive, so try at your own risk!

Thinking further afield though, there are some considerations we need to be aware of when using Node.js – it may be worth spending time setting up tools such as Node, but only if our project requirements warrant it. To understand the implications of using Node, and why it may not be the ideal approach, let's take a moment to consider this in more detail.

Using a Template – an Epilogue

Over the last few pages we've worked our way through the basic steps of how one might automate the process of creating a Ractive-based plugin. Although there are a lot of steps involved in setting something like this up, many of these steps would be a one-off, and that Grunt will take care of most of the process once it is operational.

Seems pretty reasonable, right? Well – there is a sting in this tale: what if I were to say that using Grunt isn't a favored approach? Yes – you might well think I've really lost my marbles, so let me explain why using Grunt requires careful consideration.

There is something to be said for using Grunt (or a similar task runner) – the core plugin itself can easily be written by hand, but if we decide to use Grunt to automate the creation of our plugin, we can then extend the `package.json` file to include tasks such as testing, maintaining semantic versioning, and linting our code. There is also the process of uploading our code to a repository such as NPM or GitHub too – part of using open source software means we should give back to the community where possible!

However, the flip side of this is the need to learn yet more technology – if our plugin is only a dozen lines long, for example, then it will seem like overkill if we have to use GitHub, NPM, Node.js, and the like. After all, why add in all this extra work, if all we really need is a text editor and a copy of Ractive to develop, test, and prove our plugin works?

The morale of this little epilogue is that using a tool such as Grunt shouldn't be discounted outright, without at least considering the wider picture. If we already have elements in place such as Grunt, then it may make sense to incorporate an automated process. This is particularly true if we want to make use of a plugin such as `grunt-ractive-compile` (`https://www.npmjs.com/package/grunt-ractive-compile`) to compile our templates at the same time. If, however, we only need a couple of plugins for internal use only, then going to the extent of setting up Grunt may be something for another time.

Okay – let's change tack: over the course of this book, we've covered most of the plugin types that we can create within Ractive. There are a couple left that we have yet to explore; we'll cover the use of partials a little later in this chapter, but for now let's focus on interpolator plugins and how they operate within Ractive.

Creating Interpolator Plugins

Our next plugin type is arguably one of the simplest available for Ractive – when you start to use `ractive.animate()` more, you'll soon find that the ability to only work with numbers will become a trifle limiting! There is a way to fix this, which borrows from the mustache functionality we've already seen – how about interpolating our code?

What, I hear you ask, is interpolation? Well, it's the ability (in this case) to animate from one value to another, where the value isn't a number. Think of it as an adaptor if you will – it's designed to work with `ractive.animate()`, and can handle a host of different values such as attributes or mappings, which may also not be applied immediately. Let's put this theory to the test, and create ourselves a simple plugin, to fade between two different colors, that we'll control from within a Ractive instance.

Switching Colors with an Interpolator Plugin

For our next exercise, we're going to delve into the world of mixing and managing colors – some of the maths involved can be something of a black art, so to help make it simpler, we'll make use of the chroma.js plugin, which is available from `http://gka.github.io/chroma.js/`.

To give you a flavor of what we will end up with, Figure 7-10 shows a screenshot of the finished article, prior to it beginning the transition; it starts with black text on a gray background:

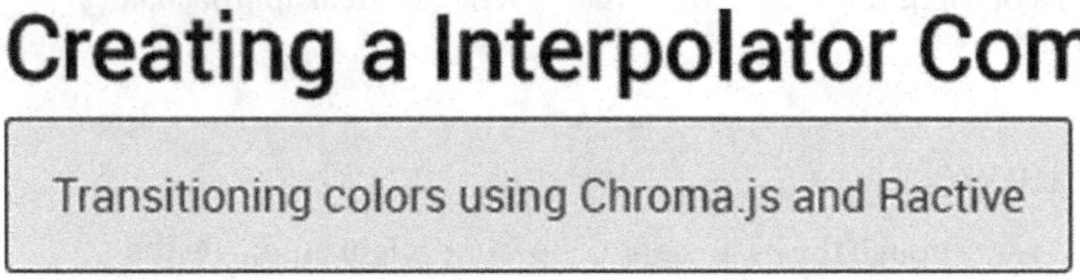

Creating a Interpolator Component

Transitioning colors using Chroma.js and Ractive

Figure 7-10.

...and Figure 7-11 shows the same demo, at the end of the transition effect; at this point it has white text on a darker gray background:

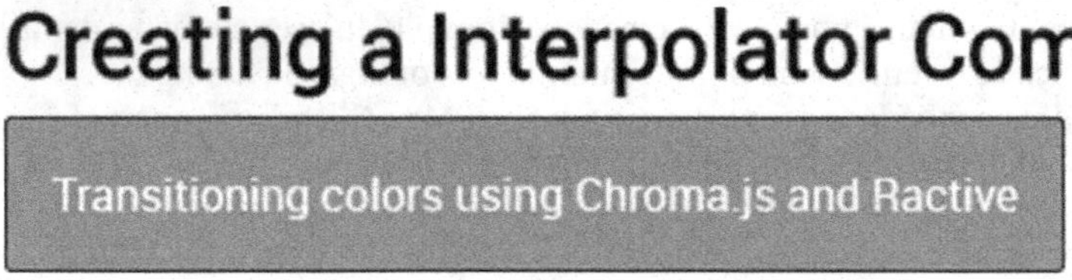

Creating a Interpolator Component

Transitioning colors using Chroma.js and Ractive

Figure 7-11. *Our interpolator in mid-transition*

This amazing little plugin abstracts most of the heavy work required when working with colors, such as converting from one format to another, or blending multiple hues into an attractive design. For the purposes of our exercise we will use various shades of gray (as this comes out best in print), but this belies the real power available when using this plugin!

CREATING AN INTERPOLATOR PLUGIN

Okay – let's make a start:

1. We'll begin by creating a new subfolder within our project folder – save it as interpolate.

2. We need to create some subfolders within the interpolate folder to store our scripts; go ahead and save them as js and css respectively.

3. Next, let's add the font files we've been using to style content – for this, extract a copy of the font folder from the previous exercise, and save this within the interpolate folder.

4. We also need copies of the Ractive library and library map files – for this, go ahead and extract copies of ractive.min.js and ractive.min.js.map from a previous exercise, and save them into the js subfolder.

5. The most important piece of media we need is the chroma.js file – download a copy from https://raw.github.com/gka/chroma.js/master/chroma.min.js, or you can use the version available on the CDNJS network or via Node.js (if you have it installed).

6. We can start adding some code at this point – open up a new text file, and add this content, saving it as interpolate.js within the js subfolder from step 2:

```
var myChroma = function ( from, to ) {
  return chroma.scale([ from, to ]);
}

Ractive.interpolators.myChroma = myChroma;

var ractive = new Ractive({
  target: 'container',
  template: '#template',
  data: {
    bg: '#e7e7e7',
    fg: '#2a2a2a'
  }
});

setTimeout( changeColor, 500 );

function changeColor () {
  ractive.animate('bg', '#9f9f9f', {duration: 1500, interpolator: 'myChroma'});
  ractive.animate('fg', '#ffffff', {duration: 1500, interpolator: 'myChroma'});
}
```

7. Save the file – our plugin is now ready for use.

At this point we can use it within our projects, although we need to register it for use within our Ractive instance. This should now be reasonably familiar, as registering interpolators uses much the same process as other plugins we've already covered in this book. For the sake of completeness though, let's run through the three options we can use to register interpolator plugins, in more detail.

Registering and Using Interpolator Plugins

Registering interpolator plugins is very easy, and uses a similar process to other plugins we've already met earlier in the book. There are three options we can use, depending on our requirements:

- We can register it as needed for each instance – we can do this using the instance's interpolators initialization property:

```
var ractive = new Ractive({
  target: 'container',
...
  interpolators: {
    chroma:  myChroma
  }
});
```

- If we want to register on a per component basis, we can do so, using the component's interpolators initialization property:

```
const MyComponent = Ractive.extend({
  interpolators: { myInterpolator }
});
```

- We may prefer to register it globally, via the `Ractive.interpolators` static property:

```
Ractive.interpolators.myChroma = myChroma;
```

With our plugin now registered, let's make use of it in a quick demo - the only step we need for this is to create our markup - for this, go ahead and add the following code to a new file, saving it as interpolate.html:

```
<!doctype html>
<html lang='en-GB'>
<head>
  <meta charset='utf-8'>
  <title>Beginning Ractive: Creating Interpolators</title>
  <link rel='stylesheet' href='css/interpolate.css'>
</head>
<body>
  <h1>Creating a Interpolator Component</h1>

  <div id='container'></div>
```

```
<script id='template' type='text/ractive'>
    <span style='background: {{bg}}; color: {{fg}}'>
        Transitioning colors using Chroma.js and Ractive
    </span>
</script>
<script src='js/ractive.min.js'></script>
<script src='js/chroma.min.js'></script>
<script src='js/interpolate.js'></script>
</body>
</html>
```

Save the file if you haven't already done so – if we preview the results in a browser, we should see a div with text fade through from one color to another, with the text changing shade too (as indicated in Figure 7-10).

So – what happened? Our plugin is probably the simplest one we've created, save for partials; more of that anon. Most of the heavy lifting in this instance is actually done by the chroma.js plugin; the key to making this work is how the interpolator plugin interacts with chroma.js and our Ractive instance. Let's dive in and see what this means in practice.

Working Through Our Demo

Our demo has something of an irony – it's at times like this when we would normally step through code to understand how it works, yet most of the heavy lifting isn't even done in Ractive! This said, there are interesting features in this demo, so let's go through it step by step.

We start with what should by now be reasonably familiar use of mustaches – there isn't anything complex here; all we are doing is specifying two placeholders inline for the background and foreground colors that we are about to use:

```
<span style='background: {{bg}}; color: {{fg}}'>
    Transitioning colors using Chroma.js and Ractive
</span>
```

Up next comes our plugin – we kick off with where the real magic happens; this puts a call out to chroma.js to scale from one color to another. Ractive helps with this when we implement the .animate() call further down the plugin – we pass in the relevant colors which are then processed by the chroma.js plugin:

```
var myChroma = function ( from, to ) {
  return chroma.scale([ from, to ]);
}
```

Before we can make use of it, we need to register it – for ease of convenience, it's registered globally in our demo, but could easily be registered at a more local level, if desired:

```
Ractive.interpolators.myChroma = myChroma;
```

We now make use of it in our Ractive instance; within our instance we pass in appropriate foreground and background colors. For the purposes of print these are grayscale in our example, don't let this stop you coming up with some original combinations! The last part of our code covers a simple function to initiate the color change; this is done through using two .animate() statements, which update the assigned colors using our interpolator:

```
var ractive = new Ractive({
  target: 'container',
  template: '#template',
  data: {
    bg: '#e4e4e4',
    fg: '#2a2a2a'
  }
});

setTimeout( changeColor, 1000 );

function changeColor () {
  ractive.animate('bg', '#9f9f9f', {duration: 5000, interpolator: 'myChroma'});
  ractive.animate('fg', '#ffffff', {duration: 5000, interpolator: 'myChroma'});
}
```

We're there – granted, it's a simple plugin, but hopefully it shows that if we're working with ractive.animate(), we're not constrained by just using numbers, which we might have had to do if we had used ractive.animate() on its own.

Let's change tack - there is one more plugin type we should explore; in a sense we've already used this type, although I'll lay good odds that you won't know where! It's a useful tool within the Ractive toolbox, so let's take a look at look at this type in more detail.

Creating Partials

Cast your mind back to Chapter 2, *Creating Templates* – yes, I know it may feel like a long time ago, but I promise there is a point to this request! Remember the demo we created, where we displayed thumbnail images of a series of cacti plants? Just to refresh your memory, this is a screenshot of that gallery effect (Figure 7-12):

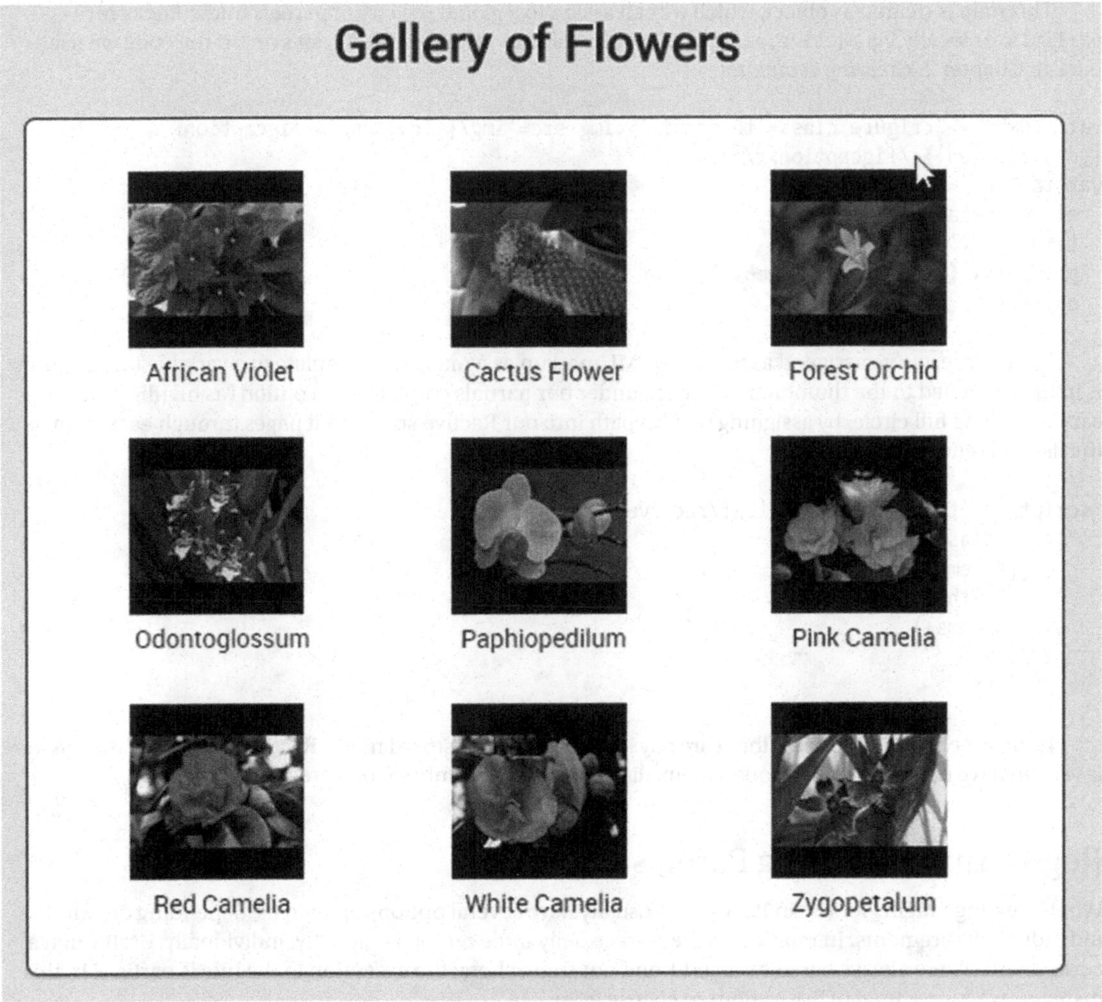

Gallery of Flowers

Figure 7-12. *(Partial) screenshot of gallery effect from Chapter 2*

The reason for going down memory lane? Well, a key part of that demo used a Ractive partial plugin – it's time we revisited this functionality!

There isn't anything special about partials – these are simply reusable pieces of code. What makes them special is that we can create a map of partials that can be reused in any project, either locally or at a global level. These partials may be as simple as a string of HTML markup, through to a simple function, or even a piece of parsed Ractive code:

```
partials: {
  stringPartial: '<p>{{greeting}} world!</p>',
  parsedPartial: {"v":3,"t":[{"t":7,"e":"p","f":[{"t":2,"r":"greeting"}," world!"]}]},
  functionPartial: function(data, p){
    return data.condition ? '<p>hello world</p>' : '<div>yes, we have no foo</div>';
  }
}
```

This map is treated as object, which we can assign to a global registry of partials under `Ractive.partials`, or locally via `ractive.partials`. To see what this means in reality, let's revisit the code we used back in Chapter 2, *Creating Templates*:

```
var thumbs = "<figure class='thumbnail'><img src='img/{{id}}.png'><figcaption>
{{description}}</figcaption></figure>";
var ractive = new Ractive({
  el: '#container',
  template: '#template',
  partials: { thumbnail: thumbs },
  data: {
```

In this case, we've assigned a string of HTML markup as a mustache template to a variable thumbs; this is in turn assigned to the thumbnail reference under our partials configuration option (as highlighted). We can then come full circle, by assigning that keypath into our Ractive script, so it pages through each item in the list and renders it onscreen:

```
<script id='template' type='text/ractive'>
    <div class='gallery'>
      {{#items}}
        {{>thumbnail}}
      {{/items}}
    </div>
  </script>
```

Here, we check first to see if there are any items in the array stored in our Ractive instance; if the answer is yes, then we need to iterate through them, displaying each thumbnail on-screen accordingly.

Registering and Using Partials

When creating plugins for use in Ractive, we usually have several options open to us, depending on our individual requirements. In most cases there are usually three options – globally, individually, or through a component. There always has to be an odd-one-out somewhere; the exception to the rule is partials! In this instance, we have a total of five options to choose from:

- We can register globally via the `Ractive.partials` static property:

  ```
  Ractive.partials.myPartial = MyPartial;
  ```

- Alternatively, we can register globally, via a non-executing script tag on the current page:

  ```
  <script type="ractive/template" id="myPartial">
    ...
  </script>
  ```

- If we're using it as part of a component, we can register it via the component's partials initialization property:

```
const MyComponent = Ractive.extend({
  partials: { myPartial }
});
```

- In some cases, it may be preferable to register on a per instance, via the instance's partials initialization property:

```
const ractive = new Ractive({
  partials: { myPartial }
});
```

- We can even register a partial In-template, using the {{#partial}} mustache, although the benefits of doing so can appear reduced, as we're not maintaining a separation of concerns in our code:

```
{{#partial myPartial}}
  ...
{{/}}
```

To bring it back to our demo, we used option 4 – option 1 or 4 would work equally well here; it all boils down to what we've talked about before, which is choosing the option that most suits your specific requirements.

Summary

A part of the appeal of Ractive is the ability to customize it using plugins - over the course of the last chapter and this, we've explored the different types available, and learned how to create some basic examples we can use as a springboard for further development. We've covered a lot of material, so let's take some time out to review what we've learned.

We kicked off by reviewing the different types of plugins we covered in earlier chapters, before moving on to creating our first decorator plugin and learning how to make it available online for others to use and improve.

Next up came a look at creating interpolator plugins; we saw how easy it is to set up a basic one, and understood that in many cases, the external plugins we call in are likely to be doing more of the heavy work than the interpolator itself! We rounded out the chapter with a recap on creating partials - we covered how we briefly got acquainted with them back in Chapter 2, before revisiting them to understand how easy it is to create and register partials for use within Ractive.

Okay - let's move on: we've come to the end of the second section of this book; to help tie things all together, we will begin to bring all the various themes into a working site, which will be the subject of our next chapter.

PART III

■ ■ ■

Putting Ractive to Use

CHAPTER 8

Using Ractive

Cast your mind back if you will – anyone remember the days of flashing marquee text, color schemes that clashed, or pages of black text on a white background (or even gray?) Thankfully those days are long since gone – the role of the user interface is crucial to the whole experience. In this chapter, we'll take a look at some examples of how well Ractive works with other libraries in the UI arena: we can really go to town!

Manipulating SVG Images with Ractive

Hands up – how many times have you needed to apply some form of effect to an image? I'll bet that it's a case of firing up your usual graphics editor, apply the filter and show the results to a customer ... only you find it's not what they want! Sound familiar?

Well, you can try applying effects such as sepia() or brightness() in your CSS styling, but there is a limit on what you can do; effects such as sepia() are fixed, so no matter what you do, you're stuck with the shade of brown that is used! To get around this, there is an alternative: we can create a longhand form of filter to apply the same effect.

Okay – I know what's coming. Why would we want to spend time creating such an effect? Well, the answer is simple: we can manipulate the color not just over the image, but at a channel level. It means that for example, if we don't like the shade of brown used, we can adjust the levels of red, blue, or green to make it warmer, colder, darker, and so on. This is just one of many effects we can apply to content – as a bonus, we can even manipulate our SVG element directly from within Ractive! It's time we got stuck into some code, so let's make a start with exploring what such a filter looks like in practice.

Creating Our Filter

When using SVG, there is a range of properties we can manipulate – for the purposes of applying filters, we need to use feColorMatrix. Put simply, feColorMatrix consists of a matrix of values of 0 to 1, which represents the different channels, as shown in this example:

```
<svg width="200px" height="200px" viewBox="0 0 200 200">
  <defs>
    <filter id="colorChange">
      <feColorMatrix
        type = "matrix"
        values="0.89 0     0     0    0
                0     0.82  0     0    0
                0     0     0.55  0    0
                0     0     0     1    0 "/>
    </filter>
  </defs>
```

© Alex Libby 2017
A. Libby, *Beginning Ractive.js*, https://doi.org/10.1007/978-1-4842-3093-0_8

```
<image xmlns:xlink="http://www.w3.org/1999/xlink" width="200" height="200"
xlink:href="PATH_TO_IMAGE/img.jpg" x="0" y="0" filter = "url(#colorChange)"> </image>
```

```
</svg>
```

If we alter these values, these will be translated into different shades of colors; these are then applied using the `filter = ...` reference within the `<image>` statement. There is a bit of a sting in this tale though; how does one choose what value to add?

There are a number of calculations that can be performed to arrive at this matrix, but they take a little getting used to, so they are not for everyone! Fortunately a tool has been constructed by Andres Galante, which is available at `http://andresgalante.com/RGBAtoFeColorMatrix/` - this allows us to convert a standard RGB value into a suitable color matrix. It's an easy tool to use, so let's take it for a spin, and use it to create our own version of a sepia filter, as part of the next exercise.

If you really want to get the inside track on the algebra involved, then there is a useful article by Amelia Bellamy-Royds of CSS Tricks fame; it's available at `https://css-tricks.com/color-filters-can-turn-your-gray-skies-blue/`. Be warned though – it's not light reading!

Applying Our Filter to an Image

To create and apply a filter is a relatively straightforward process – the code required is largely the same for different types of filter, and we just have to adjust the values used to render our chosen shade. To see what I mean, let's work through the steps required to create and apply our own sepia filter, using Ractive:

CREATING AN SVG FILTER

1. We'll start by getting our sepia matrix code – go ahead and browse to `http://andresgalante.com/RGBAtoFeColorMatrix/`, then enter each of these values into the respective fields: Red - 145, Green - 86, Blue - 26.

Alpha is already set to 1, so this value can be ignored for now.

---

2. Take a copy of the code displayed in the black window for safekeeping; we will use this later in the demo.

3. We now need to create a folder in our project area – save it as `filter`.

4. Next, go ahead and create three new subfolders within the filter folder – these should be labeled as `img`, `js` and `css` respectively.

5. We need to add copies of `ractive.min.js` and `ractive.min.js.map` to the `js` subfolder – you can copy these from any `js` subfolder in the code download that accompanies this book.

6. Fire up your text editor, then in a new document, add the following code:

```
<!doctype html>
<html lang='en-GB'>
<head>
  <meta charset='utf-8'>
  <title>Beginning Ractive: Applying SVG Filters using Ractive</title>
  <link rel="stylesheet" href="css/filters.css">
</head>
<body>
  <h1>Applying SVG Filters using Ractive</h1>
  <div id='container'></div>

  <script src='js/ractive.min.js'></script>
  <script src='js/filter.js'></script>

</body>
</html>
```

7. Save this as `filter.html` into the root of our `filter` folder.

8. We now need an image to use for our demo – I've chosen to use `camera3.jpg` from the slideshow demo we created back in Chapter 6, but you can use any you wish; please adjust the CSS accordingly.

9. It's time for the key part of our demo – creating our filter! For this, we will use the value RGBA(145, 86, 26, 1), which is a shade of sepia. Go ahead and add the following code to a new file, saving it as `filter.js` in the `js` subfolder we created in step 2:

```
var ractive = new Ractive({
  target: '#container',
  template: `<svg>
  <filter id="sepia">
    <feColorMatrix type="matrix"
      values="0.57  0     0     0     0
              0     0.34  0     0     0
              0     0     0.1   0     0
              0     0     0     1     0 "/>
  </filter></svg>
<div id="border"><img src="{{img}}" id="sepia" width="{{width}}%"
height="{{height}}%"></div>`,
  data: {
    width: 110,
    height: 100,
    img: "./img/camera.jpg"
  }
});
```

10. At this stage, our demo will operate, but it won't look great; to really finish it off, let's add some simple styling to complete the effect. For this, go ahead and add the following styles to a new document, saving it as `filter.css` in the `css` subfolder:

```css
@font-face {
  font-family: 'robotoregular';
  src: url('../font/Roboto-Regular-webfont.woff') format('woff');
  font-weight: normal;
  font-style: normal;
}

body { font-family: robotoregular, sans-serif; padding: 2rem;
font-weight: 200; }

#border {
  border: 5px solid #fff;
  box-shadow: 0 3px 6px rgba(0,0,0,.25);
  width: 640px;
  height: 423px;
}

#sepia { filter: url('#sepia') brightness(250%); }

svg { display: none; }
```

If we save and then preview the results, we should see something akin to the screenshot shown in Figure 8-1:

Applying SVG Filters using Ractive

Figure 8-1. *Applying a sepia tone using SVG filters*

At this stage, I am sure you will have lots of questions – this demo highlights a number of useful techniques, so let's explore what happened in more detail.

Understanding How Our Filter Works

I have a little confession to make – some of you may have noticed that this chapter is meant to be about using Ractive with other libraries … and yet in our demo we've not used any! There is a good reason for this – let me explain.

At its core, Ractive is JavaScript based – this means that we can use any number of different JavaScript-based libraries, such as ColorThief, which we used back in Chapter 3. There is nothing wrong with this approach, although it's another resource to pull in – sometimes it's not necessary!

Ractive plays very well with SVG by itself; we can edit many of the properties within a SVG element, without the need for additional help. To prove this, we used standard mustaches to define the image to be used, along with the width and height properties. The values can then be manipulated using the `Ractive` object, as shown in Figure 8-2:

```
> ractive.set("height", "50%")
< ▶ Promise {[[PromiseStatus]]: "resolved", [[PromiseValue]]: undefined}
> |
```

Figure 8-2. *Altering the properties of our sepia image*

This aside, we started by applying a filter, to the #sepia element thus:

```
#sepia { filter: url('#sepia') brightness(250%); }
```

This is then referenced within the SVG element; to apply our custom filter, we must use a `url(...)` value, as we are effectively applying a named element that already exists on the page (and that #sepia is a pointer to that element). In this instance though, we're also applying a `brightness()` filter too – the original image comes out very dark, so this brightens up the image to more acceptable levels (sorry – pun intended!).

Our demo is very simple though – there is so much more we can do when manipulating SVG filters using Ractive! For example, how about connecting some (or all) of the values in the color matrix to sliders, so you can individually fine-tune a selected color using the GUI?

If using feColorMatrix has piqued your interest to learn more, then have a look at Una Kravets's article on the *A List Apart* website at `http://alistapart.com/article/finessing-fecolormatrix`; it explores the principles behind how we can manipulate this property to great effect.

Let's move on from here – we can always create our own styling designs, but on occasions we may be forced to use a pre-built theme, such as one from the Semantic UI library. You might at first think this is an issue, but no – it's easy enough to achieve: let's dive in and see what this means in practice.

Applying Semantic UI Themes

Cast an eye over the Internet, and I'll lay good odds that you will come across dozens of different frameworks that attempt to style elements in their own particular way. Of course, we have the father of them all in the form of Bootstrap; others include Foundation (Zurb), Pure (by Yahoo) or UIKit by YOOtheme.

One framework that comes to mind though is Semantic UI - available from `http://www.semantic-ui.com`, this provides clean, responsive layouts, using human-readable HTML markup. It's easy enough to use by itself, but what happens if we want to use it with a library such as Ractive? You would be forgiven for thinking it might require something special in our configuration - not this time! Sure, we could create a decorator plugin, but for simple usage (at least), this isn't necessary. To see what this means in practice, let's get stuck into a simple demo.

Applying Semantic UI Manually

For our next demo, we're going to create a simple example that adds a button to the page; we'll link in a copy of Semantic UI and set our template to apply the relevant styles to our button.

APPLYING SEMANTIC MANUALLY

Let's make a start:

1. We'll start by firing up a browser, then navigating to `https://www.codepen.io`.

2. In the HTML pane, go ahead and add the following code:

```
<div id="target"></div>

<script id="template" type="text/ractive">
  <button class="ui button">
    Welcome, {{name}} !
  </button>
</script>
```

3. We need to add a small styling tweak, purely to center our demo more on the page – for this, add the following style rule to the CSS pane:

```
body {
  margin-left: 100px;
  margin-top: 50px;
}
```

4. To make it all work, we need to add our obligatory Ractive instance – for this demo, we only need to focus on providing the data; go ahead and add this into the JS pane:

```
var ractive = new Ractive({
  target: '#target',
  template: '#template',
  data: { name: 'world' }
});
```

5. We're almost there – if we run the demo now, it will error; we need to add in a link to the Ractive library, along with jQuery and Semantic UI. For this, click on Settings ⏐ CSS, then add in the link for Semantic UI as indicated in Figure 8-3:

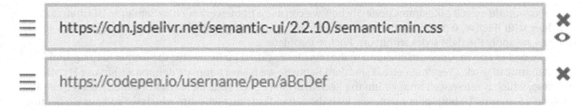

Figure 8-3. *Link for Semantic UI CSS*

6. We need to add in three links – one for jQuery, one for Semantic, and one for Ractive; these can be added on the JavaScript tab within Settings, using the details shown in Figure 8-4:

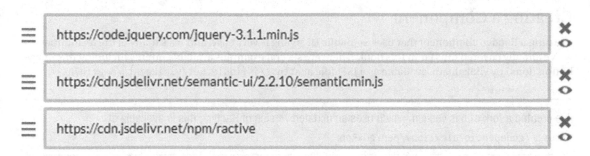

Figure 8-4. *Links for Semantic demo*

7. Click on Close, then let it refresh – it will display a button, as shown in Figure 8-5:

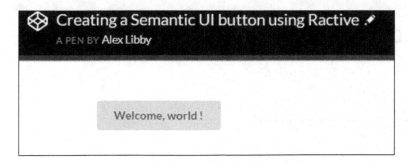

Figure 8-5. *Displaying a Semantic UI button created using Ractive*

You can see our simple demo in a Codepen – go ahead and browse to `https://codepen.io/alexlibby/pen/BdOzyP`, to view it in action.

Our simple exercise illustrates perfectly how we can use a framework such as Semantic UI when working with Ractive; it proves that we don't need to set up anything special within our configuration, as long as we apply the right styles within our Ractive template.

We had to add in jQuery, in addition to the two files required for Semantic; the former are required for Semantic to work. Everything else is standard Ractive – we have a template defined within our HTML markup, which is referenced from within the Ractive instance. The code includes the same styles required to style a Semantic UI button; our template includes a standard mustache into which we add our welcoming message, which can be changed at a later date if needed.

Let's take this a step further – we can, of course, style elements individually using Semantic (which may work for some uses), but this is not the best use of our time or resources.It's likely though that our simple proof of concept won't scale well with other interactive components from the library. Instead, let's focus on turning this into a reusable component; the great thing is that this doesn't need a huge amount of work either! Let's take a look at what we need to do, in more detail.

Creating a Component

Creating a Ractive component that uses Semantic UI styling is very easy, and uses many of the techniques we've already covered thus far in this book. There are several examples available online, including this image button demo by vikikamath, available as a JSFiddle at `http://jsfiddle.net/vikikamath/6wgzfu7h/3/`.

I've created a fork of this version, which uses an updated version of Ractive; this is available at `https://codepen.io/alexlibby/pen/gGxRob`.

We have to define our usual template that contains a placeholder mustache for the button text; the key to making it work is incorporating the right styles from Semantic within our component. This will render our button, once we link in the Semantic UI style sheet. To see it in action, let's create a demo that illustrates how easy it is to incorporate Semantic UI; the screenshot in Figure 8-6 shows the finished article:

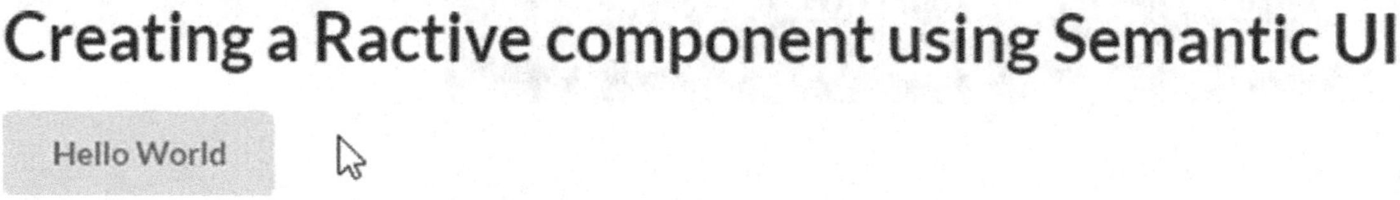

Creating a Ractive component using Semantic UI

Hello World

Figure 8-6. *A Ractive button component that uses Semantic UI*

Time we got started with writing some code! Without further ado, let's make a start:

CREATING A COMPONENT USING SEMANTIC UI

1. We'll start by creating a new folder called `semantic` – save this into our usual project area.

2. Within this folder, go ahead and create a new subfolder marked `js`; this should be stored within the `semantic` folder.

3. In a new document, add the following code and save it as `suibutton.js` within the `js` subfolder:

```
const SUIButton = Ractive.extend({
  template: `
    <button class="ui button">{{ message }}</button>
  `,
  data: { message: 'Hello World' }
});

const ractive = Ractive({
  target: "#container",
  template: `
    <SUIButton />
  `,
  components: { SUIButton }
});
```

4. From a copy of the code download that accompanies this book, extract and copy the contents of the `js` subfolder for this demo, into the `js` subfolder created in step 2. This contains the two Ractive library files, the Semantic UI core library and a copy of jQuery.

5. Repeat step 5, but this time with the `css` subfolder that is in the code download; this contains the Semantic UI theme file that we need for our demo.

6. We need to add some slight tweaks to our CSS – these are not essential, but will make the demo look a little more polished! Go ahead and add the following styles to a new file, saving it as `styles.css` within the `css` subfolder of the `semantic` folder we created at the start of the exercise:

```
@font-face {
  font-family: 'robotoregular';
  src: url('../font/Roboto-Regular-webfont.woff') format('woff');
  font-weight: normal;
  font-style: normal;
}

body { font-family: robotoregular, sans-serif; margin: 20px; }
```

7. To complete our demo, go ahead and copy across the font folder to the same semantic subfolder we created at the start of our exercise.

8. At this point if we save all of our files then preview the results, we should see something akin to the screenshot shown in Figure 8-6 on the previous page.

For anyone who knows me personally, I'm a great believer in the KISS principle, or "keep it simple..." - you get the idea! There is something about Semantic UI that makes it particularly appealing; it's one of those frameworks where emphasis is very much on keeping code clean and readable. It prides itself on offering "the same benefits as BEM or SMACSS, but without the tedium"; like I said, anything for an easier life!

Our demo uses the same principles that we've already covered, in terms of component development; we set up a template with an appropriate mustache for the button text. We then reference this as <SUIButton>, which is the name of our component, when linking it into our Ractive instance. We might consider writing a decorator plugin to help manage styling, but is there a need? As long as we have the Semantic UI classes set in our template:

```
template: `
  <button class="ui button">{{ message }}</button>
`,
```

...then there isn't any need to create anything more special to manage styling within our component.

Now – talking of components: there are dozens of other frameworks available online; we've already looked at one of the simpler ones in the form of Semantic, but what about that well-known daddy, or Bootstrap? We can absolutely make use of it within Ractive; so much so, that a component has been created for managing Bootstrap and Ractive. I feel another demo coming, so let's dive in and take a look at how to put it into practice.

Working with Bootstrap

If you've spent any time developing for the Web, then it's very likely you will have come across Bootstrap in some form or other. It's a great tool to help quickly develop prototypes, although care needs to be taken with adding all of the classes that are frequently needed!

Leaving this aside for the moment, we can easily make use of it within a Ractive instance. There are two ways to achieve this – we can either simply apply the classes in our code, or we can make use of the pre-created components already available within the ractive-bootstrap plugin for Ractive, available from http://dagnelies.github.io/ractive-bootstrap/. We worked through the former route when using Semantic UI in the previous exercise; Bootstrap can be added in the same fashion. This time around, let's look at the second option in more detail.

Adding Bootstrap to a Ractive Instance

For our next exercise, we'll work through a simple demo that configures a series of buttons to display the various states and messages that are associated with Bootstrap.

It's worth noting that there are some differences in terms of naming conventions used in this plugin. For example this plugin uses <btn> as the basis for implementing a button, rather than the more standard <button> markup; the principles for styling are still the same.

ADDING BOOTSTRAP TO RACTIVE

Okay – let's get started:

1. We'll begin by creating a new folder in our project area – save it as bootstrap.

2. Next up, go ahead and extract a copy of the bootstrap folder from the code download that accompanies this book – copy over the js, css and font folders to our new project folder created in step 1.

3. We can now add in the markup for our project – in a new file, add the following code, saving it as bootstrap.html at the root of our bootstrap folder. We will go through it section by section, beginning with linking in the files (and styles) needed for our demo:

```
<!doctype html>
<html>
  <meta charset='utf-8'>
  <title>Beginning Ractive: Working with Bootstrap</title>

  <link rel="stylesheet" href="css/bootstrap.min.css">
  <link rel="stylesheet" href="css/bootstrap-theme.min.css">
  <style>
    #container { margin-left: 10rem;  margin-top: 5rem; }
  </style>

  <script src="js/jquery.min.js"></script>
  <script src="js/bootstrap.min.js"></script>
  <script src='js/ractive.min.js'></script>
  <script src='js/ractive-bootstrap/bin/ractive-bootstrap.js'></script>
</head>
```

4. Next up comes the bulk of our markup – this adds in the container and Ractive script / template, which includes each of the buttons:

```
<body>
  <div id="container"></div>

  <script>
    var ractive = new Ractive({
      el: '#container',
      template: `
        <btn href="#buttons">Button as a link</btn>
        <btn onclick="alert('bar')">Button with onclick event</btn>
        <btn active="true">Active</btn>
        <btn disabled="true">Disabled</btn>

        <p></p>
```

```
              <btn type="default">Default</btn>
              <btn type="primary">Primary</btn>
              <btn type="success">Success</btn>
              <btn type="info">Info</btn>
              <btn type="warning">Warning</btn>
              <btn type="danger">Danger</btn>

         });
       </script>
     </body>
     </html>
```

5. Save the file – if we preview the results in a browser, we should see something akin to the screenshot shown in Figure 8-7:

Figure 8-7. *Implementing Bootstrap styling in Ractive*

It's a simple example, but a perfect illustration of how we can make use of what must surely be the granddaddy of all frameworks! If you look at the code in more detail, you will see that I've added three examples of mustaches; this is to show that we can use either mustaches or insert the text straight into the template. Using the former though means that we can manipulate the content using Ractive at a later date.

It's worth taking time to look at the other examples available on the bootstrap-ractive site; in all instances, we simply apply the same classes as used in vanilla Bootstrap, which are then interpreted by Ractive.

Okay – let's step things up a notch: so far, our demos have been relatively simple. However, there will come an occasion where we need to reference larger amounts of data; how would we do this using Ractive? Let's dive in and find out, using the example of a route planner to see how we can access data.

Building a Route Planner

London … I've spent many a happy hour visiting places such as Covent Garden, Leicester Square, Whitehall, visiting the famous Foyles bookstore on Charing Cross Road, and more – it certainly brings back plenty of memories! But I digress – why though have I brought up the subject of London? The answer is simple: our next demo will be to display the route details of a typical journey through London.

At the core of this demo are the route details – anyone visiting London might make use of the route planner provided by the capital's transport authority, Transport for London. This comprehensive tool is perfect for researching the best route from A to B; it even includes details of any walking you will have to do, if a particular road is not served by public transport.

At the heart of this tool is an API that is available, although one must register to use it; it provides a wealth of detail that can be viewed in JSON format, although it isn't the easiest to read in its raw format! We're going to make use of the data within to construct a simplified version; the data used will be based on traveling from Euston Station (north London), to the world-famous Leicester Square Odeon cinema in central London. To give you a flavor of what to expect, Figure 8-8 shows a screenshot of the finished article:

JOURNEY RESULTS

From: **London NW1 2DU, United Kingdom**

To: **Leicester Square, London WC2H 7JY, United Kingdom**

Arriving: **19:00**

Duration: **22 minutes**

Journey Start Time: **18:34**

Journey End Time: **18:56**

Summary:

9 mins — Walk to Euston Station

5 mins — **Northern line** to Leicester Square Station

8 mins — Walk to 14 Leicester Square

 18:34: London NW1 2DU, United Kingdom

9 mins

Walk to Euston Station

⊕ View details

Figure 8-8. Our finished route planner

This demo is based over several sections, as there is a lot to get through – we'll start with setting up some of the prerequisites for our demo.

Setting Up the Prerequisites

For our demo, we need to make use of a few tools - most of these are available as online versions, but we will also make use of one tool that will be in the code download that accompanies this book. The tools we will use are the following:

- Sassmeister – we can use standard CSS, but Ractive will work equally well with code generated by a CSS preprocessor such as Sass. For convenience, we will compile it manually using the online playground for compiling SASS, which is available at `https://www.sassmeister.com`. If we want to use Sass more, then it's worth looking at other tools such as node-sass (`https://github.com/sass/node-sass`, requires Node.js), or Crunch (`https://getcrunch.co/`).

- MomentJS– this can be downloaded from `http://momentjs.com/downloads/moment.min.js` - a copy of it is already included in the download for this book.

- In addition, the following tools were used to create this demo – it's worth taking a look at them, as they will be useful if you want to develop this example in the future:

- Spritepad – available at http://spritepad.wearekiss.com/, this is a perfect tool for creating and downloading image sprites. The tube / walking images that we will extract from the code download for this book were created using a single sprite generated from this tool.

- ColorHexa – available at http://www.colorhexa.com, this is ideal for obtaining the names of individual colors; this was used to create the variable names used in the Sass style sheet for this exercise.

Okay – as one might say if studying temperal mechanics, "it's time...." – let's dive in and set up our markup for this demo.

Constructing the Planner Markup

The first stage of our demo is to create the markup we need for our demo – there is nothing special in this code; it simply specifies a container for our Ractive instance, and references the various code libraries we will use in this demo:

JOURNEY PLANNER 1: THE MARKUP

1. We'll start by setting up a folder for our project – save this as `journey` within our project area.

2. Next, let's go ahead and in our markup; for this, add the following code to a new document, and save it as `journey.html` at the root of the `journey` folder:

```html
<!doctype html>
<html>
<head>
  <meta charset='utf-8'>
  <title>Beginning Ractive: Displaying Route Details</title>
  <link rel="stylesheet" type="text/css" href="css/journey.css">
</head>
<body>
  <h2>JOURNEY RESULTS</h2>
  <div id="container"></div>

  <script src='js/ractive.min.js'></script>

  <script src='js/moment.min.js'></script>
  <script src='js/journey.js'></script>
</body>
</html>
```

3. Before we get stuck into creating our Ractive instance, we need to get the relevant libraries set up for use; for this, go ahead and extract copies of the `font`, `img`, `css` and `js` folders from the code download that accompanies this book. Save all three to the root of our `journey` folder created in step 1.

That's the easy part done – now for our Ractive instance! This is the most important part of our demo, so without further ado, let's dive in and see what we need to set up in more detail.

Building Our Ractive Instance

Our fictional journey starts at Euston Station in northern London, and will end at the world-famous Leicester Square Odeon cinema, in time to attend one of the premiere movie showings that regularly take place at this cinema.

For this, we will assume that our arrival time will be 19:00hrs (the API requires 24hr clock), and that we will use the postcodes as our reference points:

- Euston Station, north London - NW1 2DU;

- Leicester Square Oden Cinema, Leicester Square - WC2H 7JY

... as the start and endpoints of our journey. For convenience, our demo will use the Journey Results API, available at https://api.tfl.gov.uk/swagger/ui/index.html?url=/swagger/docs/v1#!/Journey/ Journey_JourneyResults; we will focus on the display of the content only, up to a point where we can then reference individual data element using a ractive.get() or ractive.set() statement. The demo could then be developed to reference a stand-alone JSON file if desired (more on this anon).

With that out of the way, let's take up where we left off from the previous part of this exercise, and focus on setting up our Ractive instance and associated code.

JOURNEY PLANNER 2: THE RACTIVE INSTANCE

1. In a new document, go ahead and add the following lengthy code – save the file as journey.js, into the js subfolder we copied back in the first part of this exercise. We will go through this code section by section, starting with the creation of the station list for the second leg of our journey:

```
var stations = [
  { name: 'Warren Street Stn / Tottenham Court Rd' },
  { name: 'Goodge Street Station' },
  { name: 'Tottenham Court Road Station' }
];
```

2. Add in the following immediately below, leaving a line free – this takes care of formatting dates and times that are used in our demo:

```
function fmtDateTime(dateValue) {
  return moment(dateValue).format('MMMM Do YYYY, H:mm');
}

function fmtTime(timeValue) {
  return moment(timeValue).format('H:mm');
}

function fmtTimePlus(timeValue, timePlus) {
  return moment(timeValue).add(timePlus, 'minutes').format('H:mm');
}
```

3. Next up comes our Ractive instance – we start with the obligatory initial configuration and the initial summary of our journey (shown top right in the demo):

```
var ractive = new Ractive({
  target: '#container',
  template: `
    <div id="summary">
      <span id="legs">Summary:</span>

      <p class="time">{{legs.leg1.duration}} mins</p><span class="{{legs.leg1.
      travel}}-icon"></span><p>{{legs.leg1.summary}}</p><br>
      <p class="time">{{legs.leg2.duration}} mins</p><span class="{{legs.leg2.
      travel}}-icon"></span><p class="line">{{legs.leg2.description1}}</p> <p
      class="l2end">to {{legs.leg2.end}}</p><br>
      <p class="time">{{legs.leg3.duration}} mins</p><span class="{{legs.leg3.
      travel}}-icon"></span><p>{{legs.leg3.summary}}</p><br>
    </div>
    <!------------------------------------------------------------------------>
```

4. We then need to add in this block of code – this takes care of displaying our initial request details (top left in the demo):

```
<div id="request">
  <p>From: <span class="info">{{journeyStart}}</span></p>
  <p>To: <span class="info">{{journeyEnd}}</span></p>
  <p>Arriving: <span class="info">{{desiredArrival}}</span></p>
  <p>Duration: <span class="info">{{timings.duration}} minutes</span></p>
  <p>Journey Start Time: <span class="info">{{timings.startDateTime}}</span></p>
  <p>Journey End Time: <span class="info">{{timings.arrivalDateTime}}</span></p>
</div>
<!------------------------------------------------------------------------>
```

5. Our journey comes in three legs – the first is a short walk from Euston Rail Station to the tube station:

```
<p class="banner"><span class="{{legs.leg1.travel}}-icon"></span>{{timings.
startDateTime}}: {{journeyStart}}</p>
<p class="time">{{legs.leg1.duration}} mins</p><p>{{legs.leg1.summary}}</p>
<p class="hide one">View details<p>
<div class="extra one">
  {{#each legs.leg1.direction}}
    <p class="descr">{{description}}</p>
  {{/each}}
</div>
<!------------------------------------------------------------------------>
```

6. Once at the tube station, we're going to take a ride down to Leicester Square tube; this next block takes care of rendering the details onscreen:

```
<p class="banner"><span class="{{legs.leg2.travel}}-icon"></span>{{legs.leg2.
inttime}}: {{legs.leg2.start}}</p>
<p class="time">{{legs.leg2.duration}} mins</p><p class="line">{{legs.leg2.
description1}}</p><p class="linedetail">{{legs.leg2.description2}}</p>
<p class="hide two">View details<p>
<div class="extra two">
  Intermediate stations:
  {{#each legs.leg2.stops}}
    <p class="descr">- {{name}}</p>
  {{/each}}
</div>
<!------------------------------------------------------------------------>
```

7. We're almost there – once at Leicester Square, we have a short walk to the cinema. Add in the following code to display the details on screen:

```
<p class="banner"><span class="{{legs.leg3.travel}}-icon"></span>{{legs.leg3.
inttime}}: {{legs.leg3.start}}</p>
<p class="time">{{legs.leg3.duration}} mins</p><p>{{legs.leg3.summary}}</p>
<p class="hide three">View details<p>
<div class="extra three">
  {{#each legs.leg3.direction}}
    <p class="descr">{{description}}</p>
  {{/each}}
</div>
<p class="banner">{{journeyEnd}}</p>

    ,
```

8. We have our template markup in place, now it's time to add the data! We begin with the information needed to render our original journey request and summary details (the latter also being pulled from data later in this demo):

```
data : {
journeyStart: "London NW1 2DU, United Kingdom",
journeyEnd: "Leicester Square, London WC2H 7JY, United Kingdom",
desiredArrival: fmtTime("2017-08-17T19:00"),
timings : {
  startDateTime: fmtTime("2017-08-17T18:34"),
  arrivalDateTime: fmtTime("2017-08-17T18:56"),
  duration: "22",
},
```

9. Our first leg was from Euston Rail Station to the Tube – this block contains the details we need to display onscreen:

```
legs: {
  leg1: {
    summary: "Walk to Euston Station",
    duration: 9,
    start: "40 Eversholt Street",
    end: "Euston Station",
    inttime: 0,
    travel: "walk",
    direction: [{
      description: "Continue along Eversholt Street for 140 metres",
      latitude: 51.528967648270005,
      longitude: -0.1325920386,
    },{
      description: "Turn right on to Euston Square, continue for 62 metres",
      latitude: 51.527932885860004,
      longitude: -0.13142337617,
    }]
  },
```

10. Once at Euston Tube Station, we're going on a short ride down to Leicester Square – this block takes care of rendering the details for us:

```
leg2: {
  duration: 5,
  description1: "Northern line",
  description2: " towards Morden via Charing Cross, or Kennington Station via
  Charing Cross",
  stops: stations,
  start: "Euston Station",
  end: "Leicester Square Station",
  inttime: fmtTimePlus("2017-08-17T18:34", 9),
  travel: "tube",
},
```

11. The final leg of our journey is from Leicester Square Tube Station to the cinema, in time to see the movie; add in the following to render the details on screen:

```
leg3: {
  summary: "Walk to 14 Leicester Square",
  duration: 8,
  travel: "walk",
  start: "Leicester Square Station",
  end: "14 Leicester Square",
  inttime: fmtTimePlus("2017-08-17T18:34", 14),
  travel: "walk",
  direction: [{
    description: "Continue along Cranbourn Street for 102m",
    latitude: 51.51130433573,
```

```
            longitude: -0.12851541646
        }, {
            description: "Turn left onto Leicester Square, continue for 56m",
            latitude: 51.51091162518,
            longitude: -0.12982852908
        }]
    },
    }
  }
});
```

12. Save the contents of this file – keep it open, as we will need it shortly in the next
    part of this exercise.

Phew – that was a lot of code! If you felt this was complex enough, then it's worth taking a look at the
JSON code used as a source to produce this data block; it runs to some 1800+ lines! If you managed to get
this far, then congratulations; the bad news is that we still have a little more work to do. Let's get cracking on
it, so we can see the final results in all its glory.

Adding the Finishing Touches

Although we've added the bulk of the code required to display our content, it won't look great – we need to
add some styling, and set the "View details" blocks to show or hide on a mouse click. Fortunately these steps
are a lot less complex; let's work through them:

JOURNEY PLANNER 3: ADDING FINISHING TOUCHES

1. At the bottom of journey.js file, leave a line, then add the following event handlers;
   these will take care of closing and opening the "View details" links on our page:

```
/* Click handler for opening and closing extra info */
ractive.on( 'showOne', function(context) {
  if (document.getElementById('details1').style.display == "none") {
    document.getElementById('details1').style.display = "block"
  } else {
    document.getElementById('details1').style.display = "none"
  }
});

ractive.on( 'showTwo', function(context) {
  if (document.getElementById('details2').style.display == "none") {
    document.getElementById('details2').style.display = "block"
  } else {
    document.getElementById('details2').style.display = "none"
  }
});
```

```
ractive.on( 'showThree', function(context) {
  if (document.getElementById('details3').style.display == "none") {
    document.getElementById('details3').style.display = "block"
  } else {
    document.getElementById('details3').style.display = "none"
  }
});
```

2. Next up, it's time to apply the styling – for this, open the `journey.scss` file that is in the `css` subfolder we extracted at the start of our demo.

3. Go ahead and fire up a browser window, then browse to the SASSMeister playground at `https://www.sassmeister.com`.

4. Copy and paste the contents of the file from step 2 in this part of the exercise into the left-hand pane, then wait a few seconds.

5. Once compiled, the new code will appear on the right – copy everything into a new file, saving it as `journey.css` in the `css` subfolder of our journey folder.

6. Save and close any files still open, then preview the results of our work by running `journey.html` in a browser – if all is well, we should see something akin to the screenshot we saw at the start of this set of exercises.

Hooray! We got there – granted, it's a lot of code, but it contains some useful tricks that we've already covered throughout this book. It's worth taking time out to explore these in more detail, so while you pause to catch your breath, let's take a look at them in more detail.

Understanding What Happened

Although our demo contained a fair amount of code, it is based around several key principles, in addition to the extensive use of keypath references and mustaches used to retrieve and render data on screen:

- We've used keypaths up to three levels deep, such as `{{legs.leg2.start}}`;

- On at least three occasions, we've made use of the `{{#each}}` statement to iterate through an array;

- We've linked in the Moment.js date and time library, to help format dates for our demo;

- We've used string interpolation to provide placeholders for the tube and walking icons, using the format `<span class="{{legs.legX.travel}}"></span>` to work out which icon to display.

If we take a closer look at our code, we can see the standard configuration options for our target, which is set against the `#container`; we then specify our template using backticks, which allows us to format it as it will appear on the page. It's then a simple matter of iterating through each statement, and filling in the gaps – the keypath references pull in the data from our specially constructed version of the raw JSON file produced by the journey planner.

Taking It Further

This isn't the end of the story though – could we take our demo further? Well, there are a few ideas that come to mind, although it will ultimately depend on which direction we want to develop our example. This aside, the ideas we could explore include the following:

- How about creating something that shows a mini map against each leg of our journey? Our data already includes the longitude and latitude values already, so it should be a matter of adding in placeholder HTML to call in the relevant values at the appropriate point.

- Our demo iterates through each leg manually, but this isn't the most effective way – question is, what would we need to do to make it more efficient? We could potentially use an {{#each}}...{{/each}} block, but it's likely that our code will require refactoring to allow for this change. We also have the matter of dealing with the tube entry – do we adjust the references to bring them more in line with the walking blocks?

- There is scope to turn each of the travel modes (i.e., walking, using the tube, bus) into individual components – they can be set to display the content for each leg in a consistent format, so all that we need to do is pass through the relevant data.

- As a small touch, we would change the icon against "View details" to show a minus sign when the <div> has been expanded, and a plus sign when it has been contracted; it's a minor detail, but something that customers will want to see!

- We added in a description entry, but we may want to consider turning this into a component. As it stands, this might add more code than is sensible for a one-line entry. We would need to consider adding more, or reworking the code to incorporate more into such a component, to make it more attractive as an option.

- The data we used was included directly in our Ractive instance – as a next step, we should look to load it in via Ajax, to simulate loading from an external source.

- The code structure we've created makes extensive use of keypaths that go several levels deep; this works technically (and shows the principles of how we might access the data manually). It's not the most efficient way to reference the content, though; tt would absolutely benefit from being reworked to make use of partials. It would likely require the use of {{>yield}} or {{>content}}, to cater for the different types of travel required, such as walking or taking the Tube. The code we've used illustrates how we might

This is just a small selection of the ideas that come to mind – the format we've used is very manual, but it is enough to show how we might render the data initially. It's up to us to come up with more efficient ideas, based on client requirements!

207

Summary

Working with Ractive can be a real joy, once we get accustomed to how it manages data - the only question we need to answer is how can we make the best use of it? Fortunately Ractive works well with a host of different technologies - we've already made use of plugins and the like; in some cases we don't even need to set up anything special. Throughout the course of this chapter, we've explored some examples of where Ractive can be used, so let's take a moment to review what we have learned.

We kicked off with a little foray into manipulating images with SVG filters; we learned how standard filters don't allow us the ability to manipulate individual color channels, and that we can use Ractive to set up our target image. We then moved onto working with Semantic UI themes; we explored how easy it is to add the theme library to a Ractive instance, as long as we referenced the appropriate CSS attributes in our code. We then discussed how setting up this styling manually isn't the best use of our time; instead, we explored how we can turn a simple element such as a button into a suitably styled component that uses Semantic UI.

Next up came a simple demo in the form of adding Bootstrap - we understood how we can apply the same principles as we used with Semantic, to incorporate Bootstrap theming. We then covered an alternative method, in the form of the ractive-bootstrap plugin that will do much of the heavy lifting for us; it was simply a matter of applying the right components and classes at the appropriate point.

We then rounded out the chapter with a long demo that created a route planner using Ractive; this brought together a number of the concepts we've touched on earlier such as string interpolation, use of the {{#each}} block, and referencing content using keypaths. We worked through the initial preparation and construction phases, before finishing it off with some additional tweaks. As a final stage, we explored how this demo worked in more detail, before understanding some of the key ways in which we can extend this demo as part of any future development.

Phew - we've certainly covered a lot! However our journey doesn't end here - over the course of the next two chapters, we will work on developing a more complete example. Chapter 10 will see us build a working shopping cart using Ractive, but before we get there, we need somewhere to host it - this will be the subject of our next chapter.

CHAPTER 9

■ ■ ■

Putting It All Together

Up until now, we've covered a lot of content – it's time to pull it all together! Over the course of this chapter and the next, we'll touch on some of the elements that we've explored over the course of the book so far, to create a working example that shows how Ractive can operate when used in a more complex solution.

Setting Our Requirements

Over the course of this book, we've covered a host of different concepts that make up Ractive; it's time we put some of them together, to form a more practical example! It seems only sensible to set up something such as an online store, and given the subject of this book, why not base it on a book store? Yes, I may be old fashioned, but there is something about thumbing through a technical book that is still appealing ... but I digress – it's time we introduced our next project.

Our client (the e-commerce manager of a publisher), has become intrigued by the subject of a new book on RactiveJS. He wants to try protoyping a version of their online shop – it must perform well, be easy to use, and won't take too much time to make. At this stage he is not upset if every element doesn't work; it's more about appearance. Given what we've learned about how we can put together Ractive applications, it seems the ideal opportunity to try it out and show our client what they want as a demo.

Sound familiar? To sum up, we need to produce the following:

- A suitable template that can be used as a basis for pages;
- Some dummy text and images to represent suitable content for elements on the front page;
- A basic working cart, which can select a book, add it to the cart, and allow it to be checked out ready for payment.
- In addition, we're going to throw in a bonus – we'll use the relatively new Payments API to form a basic checkout process that can be added to the cart.

© Alex Libby 2017
A. Libby, *Beginning Ractive.js*, https://doi.org/10.1007/978-1-4842-3093-0_9

To help simplify matters, we will focus on the basic page template and front page content in this chapter; we will cover the cart functionality in Chapter 10, *Creating a Shopping Cart*. To give you an idea of how our finished article might look, Figure 9-1 shows a (partial) screenshot of the homepage in action:

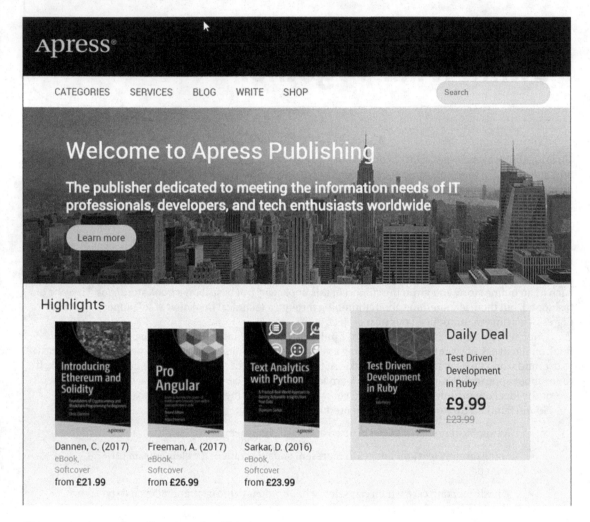

Figure 9-1. Screenshot of our completed homepage

The sharp-eyed among you will of course notice the more than passing similarities to the website for the publisher of this book; this is intended, as we will borrow elements to help mock up our design. Okay – enough chat: time we got stuck in! We have a fair amount of code to cover over the course of this chapter, so we'll start by setting up our environment, and assembling the relevant media and supporting files ready for constructing our site.

Getting Prepared

It goes without saying that a key part of setting up any website is a well-laid out structure; a website whose content and media are not stored properly will only become a real pain to manage! To help with this, we need to run through a few steps, so that our folder structure and media files are all set up, before we begin development.

```
GETTING PREPARED
```

1. In our project area, go ahead and create a new folder called website.

2. From a copy of the code download that accompanies this book, extract copies of the fonts and img folders, and then save them in the website folder created in the previous step.

3. We will need somewhere to store our styling, so go ahead and create a folder called css within the website folder.

4. We will of course need to use Ractive, so for this, go ahead and create a new folder called js and store it within the website folder we created in step 1.

5. At this point we need to add in the core ractive.min.js and ractive.min.js.map source map files too – go ahead and extract copies from the code download that accompanies this book, and drop them into the js subfolder we have just created.

6. Now that our media and folder structure is good to go, let's move on and make a start with creating the framework that will become the basis for our site.

Creating the Basic Container

Over the course of this book, we've worked through an array of different exercises, but probably not one as short as the one we are about to complete! Our next exercise is a simple two-step process – we need to set up the markup that will form the basis for our site; it won't look much at present, but we will address that shortly when we start to implement our Ractive instance.

```
CREATING THE BASIC CONTAINER
```

Let's make a start:

1. In a new document, go ahead and add the following code:

```html
<!doctype html>
<html>
<head>
  <meta charset='utf-8'>
  <title>Beginning Ractive: Creating a Site Template</title>
  <link rel="stylesheet" type="text/css" href="css/styles.css">
</head>
<body>
  <div id="container"></div>
  <script src='js/ractive.min.js'></script>
  <script src='js/website.js'></script>
</body>
</html>
```

2. Save this as index.html at the root of our project folder – our markup is now in place.

Our code so far doesn't need much explanation: we're setting a basic <div> as our container, along with links to Ractive and our style sheet; we will use this container to populate content from within Ractive.

You will notice that we haven't included a <script type="text/ractive"> statement in our code; most of the template and functionality will be populated from within our Ractive instance, so this isn't necessary. With this in mind, let's turn our attention to setting up our Ractive instance, and begin to populate it with a suitable template and content.

Setting Up Our Data

The old adage that "data is king" remains true – given the ability to manage data updates automatically, it's important that we get our data structure right in Ractive! Maintaining suitable data should be a continual process – this is not just to keep content fresh, but also to make sure that our content is suitably structured, and that old content is removed at the appropriate time.

That said, there are some standard configuration options that we must apply in any Ractive instance, although not always in the same format each time. To see what I mean, and as part of the next exercise, we will set up our principal Ractive instance, and begin configuring it for use in our demo.

SETTING UP OUR DATA

1. We'll start by setting up our new Ractive instance – for this, go ahead and add the following to a new file, saving it as website.js within the js subfolder of our project area.

```
var ractive = new Ractive({
  target: '#container',
  template: website,
  components: { APFooter, APPublish, APSubscribe },
});
```

2. Our site won't be of any use without data, so to fix this, add the following code immediately after the components: {...} entry in the previous step. There are a few lines involved, so we'll break it down into sections, starting with the initialization of data for our header and menu:

```
data: {
  title: 'Welcome to Apress Publishing',
  strapline: 'The publisher dedicated to meeting the information needs of IT
  professionals, developers, and tech enthusiasts worldwide',
  about: 'Learn more',
  menu: headermenu,
```

3. Next up comes the books data block – this is used to populate the Highights cartridge at the top of our homepage:

```
books: [{
  img: "img/highlight1.jpg",
  author: "Dannen, C. (2017)",
  format: "eBook, Softcover",
  price: "£21.99",
```

```
},{
  img: "img/highlight2.jpg",
  author: "Freeman, A. (2017)",
  format: "eBook, Softcover",
  price: "£26.99",
},{
  img: "img/highlight3.jpg",
  author: "Sarkar, D. (2016)",
  format: "eBook, Softcover",
  price: "£23.99",
}],
```

4. The third cartridge in our site will be reserved for displaying categories of books sold by Apress Publishing; for this, we will use an array to populate the names of each category:

```
categories: catlist,
```

5. For now, the final data block will be given over to displaying a daily deal – we'll set up details of our chosen book at this point:

```
daily: {
  img: "img/daily.jpg",
  title: "Test Driven Development in Ruby",
  discount: "£9.99",
  oldprice: "£23.99"
}
}
```

6. Save the file – leave it open for now, as we will continue using it shortly.

If we try to preview the results at this stage, our page won't really show anything of note. Indeed, it is more likely to display an error – how come?

Well, if we take a look at the code carefully, we should be able to spot some issues with missing content. This is entirely planned – there are some sections we need to add into our code, such as data for our menu and for the category list. This is an easy fix to implement – let's dive in and take a look.

Filling in the Gaps

We have a host of different sections we need to add to our page as content; these include blocks such as a category list, subscribe call to action, and highlighted books.

However, before we can add these in, there are three pieces of code we need to add to support this and fix some of the errors shown from the previous exercise.

FILLING IN THE GAPS

Let's dive in:

1. Revert back to the `website.js` file we had open in the previous exercise, then add the following array block at the top of the file, before the `var ractive = new Ractive...` line:

```
var headermenu = [
  { name: 'Categories', link: '#' },
  { name: 'Services', link: '#' },
  { name: 'Blog', link: '#' },
  { name: 'Write', link: '#' },
  { name: 'Shop', link: '#' }
];
```

2. Next, leave a line then add the following array block – this takes care of the category list subject headings:

```
var catlist = [
  { name: 'Apple & iOS' },
  { name: 'Big Data & Analytics' },
  { name: 'Business Databases Enterprise Software' },
  { name: 'Game Development' },
  { name: 'Graphics' },
  { name: 'Hardware & Maker' },
  { name: 'Java' },
  { name: 'Machine Learning' },
  { name: 'Microsoft & .NET' },
  { name: 'Mobile Networking & Cloud' },
  { name: 'Open Source Programming' },
  { name: 'Python' },
  { name: 'Security' },
  { name: 'Web Development' }
];
```

3. Finally – and yes, this is where things will begin to get interesting – we need to add in a single variable; this is the basis for our template:

```
var website = ``;
```

■ **Note** We've used back ticks in this code block, which is for convenience purposes only – it is to allow us to lay out the template as it will appear on the page. In an ideal world, we should choose which JavaScript standard we want to use, for consistency; If the preference is to use normal quotes (i.e., an older standard of JavaScript), then spaces must be removed from the HTML markup to avoid any errors.

---

4. At this point go ahead and save the file – keep the file open for now, as we will continue using it in the next part of our marathon exercise.

We're now ready to build our template! Before we do so, there is an important point we should cover off – the use of arrays. In the case of the category listing, the most effective route to displaying this is to use the {{#each}} keyword, as each heading uses the same style; this allows us to use an array to store the information. We're using a similar principle for the menu, although we are referencing each menu heading directly.

Okay – let's move on: over the course of the next few pages, we will work our way through adding each block. A screenshot of each section will be displayed, followed by the code required to make it work in the template. There are a few blocks involved, so without further ado, let's dive in and make a start on adding content.

Implementing the Design

This is the stage where we can begin to fill out our template, and turn it into something more recognizable; the great thing about Ractive (as we will see later), is that we can begin to turn each section into its own component, which makes it neater (and easier) to add in to the overall design.

We will split the addition of content into two parts – the initial part will add in some blocks manually such as the Highlights section; we will then move onto styling the site, before returning to add the remaining blocks as individual components.

A completed version of the code is available in the js subfolder, within the code download that accompanies this book – it's in the file marked website.js.

There is a fair amount to cover, so let's make a start – we will cover the construction in sections, starting with the header and menu system; this will make it easier to see what is happening at each point in the journey.

Adding the Header and Menu

The first block we will add is a header – this will contain the Apress Publishing logo, our menu and search, and a header banner. A screenshot of how this will look once the styles have been added is displayed in Figure 9-2:

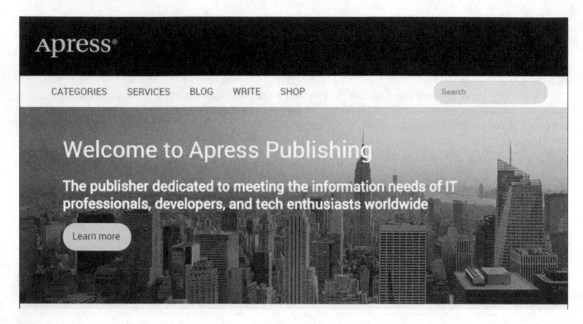

Figure 9-2. The completed header

The code for this block is as follows:

ADDING THE HEADER AND MENU

1. Revert back to the website.js file we have had open over the last few exercises, and look for this line, on or around line 26:

   ```
   var website = ``;
   ```

2. Go ahead and add the following code in between the backticks – this contains our header image, search box and menu, along with a suitable welcome message:

   ```
   <header>
     <div id="top"><img src="img/logo.svg"></div>
     <p class="search"><input type="text" name="search" placeholder="Search"> </p>

     <nav>
       <ul id="menu">
         <li class="item"><a href="{{menu[0].link}}">{{menu[0].name}}</a></li>
         <li class="item"><a href="{{menu[1].link}}">{{menu[1].name}}</a></li>
         <li class="item"><a href="{{menu[2].link}}">{{menu[2].name}}</a></li>
         <li class="item"><a href="{{menu[3].link}}">{{menu[3].name}}</a></li>
         <li class="shop"><a href="{{menu[4].link}}">{{menu[4].name}}</a></li>
       </ul>
     </nav>
   ```

```
<section id="head-img">
  <div>
    <h1>{{title}}</h1>
    <h2>{{strapline}}</h2>
    <a href="about.html">{{about}}</a>
  </div>
</section>
</header>
```

3. Save the file – keep it open, as we will move onto adding the next block shortly.

If we preview the results, we should start to see some content rendered onscreen, but it will look awful! This will be fixed once we start to tackle the styling; we will switch to this, once we've added a couple more sections, beginning with the Highlights.

Displaying Highlights and the Daily Deal

Now that our header image is in place, we can begin to set up the first content block in our demo – this will serve the book Highlights and Daily Deal. A screenshot of how this will appear in the finished article is shown in Figure 9-3:

Highlights

Dannen, C. (2017)
eBook,
Softcover
from **£21.99**

Freeman, A. (2017)
eBook,
Softcover
from **£26.99**

Sarkar, D. (2016)
eBook,
Softcover
from **£23.99**

Figure 9-3. *Highlights and Daily Deal*

The code for this is a little more complex, but only marginally – we now make use of the {{#each}} block that we alluded to at the end of Filling in the Gaps, from earlier in this chapter. Let's take a look:

ADDING THE HIGHLIGHTS BLOCK

1. Switch back to the `website.js` file we had open just now – leave a line blank, then add the following block of code immediately below this blank line:

```
<section id="highlights">
  <h3>Highlights</h3>
  <ul>
   {{#each books}}
      <li class="item">
        <div class="book"><img src="{{img}}"></div>
        <div class="info">{{author}}</div>
        <div class="format">{{format}}</div>
        <div class="info">from <b>{{price}}</b></div>
      </li>
     {{/each}}
     <li id="daily">
       <h3>Daily Deal</h3>
       <div class="info">{{daily.title}}</div>
       <div class="discount">{{daily.discount}}</div>
       <div class="oldprice">{{daily.oldprice}}</div>
       <div class="book"><img src="{{daily.img}}"></div>
     </li>
  </ul>
</section>
```

2. Save the file – leave it open for now, as we will continue with it shortly.

At this point we will have the Highlights books listed, along with a Daily Deal – we make use of a standard unordered list, but use mustache placeholders to reference the details about each book.

Notice a difference in the style of how the book details are called? The first one doesn't need to use a full keypath – this is taken care of by the {{#each books}} reference, so a value such as {{img}} becomes {{books.img}}. With the latter format, as we are only referencing one book, we can call the properties directly instead.

Adding a Categories List

An essential part of any bookstore will be a list of categories – after all, how can we find a product if there are no groups set up? The real functionality for this takes place in the cart itself, but for now, we can mock up a suitable category list using the {{#each}} method and the catlist array we created earlier in the chapter. To give a flavor of what this will look like once completed, a screenshot of the finished article is displayed in Figure 9-4:

Browse our categories

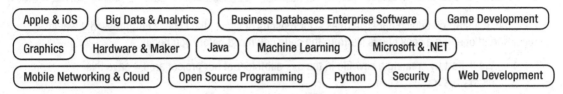

Figure 9-4. Categories listing

Let's explore the code in more detail:

ADDING THE CATEGORIES BLOCK

1. The Categories block will slot in immediately after the Highlights section – leave a blank line, then add the following code in or around line 71:

    ```
    <section id="categories">
      <h3>Browse our categories</h3>
      <ul>
        {{#each categories}}
          <li class="item">{{name}}</li>
        {{/each}}
      </ul>
    </section>
    ```

2. Save the file, but don't close it – we will return to it momentarily.

A small point of note – the {{#each}} method that we alluded to earlier is highlighted in the above code; this means we don't have to provide a full keypath reference to each piece of information, as the {{#each}} block will work out what should be imported when it is processed by Ractive.

Okay – let's move on: as promised, we will cover the remaining blocks shortly, but for now, we're going to turn our attention to adding some styling for the blocks that are now in place. This approach might seem a little odd, but stay with me on this – it will all fall into place once we add in the remaining cartridges later in this chapter!

Adding Styles

Over the course of the next couple of pages, we have a whole host of styles we need to add, in order for our demo to resemble something presentable – without them, well ... let's just say it will look awful!

The great thing about Ractive though is that it encourages a modular approach to development – it means that we can either store CSS styling within a central style sheet, or with each component. There are advantages to both, and equally there are reasons as to why this approach isn't so useful; for now, we'll take a mixed approach where some of our styling will be in a central style sheet, and some with each component.

ADDING STYLES

Let's make a start on adding our style rules – for reasons of space, the code is compressed; I would recommend opening a copy of this file from the code download before you begin:

1. We'll start by creating a new file in the `css` subfolder of our project area – save this as `styles.css`.

2. Next, go ahead and add the following blocks of code – our style sheet is fairly lengthy, so we will go through it section by section, starting with some base styles for our container and homepage:

```css
@font-face { font-family: 'robotoregular'; src: url('../fonts/Roboto-Regular-webfont.woff') format('woff'); font-weight: normal; font-style: normal; }
body { font-family: robotoregular, sans-serif; }
section { width: 100%; min-height: 100px; }
h1, h2 { color: #fff; }
h1 { font-size: 2.42857rem; font-weight: normal; }
li { display: inline-block; padding: 0 0.9375rem 0 0.9375rem; }
a { text-decoration: none; color: #6e6e6e; }
#container { border: 0.0625rem solid #000; width: 59rem; margin: 1.875rem auto 1.875rem auto; }
```

3. Next up comes the header image – go ahead and add the following two style rules to take care of the Apress logo and black border at the top of our page:

```css
#top { width: 100%; background-color: #000; color: #fff; }
#top img { height: 2rem; margin: 2.3rem 0 1.7rem 1.65rem; }
```

4. We can't have a site without some form of menu, so we'll add in styling for a simple one-level affair:

```css
#menu li { text-transform: uppercase; }
#menu li a:hover { border-bottom: 0.25rem solid #ffcc00; padding-bottom: 0.75rem; }
```

5. This is where we start to get into the site content; next up is the header image section. For this, add the following rules that will insert an image and correctly place it (and the message within) on the page:

```css
#head-img { background-image: url(../img/header.jpg); height: 21rem; width: 100%; }
#head-img div { line-height: 1.875rem; padding: 1.5625rem 0 0 4.6875rem; width: 43.4375rem; }
#head-img div a { padding: 0.4375rem 0.625rem 0.625rem 0.4375rem; background-color: #ffcc00; border-radius: 2.375rem; display: block; width: 6.25rem; text-align: center; }
```

6. The first cartridge below the welcome image is the Highlights section – for this, we need to add in rules to take care of the simple list we've created:

```
#highlights { background-color: #f7f7f7; padding-top: 1.5625rem; }
#highlights h3 { color: #1a1a1a; font-size: 1.51429rem; margin-left: 1.875rem;
line-height: 1.25rem; }
#highlights ul { padding-bottom: 3.125rem; }
#highlights .book img { width: 8.125rem; height: auto; }
#highlights .format { color: #999; width: 6.25rem; font-size: 0.875rem; }
```

7. Our page has a Daily section, where a book is selected to be on special offer; for this, we need a set of styles to position the block, and add color to the title, information, price, and discounted price:

```
#daily { width: 17.5rem; height: 13.125rem; float: right; padding: 1.875rem
0.9375rem 0.9375rem 0.9375rem; background-color: #e6e6e6; margin: -1.25rem
4.375rem 0 2rem; position: absolute; }
#daily h3 { color: #1a1a1a; font-size: 1.51429rem; margin-left: 1.875rem; line-
height: 1.25rem; position: absolute;
padding-left: 7.5rem; margin-top: 0.125rem; }#daily .info { position: absolute;
padding-left: 9.375rem; margin-top: 2.5rem; width: 5.3125rem; }
#daily .discount { font-weight: bold; font-size: 1.71429rem; position: absolute;
padding-left: 9.375rem; margin-top: 6.875rem; }
#daily .oldprice { text-decoration: line-through; color: #999; float: left;
position: absolute; padding-left: 9.375rem; margin-top: 9.0625rem; }
```

8. Our shop won't sell books from just one category – this would soon get very boring! Instead, we should have a list of multiple categories; the style rules take care of their appearance on the page:

```
#categories { background-color: #ffffff;  padding-bottom: 0.5rem; }
#categories h3 { color: #1a1a1a; font-size: 1.51429rem; margin-left: 1.875rem;
line-height: 1.25rem; }
#categories li { border: 0.0625rem solid #4d4d4d; border-radius: 0.9375rem;
padding: 0.3125rem 0.9375rem 0.3125rem 0.9375rem; margin: 0.3125rem; }
```

9. What is a site without some form of search facility? It would soon lose customers – our mockup therefore has one in the title bar, which we style using the following rules:

```
.search { color: #fff; float: right; line-height: 3.125rem; padding-right:
0.9375rem; }
.search input { background-color: #e6e6e6; padding-top: 0; padding-bottom:
0; position: relative; border-radius: 1.21429rem; height: 2.5rem; padding:
0.71429rem 0.78571rem 0.78571rem; border: 0.07143rem solid #d9d9d9;
box-sizing: border-box; margin-right: 1.25rem; }.search input:active, input:focus
{ background-color: #ffffff; outline: none; }
```

10. Save the file – we can close it for now, as we don't need it immediately.

Phew! We have an extensive list of styles in place, which covers most of the components we've developed for our mockup. However, if we were to look in the version of our style sheet that is in the code download that accompanies this book, we will see some differences – with good reason.

The modular nature of Ractive means that we can develop components for our site; these can then be reused as created, or (if we develop them the right way), as a basis for new components, or to display different information. We've developed some of the components required for this site, so we have moved their styling rules into each component, and commented out the original code in the style sheet.

The key point here though is that we can choose how we style these components; in one sense, it's better to host the appropriate rules within the component, to help maintain that sense of modularity. However, this comes at the cost of losing the ability to minify code (particularly that which is in one location) – there is no right or wrong answer, but it does mean that we have to decide on an approach that best fits our needs, and one which remains consistent throughout the site.

Leaving aside the bigger picture for now, we will use a mix of both approaches in our demo – some styles will be added manually, and others will come via components. This latter approach is the next step in our development, so let's dive in and start creating the missing components for our site.

Creating Reusable Components

Remember how we added styles for most of the elements on the page, but that we wouldn't be covering all of them?

Well, there is a simple reason for this – we've generated a template within our Ractive instance; this works well, but it isn't the most effective way to create our site. Instead, we can assemble components based on our existing code; to show you how this would work, we're going to add the remaining elements using this method. We'll take a look at the Subscription option and footer shortly, but for now, let's focus on setting up the Publishing cartridge first.

Adding the Publishing Cartridge

The first of three components that we will create for our site is the Publishing cartridge – this is simply an advert encouraging potential authors to write for Apress. A screenshot of the finished article is shown in Figure 9-5:

Figure 9-5. *Publishing with Apress catridge*

The code to create this is very straightforward – in the main we use standard mustaches to render our content on screen; this is refined using styles that are defined within our component. Let's take a closer look.

ADDING THE PUBLISHING CARTRIDGE

1. Revert back to the `website.js` file we had open in the previous exercise, then leave a line after the closing `</section>` in the categories block (on or around line 80), and add the following line:

   ```
   <APPublish />
   ```

2. Leave two blank lines after the closing backtick and semicolon (`` ` ``;) on or around line 83, then go ahead and add the following code:

   ```
   /* Publish */
   const APPublish = Ractive.extend({
     template: `
       <section id="publish">
         <h3>{{title}}</h3>
         <p class="info">{{info}}</p>
         <p class="proposal"><a href="#">{{proposal}}</a></p>
       </section>  `,
     css: `
       #publish { background-color: #f7f7f7; background: url(img/publish.jpg);
       background-position: center center; background-repeat: no-repeat; background-
       size: cover; position: relative; height: 225px; }
       #publish h3 { color: #fff; font-size: 1.51429rem; margin-left: 1.875rem;
       line-height: 1.25rem; width: 25rem; position: absolute; margin-top:
       2.8125rem; margin-left: 1.875rem; font-weight: 300; }
       #publish .info { color: #fff; width: 39.375rem; position: absolute; margin-
       top: 4.6875rem; margin-left: 1.875rem; }
       #publish .proposal a { padding: 10px; padding-top: 0.4375rem; background-
       color: #ffcc00; border-radius: 2.375rem; display: block; width: 9.6875rem;
       text-align: center; text-decoration: none; padding-bottom: 0.4375rem; margin-
       left: 1.875rem; position: absolute; margin-top: 9.6875rem; }
       `, data: {
       title: 'Publishing with Apress',
       info: 'We build strong partnerships with our authors. Apress offers authors
       the chance to work with a publisher with the marketing, distribution, and
       commercial weight of a major player while maintaining the spirit of an
       independent publishing house.',
       proposal: 'Submit a proposal'
     }
   });
   ```

3. We also need to amend our `components` object in the main Ractive instance – for this, open up `website.js`, then add this line as indicated:

   ```
   template: website,
   components: { APPublish },
   ```

4. Remember to save the file – keep it open for now, as we will resume editing in it shortly. If we preview the results in a browser, we will see our Publishing element appear as a new component on the page.

It's worth taking time to review this code in a little more detail – the beauty of Ractive means that we have a simple template we can use to turn almost any standard code into a basic Ractive component.

It may not look straightforward at first, but if we dial down the content in this component, we are left with the following:

```
/* Publish */
const APPublish = Ractive.extend({
  template: `... `,
  css: `...`,
  data: {
    <keypath reference>: <value>,
    ...
  }
});
```

We don't need anything more complicated than this for our project – if we create from scratch, then we can move existing HTML markup into the template section. Any pieces of information within can be replaced with the appropriate mustache, and the data for that stored within the data block. We can then apply styles to our component as desired – note that this may lead to duplication, so it's important to ensure that we take care over which styles are used in our component.

Okay – we have our Publish component in place; we have two more to add, in the form of the Subscription option and the site footer. Let's take a look at the subscription option as our next component – hopefully it will illustrate that we can use the same principle to produce multiple basic components within Ractive.

Adding a Subscription Option

Our next component is to add a "subscribe to our newsletter" option – it's enough to mock it up for the purposes of our demo, but in reality this would need to tie in with code that accepts a valid email address and stores it for sending out newsletters. That aside, Figure 9-6 shows a screenshot of how our finished component will appear in our mockup:

Figure 9-6. *Our Subscribe component*

As with the previous component, the code to create this is very straightforward. In the main we use standard mustaches to render our content on screen; this is refined using styles that are defined within our component. Let's take a closer look:

ADDING A SUBSCRIPTION OPTION

1. Revert back to the website.js file we had open in the previous exercise, then add this line of code immediately after `<APPublish />`, on or around line 81:

```
<APSubscribe />
```

2. Leave two blank lines after the closing brackets from the APPublish component, then add the following code; the first part deals with the template for our component:

```
/* Subscribe */
const APSubscribe = Ractive.extend({
  template: `
    <section id="subscribe">
      <h3>{{title}}</h3>
      <p class="intro">{{intro}}</p>
      <form id="subscribe-form">
        <label>Email Address:
          <input type="email" value="">
          <input type="submit" class="signup" value={{signup}}>
        </label>
      </form>
      <div class="advert"></div>
    </section> `,
```

3. The second part takes care of the styles we will use to render our component:

```
css: `
  #subscribe { background-image: url(img/advert.jpg); width: 29.375rem; height:
  16.125rem; margin: 0.9375rem; background-size: cover; background-position:
  center; background-color: #333333; }
  #subscribe h3 { color: #1a1a1a; font-size: 1.51429rem; margin-left: 1.875rem;
  line-height: 1.25rem; float: left; position: absolute; padding-left: 31.25rem;
  margin-top; 3.125rem; width: 40rem; margin-bottom: 0.5rem; }
  #subscribe .intro { margin-left: 1.875rem; margin-top: 7.8125rem; line-height:
  1.25rem; float: left; position: absolute; padding-left: 31.25rem; width:
  15.625rem; }
  #subscribe label { margin-left: 1.875rem; float: left; position: absolute;
  padding-left: 31.25rem; width: 15.625rem; margin-top: 3.125rem; margin-top:
  3.625rem; }
  #subscribe label input { margin-top: 0.3125rem; }
  #subscribe input[type=submit] { margin-left: 1.875rem; line-height: 1.25rem;
  float: left; position: absolute; padding: 0.625rem; padding-top: 0.4375rem;
  background-color: #ffcc00; border-radius: 2.375rem; display: block; width:
  6.25rem; text-align: center; text-decoration: none; padding-bottom: 0.4375rem;
  margin-left: 12.0625rem; margin-top: -2rem; color: #6e6e6e; }
```

4. These remaining few lines define the data that will be displayed within our component:

```
data: {
    title:  'Subscribe to our newsletter',
    intro: 'Stay up to date on daily deals, discount promotions, events & new
    releases. Save up to 90% on eBook purchases.',
    signup: 'Sign up now'
  }
});
```

5. We also need to amend our components object in the main Ractive instance – for this, open up `website.js`, then amend this line as indicated:

```
components: { APFooter, APPublish, APSubscribe },
```

6. Remember to save the file – keep it open for now, as we will resume editing in it shortly.

If we take a careful look at the code, we can see we've made use of the template and principles outlined in the previous exercise – it should show that we don't need anything complex for a basic component such as our one!

There is a proviso though: we've not touched the code required to accept, validate, and store the email address for our newsletter. If we were developing this to a full working version, then we can use an email validation plugin that we would link in to our component, then add additional code to take care of storing the email address separately. Let's move on – we have one more component to add, in the form of a footer. This will finish off the mockup; let's dive in and see what is required to get it working in more detail.

Finishing with a Footer

Although this component will appear to be simpler to implement than the previous two examples, it still makes use of the same principle as before – defining the `template`, `css`, and `data` options. To give a flavor of how it will appear, Figure 9-7 shows a screenshot of the finished article:

Figure 9-7. Our finished footer

At the risk of sounding like a broken record (!), the code to create this is very straightforward. As before, we use standard mustaches to render our content on screen; this is refined using styles that are defined within our component. Let's take a closer look.

ADDING A FOOTER

1. Revert back to the `website.js` file we had open in the previous exercise, then on a new line immediately after `<APSubscribe />`, add the following: `<APFooter />`

2. Leave two blank lines after the closing brackets from the APSubscribe component, then add the following code:

```
/* Footer */
const APFooter = Ractive.extend({
  template: `
    <footer>
      <p><img src="img/logo.svg"></p>
      <p>{{message}}</p>
    </footer>
  `,
  css: `
    footer { background-color: #000; line-height: 2.375rem; padding-left:
    1.25rem; color: #6e6e6e; }
    footer p { width: 23.75rem; display: inline-block;}
    footer p:nth-child(1) { width: 10rem; }
    footer p img { vertical-align: middle; padding-right: 2.1875rem; }
  `, data: { foo_message: '© Apress 2017 | Terms & Conditions | Privacy Policy' }
});
```

3. We also need to amend our components object in the main Ractive instance – for this, open up website.js, then amend this line as indicated:

```
components: { APFooter, APPublish, APSubscribe },
```

4. Remember to save the file – once this is done, we can close it, as we don't need it for now.

Our site mockup is now complete – if all is well, we should see something akin to the screenshot shown in Figure 9-1 near the beginning of this chapter. It's still a long way from something we can present as a fully working solution for use by customers, but it will at least give our client an idea of how their site will look when it is completed.

Okay – let's change tack: now that our site mockup is completed, there are a few key points we need to explore in more detail. One of the key strengths of Ractive is its ability to update data on the page quickly; let's take a moment to see how this works on our completed demo.

Updating the Site

Over the course of the last few pages, I've extolled the virtues of Ractive's legendary data management skills – it's time to put them to the test!

For anyone who has spent any time working with jQuery (or even JavaScript), then they will be used to having to work out which element contains text that needs to be updated. Trouble is, what if the data is in an element that isn't easily accessible? Sure, we could use the likes of .next(), .parent(), or .children(), but this becomes messy. This is where Ractive comes into its own – data is stored in JSON format within the Ractive instance, so it becomes a cinch to update text. Let's put this to the test in a simple demo.

UPDATING THE SITE

1. Open up a browser session, then run index.html to view our demo.

2. Go ahead and enter this command at the console, then press Enter:

   ```
   apsubscribe = APSubscribe.defaults.data;
   ```

3. With the data block defined as a variable, now enter this command at the console:

   ```
   apsubscribe.sub_title;
   ```

So, what did these two lines of code produce? We can see the results in Figure 9-8:

```
> apsubscribe = APSubscribe.defaults.data
<  {sub_title: "Subscribe to our newsletter", sub_intro: "Stay up
 ▶ to date on daily deals, discount promotion… new releases. Save
   up to 90% on eBook purchases.", sub_signup: "Sign up now"}

> apsubscribe.sub_title
<  "Subscribe to our newsletter"

> |
```

Figure 9-8. *Searching for data*

All we did is to retrieve the title of our Subscribe block - this initially returned the three entries within it, but then returned just the title entry when we ran the second command. It's important to note though that we registered this globally.

Let's take this up a notch – what if the data is inside a component? No problem – try entering this line into the console:

```
ractive.findComponent('APPublish').set("pub_title", "Bienvenue à Apress Publishing");
```

Take a look at the Publishing component on the page – notice anything different?

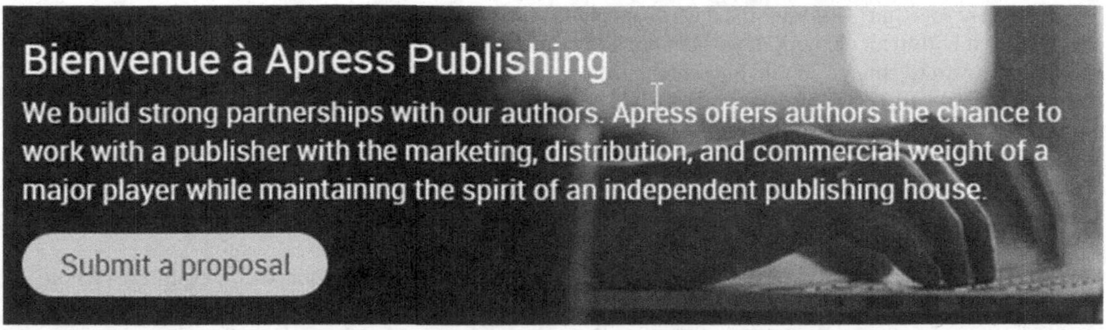
Bienvenue à Apress Publishing
We build strong partnerships with our authors. Apress offers authors the chance to work with a publisher with the marketing, distribution, and commercial weight of a major player while maintaining the spirit of an independent publishing house.
Submit a proposal

Figure 9-9. *Translating content into French...*

Hopefully you will see that the title has been translated into French - it's worth noting that we can achieve the same result by modifying our call to the APSubscribe component, thus:

```
<APSubscribe sub_title="Bienvenue à Apress Publishing" />
```

Okay - how about we something else: a quick trip back to my favorite country, Denmark, would give us this, as shown in Figure 9-10:

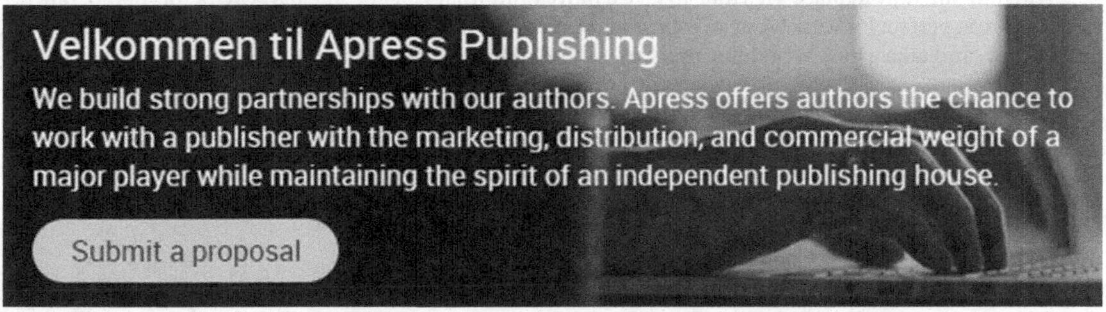
Velkommen til Apress Publishing
We build strong partnerships with our authors. Apress offers authors the chance to work with a publisher with the marketing, distribution, and commercial weight of a major player while maintaining the spirit of an independent publishing house.
Submit a proposal

Figure 9-10. *...or Danish*

To prove it really is this simple to update content, we can see the results of changing both elements within the console, as indicated in Figure 9-11:

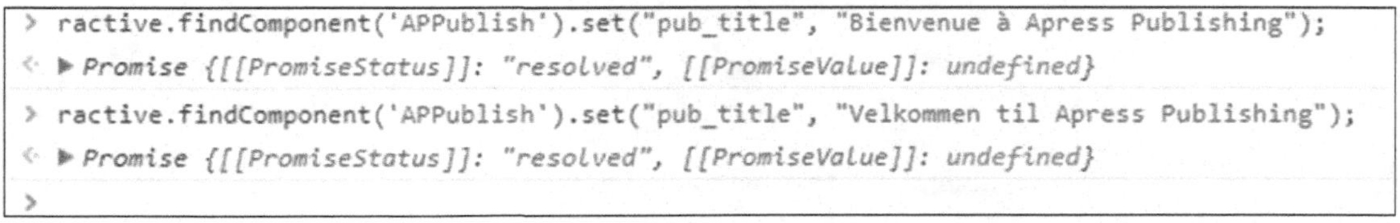
> ractive.findComponent('APPublish').set("pub_title", "Bienvenue à Apress Publishing");
< ▶ Promise {[[PromiseStatus]]: "resolved", [[PromiseValue]]: undefined}
> ractive.findComponent('APPublish').set("pub_title", "Velkommen til Apress Publishing");
< ▶ Promise {[[PromiseStatus]]: "resolved", [[PromiseValue]]: undefined}
>

Figure 9-11. *Running the code in console*

How easy was that? Gone are the days of having to work out which class or selector to use, in order to update text within an element. If we plan our site properly (and I am sure you will do this!), then every element we want to change should be available within our Ractive instance. As long as each instance of that component has a unique name, then it alone will be updated; if we have multiple instances with the same name, then they will each be updated.

Summary

Creating a site using Ractive can be a real joy - throughout the course of this book, we've explored a whole host of different features from the Ractive library, and brought many of them together to create a basic working demo of a site. Let's take a moment to review what we've covered throughout this chapter.

We kicked off by setting out our requirements, before working through some simple housekeeping to help get our workspace set up. We then began coding the basic container for our site, before setting up data in our Ractive instance.

Next up came the initial part of the design - we first added the header and menu, before building the Highlights, Daily Deal, and Categories cartridges.

We then moved onto styling the code so far - we explored how this might be achieved by either manually adding styles, or (as we see later in the chapter), incorporating the styles into each component.

We then rounded out the chapter by adding the three remaining blocks as components, before taking a look at how we might update the site's data, as a precursor to implementing facilities such as language localization.

With our site now in place - it's time to take a move onto what will become part two of this demo: our cart. Ractive is perfect for working in an e-commerce environment, so without further ado, let's continue on our journey, and take a look at building that cart, as the subject of the next chapter.

CHAPTER 10

■ ■ ■

Creating a Shopping Cart

One of the key strengths of Ractive is repetition – and no, I don't mean in code! In this instance I'm referring to instances where we need to display a series of items on the page, using the same format. A perfect example of this is in a shopping cart – we have to display products, prices, descriptions, and so on, so why not use Ractive? Over the course of this chapter, we'll work through the steps needed to create such a cart, which you can use as a basis for future projects.

Setting the Scene

In this modern age of the Internet, shopping online has dramatically increased over the last few years; a key part of this is the increasing use of mobile devices to browse for and purchase goods and services online. For some countries, this is currently over 60% (Italy), with others such as Indonesia reaching as much as 90%! It's therefore essential to have a performant site if one is to survive in retail.

For the third and final project of three in this book, we will use Ractive to create our product catalog and cart demo. We introduced the first part of this, in the form of the template page we created in Chapter 9 - Ractive's ability to manage updates to data (such as quantities), or adding and removing products from the cart, makes it perfect for creating shopping carts. To help set the scene, there are a few points we need to cover:

- Creating a fully fledged system is outside of the scope of this chapter; indeed, one could easily write a book in its own right, and still not cover everything needed! We will focus on the core cart functions, stocking of our catalog, and adding or removal of products from our cart.

- Our final solution will **not** be production ready – it will require further development before it would be ready to earn revenue. We will explore some of these areas toward the end of the chapter.

With this in mind, let's make a start – as with any project, there is usually a little housekeeping before we can get stuck into code; this one is no exception! Let's take a look at what we need to do first, before we can start creating our code.

© Alex Libby 2017
A. Libby, *Beginning Ractive.js*, https://doi.org/10.1007/978-1-4842-3093-0_10

Creating Our Cart

Over the course of this chapter, we will create a fair amount of code; before we get started on this, there is a little housekeeping we should take care of first:

SETTING UP OUR WORK AREA

1. We need to set up a few folders to store our media and code – for this, go ahead and create a folder called `shop`.

2. Inside this folder, add four new folders – save them with the names `css`, `fonts`, `img` and `js` respectively.

3. We need a set of images to represent the books we will be selling – there is a set prepared within the `img` folder in the code download that accompanies this book. Go ahead and copy the contents of the `img` folder to the `img` folder we created in step 1.

At this point, we are ready to start creating our shopping cart. Our demo will work perfectly well from the browser, if loaded from the filesystem. However, if we want to take things further, there are a couple of optional extra steps we can take:

- Toward the end of the chapter, we will take a look at adding a payment facility for our shopping cart. We can of course feed through to a service such as PayPal, but I'm all about pushing the boat out; we will try out the new Payment Request API to handle the initial payment request. It's worth noting that this is an experimental API, so it will change over time; I strongly recommend checking compatibility / the current standards if you decide to use this in other projects.

- To create an optimal solution, I would recommend installing a local web server if you can; there are dozens available, but feel free to use your existing one, if you already have one installed. This step isn't obligatory; if circumstances dictate that you can't install it, then the demo will work fine from the local filesystem.

To get a flavor for what we will develop throughout this chapter, Figure 10-1 on Page 3 shows a screenshot of the finished article. Okay – we're all set; it's time to get coding! Over the course of the chapter, there is a fair amount of code to cover, so we will explore it section by section, beginning with setting up the data to be used in our shop.

Setting Up Our Data

A shop without a catalog is like a car without wheels - it won't be going very far! We clearly need to create something; for our demo, we will set up data records for a series of books on random topics, as published by Apress, and as illustrated in Figure 10-1:

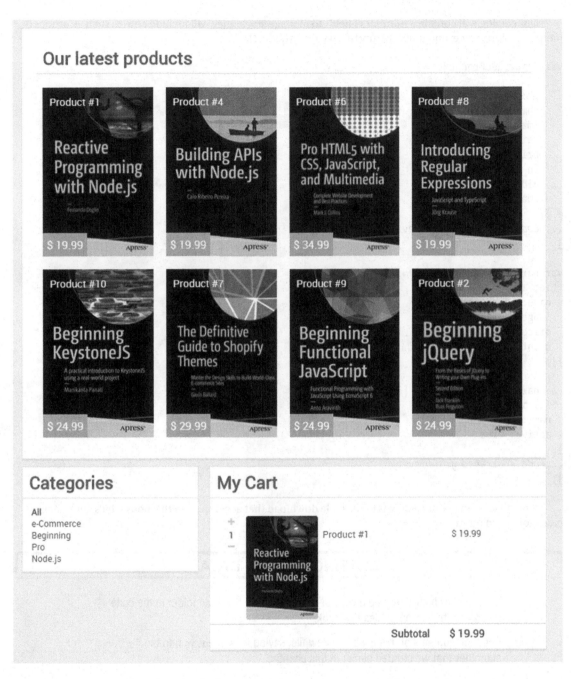

Figure 10-1. *A screenshot of our finished cart*

Our catalog will contain a number of fields to manage stock; they will include entries such as product name, category, price, and unit quantity (used within the cart):

```
var hardcodedProducts = [
  {
    id: 1,
    name: 'Product #1',
    image: './img/book1',
    category: 5,
    price: '13.20',
    in_cart: true,
    hidden: false,
    quantity: 1
  },
... code shortened for brevity
];

var hardcodedCartProducts = [{
  id: 1,
  name: 'Product #1',
  image: './img/book1',
  price: '13.20',
  quantity: 1
}];

var hardcodedCategories = [{
  id: 1,
  name: "All",
  active: true
},
...code shortened for brevity
];
```

The full version of our catalog is in the code download that accompanies this book – let's get it set up ready for use in our demo:

SETTING UP OUR DATA

1. We will start by opening up a copy of data.txt from the code folder in the code download that accompanies this book.

2. Copy the contents of this file into a new file, saving it as shop.js into the js subfolder that we created earlier in this chapter.

Our data is now ready for use – trouble is, it won't be of any use without something to manage it! Let's start to fix that by adding markup that will be the basis for our product catalog.

Creating Our Catalog Page

The next stage in construction is to add our markup – there is nothing special or out of the ordinary; it is plain HTML. The code will be split into three sections: one to cater for the catalog, the second to host the cart, and the third to manage filters.

ADDING OUR CATALOG PAGE

We'll continue with adding code:

1. For this part, go ahead and create a new file at the root of the shop folder called `index.html` – add the following code:

```
<!doctype html>
<html>
<head>
  <meta charset='utf-8'>
  <title>Beginning Ractive: Creating a Shopping Cart</title>
  <link rel="stylesheet" type="text/css" href="css/shop.css">
</head>
<body>
  <main class="main">
    <div class="wrapper cf">
    </div>
  </main>
</body>
</html>
```

2. The code as it stands won't achieve much – for this, we need to add in the various blocks that will handle our catalog, cart, and filters. Go ahead and add the first immediately after `<div class="wrapper cf">`, which will take care of the catalog:

```
<div class="box latest-products">
  <h1>Our latest products</h1>
  <ul class="products-list cf"></ul>
</div>
```

3. Next up comes the list that will look after the cart:

```
<div class="box cart">
  <h1>My Cart</h1>
  <ul class="cart-list"></ul>
</div>
```

4. The third section will manage our category list:

```
<div class="box filters">
  <h1>Categories</h1>
  <ul class="categories-list"></ul>
</div>
```

5. Next, we need to add in our script links before the closing </body> tag – this is to prepare for the scripts that we will add shortly:

```
<script src='js/ractive.min.js'></script>
<script src='js/jquery.min.js'></script>
<script src='js/shop.js'></script>
```

6. At this stage save the file – our markup is now in place; if we ran it in a browser it won't show a great deal, but this is to be expected!

The next stage is for us to add our functionality; we will kick off with adding our core Ractive instances, before adding in our cart observer and event handlers.

Implementing the Cart

The next exercise is where things will begin to get interesting – over the next few pages, our shop will start to take shape, as we begin to create the code for our demo.

For our demo to operate correctly, we need to add three Ractive instances – this is more than we've ever added before to a demo, but as long as we manage them correctly, they won't conflict with each other. The instances we add will take care of the product list (or catalog), our shopping cart, and the category list. Let's continue with adding code:

IMPLEMENTING THE CART

1. If it isn't already, reopen the shop.js file, then add the following code immediately before var hardcodedProducts = [, leaving 2 free lines between the existing data block and our Ractive instance block:

```
$(function () {

    var ProductList = new Ractive({
        el: '.products-list',
        template: '#product_item',
        data: {products: hardcodedProducts}
    });

    var Cart = new Ractive({
        el: '.cart-list',
        template: '#cart_item',
        data: {
            products: hardcodedCartProducts,
            subtotal: 0
        }
    });
```

```
    var Categories = new Ractive({
      el: '.categories-list',
      template: '#categories_item',
      data: {categories: hardcodedCategories}
    });
});
```

2. Save the file – if we run our demo at this point, we won't see a great deal – in fact
    we'll see an error!

What gives - surely we should start to see something displayed, right? If we take a closer look, we will see an error akin to that shown in Figure 10-2:

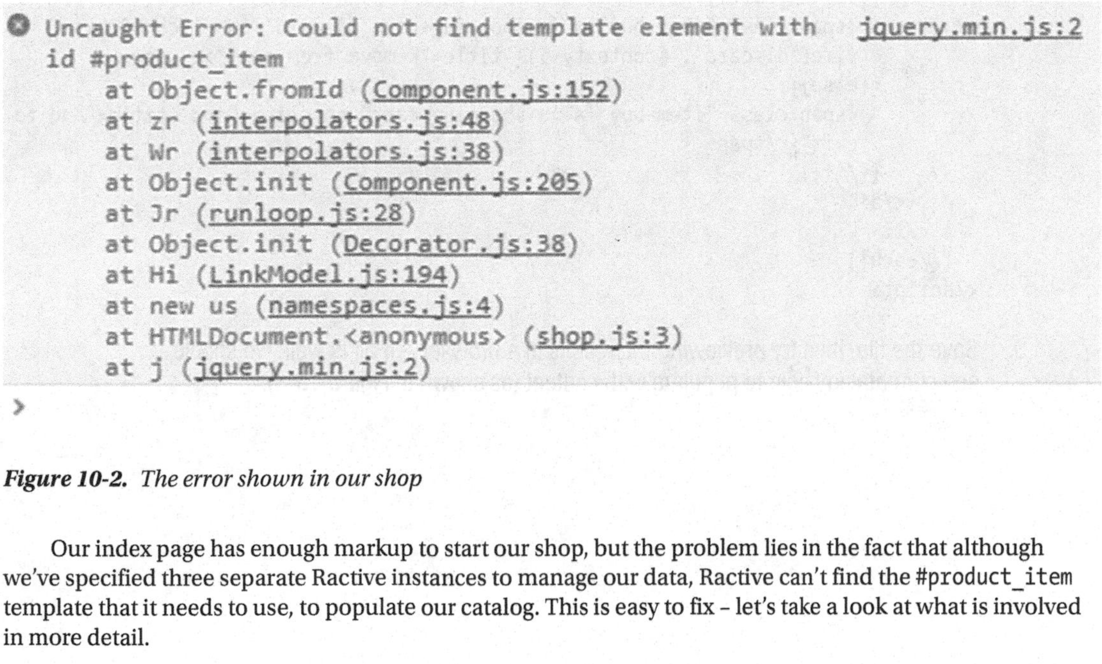

```
⊗ Uncaught Error: Could not find template element with      jquery.min.js:2
  id #product_item
      at Object.fromId (Component.js:152)
      at zr (interpolators.js:48)
      at Wr (interpolators.js:38)
      at Object.init (Component.js:205)
      at Jr (runloop.js:28)
      at Object.init (Decorator.js:38)
      at Hi (LinkModel.js:194)
      at new us (namespaces.js:4)
      at HTMLDocument.<anonymous> (shop.js:3)
      at j (jquery.min.js:2)
>
```

Figure 10-2. *The error shown in our shop*

Our index page has enough markup to start our shop, but the problem lies in the fact that although we've specified three separate Ractive instances to manage our data, Ractive can't find the #product_item template that it needs to use, to populate our catalog. This is easy to fix – let's take a look at what is involved in more detail.

Populating Our Catalog

For any Ractive instance to operate correctly, there are two core settings that need to be specified – Ractive needs to know where to render the data, and how to render it. The same applies to any component; these are after all just rebadged Ractive instances, but with potentially slightly different options!

Cast your mind back to the error we saw just now – the cause of this was a missing template in our markup, so Ractive didn't know how to render our data. Let's amend our code to fix this issue:

```
┌─────────────────────────────────────────────────────────────────────┐
│                    POPULATING OUR CATALOG                             │
└─────────────────────────────────────────────────────────────────────┘
```

1. Return to the `index.html` file we had open from the start of our demo; if you don't have it open, then go ahead and reopen it now.

2. Next, leave a line after the closing `</main>` statement, then add this block of code:

```
<script type="text/ractive" id="product_item">
  {{#each products}}
    <li class="{{ hidden ? 'hidden' : '' }} {{ in_cart ? 'in-cart' : '' }}">
      <a class="item" href="#/product/{{id}}">
        <h3 class="item-name">{{name}}</h3>
        <img class="item-image" src="{{image}}.jpg" />
        <span class="item-price">$ {{price}}</span>

        {{#if in_cart}}
          <span class="item-buy fa fa-shopping-cart discard" on-click='@this.
          fire("discard", @context, i)' title="Remove from cart"></span>
        {{else}}
          <span class="item-buy fa fa-shopping-cart" on-click="add" title="Add to
          cart"></span>
        {{/if}}
      </a>
    </li>
  {{/each}}
</script>
```

3. Save the file, then try previewing the results in a browser – if all is well, we should see our catalog begin to populate with content (as shown in Figure 10-3):

Our latest products

- ### Product #1

$ 13.20

- ### Product #4

$ 6.66

Figure 10-3. *The beginnings of our shop*

At this stage, it looks okay – inasmuch as we have content, but clearly no styling! We have reached a point where our demo is starting to take shape so let's take a moment to explore how our code works in more detail.

Understanding Our Code So Far

The bulk of our markup splits into two parts – the first part takes care of creating placeholders for each of the elements within our shop. We kick off with `.products-list`, which handles our catalog; next up is `.cart-list` (for our cart), and we finish with `.categories-list` for managing our filters.

Our first script block within the markup takes care of the product list – we use an `{{each...}}` block to iterate through the product list, and render each item on the page. Inside this block we set a class to confirm if the product should be hidden or present in our cart. This is followed by a series of statements with mustache placeholders to render product URL (required for the cart), book name, book image, and price.

With the content displayed on screen, there is one last part – we use an `{{if...}}` statement to determine if the product has already been added to the cart and could be removed, or if it has yet to be added. This simply applies some styling to indicate its current state: green to indicate it has yet to be added, and red if it is already in the cart.

So far, so good, right...? Well trouble is, our errors persist; this time we're seeing the same issue but with the `#cart_item` template. Thankfully this is the same root cause, although this time the failure is due to a missing `#cart_item` template – let's turn our attention to fixing this issue now.

Implementing the Cart and Categories

At this stage we have a catalog that contains our products, and some section titles – we won't be able to select a book yet though, as we need to finish adding our markup.

The next block of markup relates to the cart – adding this will fix the error we ended up with at the end of the previous part of our demo:

IMPLEMENTING THE CART – PART 2

1. For this part of our demo, we need to return to the `index.html` file – leave a line, then add the following code:

```
<script type="text/ractive" id="cart_item">
    {{#if products}}

    {{#each products:i}}
      <li class="item cf">
        <div class="item-counter">
          <span class="fa fa-plus" on-click='@this.fire("plus", event, i)'>
          </span>
          <span class="item-counter-quantity">{{quantity}}</span>
          <span class="fa fa-minus" on-click='@this.fire("minus", event, i)'>
          </span>
        </div>
```

```
        <img class="item-image" src="{{image}}-small.jpg" alt="{{name}}" />
        <span class="item-name">{{name}}</span>
        <span class="item-price">$ {{price}}</span>
        <span class="item-discard discard-from-cart fa fa-lg fa-trash"
        on-click='@this.fire("remove", @context, i)'></span>
      </li>
    {{/each}}

    <li class="subtotal cf">
      <span class="subtotal-caption">Subtotal</span>
      <span class="subtotal-number">$ {{subtotal}}</span>
    </li>
  {{else}}
    <li class="empty">Your shopping cart is empty.</li>
  {{/if}}
</script>
```

2. Save the file – if we preview the results at this point, we should see that the errors are now clear, although there is no change in our styling!

This block of code contains some useful concepts that deserve more explanation – we're using similar `{{each...}}` and `{{if...}}` statements as before, but this time we add in three proxy event handlers to our Ractive instances. These will fire methods when clicking on the plus or minus signs, or hit the discard icon. In each instance, we pass through the event that triggered the call, and `i`, which represents the index of the product we are manipulating in our cart.

For now, these event handlers won't operate – we need to modify our Ractive instances to respond to these proxy calls. There are several stages to this; we'll begin with adding and removing products from the cart.

Making Our Catalog Operate

At this point we now have our markup in place – it's time to make it interactive! This will come in three parts – we need to add or remove products from our cart, implement changes to update the cart contents, and add a set of filters to refine what is displayed in each book category. We'll begin with taking a look at adding or removing products in more detail.

Adding and Removing Products

A core part of any cart is, of course, the option to be able to add or remove products; otherwise we're clearly not going to be able to sell any of our books! To fix this, we need to add an event hash, or a super method – this contains both of the methods required to add or remove products from our cart. Let's take a look at the code:

ADDING AND REMOVING PRODUCTS

1. We'll start by opening up shop.js from the js subfolder that we created at the beginning of this chapter; go ahead and add this event object below the closing });
from the Categories Ractive instance, leaving a line between block:

```
ProductList.on({
    add: function (event) {

        this.set(event.resolve() + '.in_cart', true);

        Cart.push('products', event.get());
    },

    discard: function (event) {
        this.set(event.resolve() + '.in_cart', false);

        Cart.get('products').forEach(function (product, index) {
            if (event.get('id') === product.id) {
                Cart.splice('products', index, 1);
            }
        });

    }
});
```

2. Save the file – keep it open, as we will use it to add in the next two blocks shortly.

So – what happens here? In our event object (represented by the ProductList.on({...}) wrapper, we have two events: one to add products from our catalog, and the other to discard them. In our add() event handler, we trigger an update through the use of set(); this sets a class to indicate they've been added to the cart. We then push that product into the cart, using event.get() to return the values within the products array created in our markup.

Adding in products is of course only part of the story – we need to implement the ability to remove them too! This part is handled by the discard event handler; we use this.set() to identify products currently in the cart before working out which item should be removed as a result of triggering its event handler. If we get a match when comparing event.get(id) against product.id , then the product will be removed and the cart updated. We can see something of the classes that have been applied, to indicate which products are already in the basket, from the screenshot shown in Figure 10-4:

```
▼ <ul class="products-list cf">
  ▼ <li class="in-cart">
    ▶ <a class="item" href="#/product/1">…</a>
    </li>
  ▶ <li>…</li>
  ▶ <li>…</li>
```

Figure 10-4. Our catalog, indicating which products are in the basket

We're getting ever closer to a finished shop – there are two more parts we still need to add though, to complete the functionality of our shop. Before we look at that, it would seem a good point to add our styling; not only will it make our shop look presentable, but it will also help to complete some of the missing functionality within! There are a fair few styles required, so let's take a look at them in more detail.

Styling the Cart

We're almost at the end of creating our shopping cart - one of the key parts we need to add is our styling. While this will serve to make our shop look presentable, there is also an element of triggering some of the functionality in our shop. We need to use CSS to style the add or remove options in the cart, for example – without it, customers won't be able to use the cart correctly.

For reasons of space, the CSS code has been compressed – a copy of the code in expanded format is available in the code download that accompanies this book.

There is a lot of code required for this, so without further ado, let's make a start:

ADDING THE STYLING

1. We'll begin with creating a new file – save it as shop.css within the css subfolder of our shop folder, which we created at the beginning of this chapter.

2. We make use of the Font Awesome library, so for this, go ahead and extract copies of the font folder and font-awesome.min.css file, then put them into the fonts and css folders respectively.

3. Go ahead and add in each block in turn, leaving a line between each – we'll start with some initial base styles, and import the FontAwesome CSS library (used for some of the small icons):

```
@import "font-awesome.min.css";

@font-face { font-family: 'robotoregular'; src: url('../fonts/Roboto-Regular-
webfont.woff') format('woff'); font-weight: normal; font-style: normal; }
*, *:before, *:after { box-sizing: border-box; margin: 0; padding: 0; outline: 0; }
html, body { font-family: robotoregular, sans-serif; height: 100%; }
body { margin: 0; padding-top: 1.25rem; font-size: 0.75rem; background: #eeeeee;
color: #555; }
.cf { *zoom: 1; }
.cf:before, .cf:after { content: " "; display: table; }
.cf:after { clear: both; }
```

4. Next up comes some base UI styles, such as setting an opacity when hovering over each book:

```
a { color: #0098C8; text-decoration: none; }
a:focus, a:hover { text-decoration: underline; opacity: .8; }
.wrapper { width: 45.625rem; }
.main { width: 50rem; margin: 0 auto; }
.box { margin: 0.625rem 0 0; background: #ffffff; border: solid 0.0625rem rgba(0,
0, 0, 0.1); box-shadow: 0 0.125rem 0 rgba(0, 0, 0, 0.05); overflow: hidden; }
.box h1 { padding: 5px 0.625rem; margin-bottom: 0.625rem; border-bottom: solid
0.0625rem rgba(0, 0, 0, 0.1); }
.box h2 { padding: 5px 0.625rem; color: #0098C8; }
```

5. The next few styles take care of the shop catalog – both for displaying them in grid formation, and when they have been added to the cart:

```
.latest-products { width: 45.625rem; margin: 0.625rem 0; float: left; padding:
20px; }
.latest-products .products-list { list-style-type: none; }
.latest-products .products-list li.hidden { display: none; }
.latest-products .products-list li.in-cart .discard { background: #ff6347; }
.latest-products .item { position: relative; display: block; width: 9.5625rem;
height: 14.5rem; float: left; margin: 0.5625rem; }
.latest-products .item.in-cart .discard { background: #ff6347; }
.latest-products .item-name { position: absolute; z-index: 2; top: 0; left: 0;
width: inherit; padding: 0.625rem;
background: rgba(0, 0, 0, 0.4); color: #ffffff; font-weight: normal; }
.latest-products .item-image { position: absolute; z-index: 1; top: 0; left: 0;
display: block; width: inherit; height: inherit; background: rgba(0, 0, 0, 0.1); }
.latest-products .item-price { position: absolute; z-index: 3; bottom: 0; left:
0; padding: 0.375rem; font-size: 1.25rem; color: #ffffff; background: #b3b300; }
.latest-products .item-buy { transition: all 0.3s ease-out;  position: absolute;
z-index: 3; bottom: 0; right: 0;
background: #0098C8; color: #ffffff; padding: 0.8125rem; opacity: 0; }
.latest-products .item:hover span { opacity: 1; }
```

6. We can't have a shopping cart without doing something about styling the cart, so next up come the styles for our basket:

```
.cart { width: 29.375rem; margin-top: 0; float: right; margin-bottom: 1.25rem; }
.cart .cart-list { list-style-type: none; padding: 0.625rem 0; }
.cart .empty { margin:0.625rem; padding: 0.625rem; text-align: center;
background: #FFCC00; font-weight: bold; color: #000000; border-bottom: solid
0.125rem rgba(0, 0, 0, 0.1); font-size: 0.875rem; }
.cart .subtotal { border-top: solid 0.0625rem rgba(0, 0, 0, 0.15); font-size:
1.2rem; }
.cart .subtotal > * { float: left; display: block; }
```

```
.cart .subtotal-caption, .cart .subtotal-number { text-align: right; padding:
0.15625rem 0.1375rem; font-weight: bold;}
.cart .subtotal-caption { width: 19.6875rem; }
.cart .subtotal-number { width: 4.6875rem; }
.cart .item { position: relative; padding: 0.3125rem 0.625rem 0.9375rem; border-
bottom: solid 1px rgba(0, 0, 0, 0.05);}

.cart .item:last-child { border-bottom: none; }
.cart .item > * { float: left; display: block; }
.cart .item-counter { width: 2.5rem; text-align: center; }
.cart .item-counter > span { display: block; width: inherit; padding: 0.09375rem; }
.cart .item-counter .fa { opacity: .3; cursor: pointer; }
.cart .item-counter:hover .fa { opacity: 1; }
.cart .item-counter-quantity { font-weight: bold; }
.cart .item-image { width: 6.25rem; height: 8.875rem; border-radius: 0.1875rem; }
.cart .item-name { width: 10rem; padding: 1rem 0.4375rem; font-size: 1.1em; }
.cart .item-price { width: 4.6875rem; text-align: right; padding: 1rem 0.4375rem; }
.cart .item-discard { width: 1.375rem; padding: 0.375rem 0; margin: 0.8125rem 0;
text-align: center; opacity: 0; cursor: pointer; }
.cart .item:hover .discard-from-cart { opacity: .6;}
```

7. Last, but by no means least – we should add some styling for our category filters:

```
.filters { width: 245px; margin: 10px 0 0; }
.filters .categories-list { list-style-type: none; padding: 0 10px 10px; }
.filters .categories-listitem { -webkit-transition: all 0.3s ease-out;
transition: all 0.3s ease-out; padding: 2px 3px; cursor: pointer; }
.filters .categories-listitem.active { font-weight: bold; }
```

Phew – that was a fair amount of code to cover! Our shopping cart will hopefully begin to look presentable now, although it won't yet be complete; we still have some functionality to add. The next one to look at is managing the cart – after all, we can't have a cart that doesn't allow us to order more than one copy of a book, surely...?

Updating the Cart

For the next part of our project, we need to add some additional functionality to our cart – this will make use of another event object on the Cart instance. Our cart is simple enough that we only need three additional event handlers – two to change the number of copies of a book we order, and the other to remove a book if we make a mistake in choosing a particular book.

Let's have a look at what is involved:

UPDATING THE CART

1. Revert back to the `shop.js` file we had open in *Adding or removing products*, then miss a line and add the following code blocks in turn:

```
Cart.on({
  plus: function (event, index) {
    var quantity = this.get(event.resolve() + '.quantity');

    if (quantity === 9999) return;
    this.set(event.resolve() + '.quantity', ++quantity);
  },
```

2. We started with the `plus` function to take care of increasing the quantity; the `minus` function deals with reducing it if needed:

```
  minus: function (event, index) {
    var quantity = this.get(event.resolve() + '.quantity');
    if (quantity === 1) return;
    this.set(event.resolve() + '.quantity', --quantity);
  },
```

3. We sometimes make a mistake, so we can take care of this with the remove function:

```
  remove: function (event, index) {

    Cart.get('products').forEach(function (product, index) {
      if (index === product.id) {
        this.set('products.' + index + '.in_cart', false);
      }
    });

    this.splice('products', index, 1);
  }
});
```

4. When adding new books, or changing the quantities ordered, we need to reflect this in the overall price; this `cart.observe()` function will initiate a refresh when needed:

```
Cart.observe('products', function () {

  var subtotal = 0;

  this.get('products').forEach(function (product, index) {
    subtotal += product.price * product.quantity;
  });

  this.set('subtotal', (subtotal.toFixed(2)+''));
});
```

5. Save the file – at this stage, we now have an almost completed online shop! If we preview the results in a browser, then we'll be able to pick and choose books; the only step we can't do will be to filter books by category, but we will look at that shortly.

In the meantime, what's taking place in our code? The key to making the quantity buttons work lies in the use of event.resolve(); this gets a value based on resolving a given keypath. In this instance, we're looking for the value stored in the hardcodedCartProducts object – Figure 10-5 shows that by default this will return a 1, if we query the first product in our basket, using a browser console session:

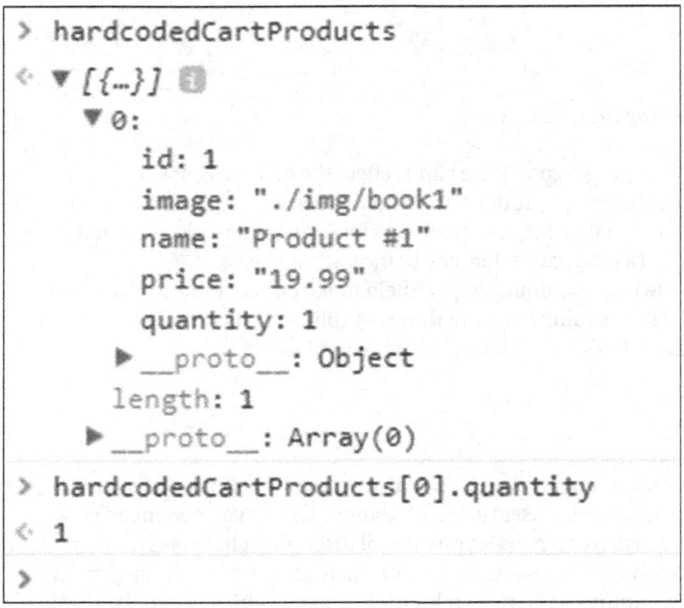

```
> hardcodedCartProducts
⟸ ▼ [{…}] 🔢
     ▼ 0:
         id: 1
         image: "./img/book1"
         name: "Product #1"
         price: "19.99"
         quantity: 1
       ▶ __proto__: Object
       length: 1
     ▶ __proto__: Array(0)
> hardcodedCartProducts[0].quantity
⟸ 1
>
```

Figure 10-5. *Querying our catalog for quantity selected*

Now, if we click on the plus sign against Product 1 in our basket (it's there by default, but any product can be used for this), clearly we will see the quantity increase. Try entering the same command as shown in Figure 10-5 - we should see our catalog show 6 items of Product 1 are in our cart, as illustrated in Figure 10-6:

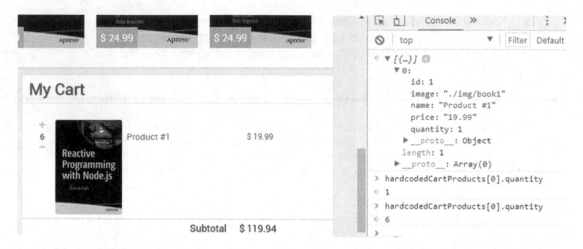

Figure 10-6. *Querying our cart, after increasing the quantity*

Adding or removing products is great, but not so good if we can't reflect the changes back to our subtotal value! Updating this is the role of the observe() function; we don't need to pass values to it, as the function retrieves each of the products within the cart, the quantities for each, and works out what the subtotal should be before updating the subtotal keypath reference in the Cart instance.

Okay – let's change tack and focus on the last remaining step: to help make our customers' lives a little easier, how about adding a filter option? This isn't going to be anything complicated; we simply hide those books that don't feature in a selected category. Let's have a look at what is involved.

Applying a Filter

Adding a filter option to any shop should be a no-brainer – trouble is, I've seen many shops add such a filter, but their implementation has been terrible! The classic issue is products that have been incorrectly classified; this might be through user error, or where there is some form of disconnect between how a retailer thinks a product should be classified, against where customers are more likely to look to find that product. This can equally be as a result of a filter that requires a full page reload when used, which also makes it slow to use.

APPLYING A FILTER

In our case, our filter will be very simple – all we do is hide those products that are not part of a chosen category. Let's take a look at what is involved:

1. We'll start by adding some additional markup to our index.html file – go ahead and open it, then add the following immediately before the three script calls at the end of file, leaving a line before that block:

```
<script type="text/ractive" id="categories_item">
  {{#each categories}}
    <li class="categories-list__item {{ active ? 'active' : '' }}" on-
    click="toggle">{{name}}</li>
  {{/each}}
</script>
```

2. We have our markup in place, but to make it work, we need to add an event handler to respond to any changes: go ahead and add the following code immediately after the closing }); of the `Cart.on()` event object, leaving a blank line in between each block:

```
Categories.on({
  toggle: function (event) {
    if (event.get('active')) {
      return;
    }

    this.set('categories.*.active', false);
    this.set(event.resolve() + '.active', true);

    ProductList.get('products').forEach(function (product, index) {
      ProductList.set('products.' + index + '.hidden', event.get('id') !== 1 &&
      event.get('id') !== product.category);
    });
  }
});
```

3. Save the file – if we preview the results, we should now have a working shop, where we can add and remove products, filter on our selected category, and have a cart that reflects any changes made to our selections.

We could call it a day at this point – after all our shop is complete, and works well. However, as anyone who knows me personally will know, I always like to push things a little further! For example, how about adding a payment option? There are other areas we can focus on too, as a means to help improve our code even further – let's begin though with setting up that payment option first.

Adding a Payment Option

Adding a payment option to any e-commerce site can be a real minefield – do we use PayPal, or another provider? Which countries do we sell to? How do we deal with VAT or other such taxes? These are some of the questions we must answer – what does one choose...?

Implementing a shopping cart can easily be the subject of a book in its own right – the choices we make will determine if the site is a roaring success, or sinks faster than a lead balloon. There is an option though, that we should consider; what if we had a cart available right now, without having to install extra software or plugins? Yes – you heard me right: we indeed have an option available now, in the form of the **Payment Request API**. This opens up some real possibilities, so let's take a moment to explore what this API is, and how we can make use of it in our projects.

Introducing Payment Request API

If you've spent any time implementing shopping carts, I suspect the one thing you will notice is that carts can come with all sorts of options – and that I'll lay good odds that many of them aren't even necessary!

Instead, why not have something simple that collects all of the data together in a unified format, ready to pass on to our payment processor? That's all good, but what if it could be in the browser already? In an age where more sales are done on mobile devices than desktops, this surely must be a good thing...

Enter the Payment Request API – this might sound complicated, but for a basic solution, there is relatively little code required to produce a workable result.

The great thing about the API is that it is designed to standardize the payment process across browsers as much as possible, support multiple payment methods, and be able to easily pass details to payment processors such as Stripe or PayPal.

There are a few gotchas to using this API, but we can work around these – we'll cover this subject in more detail toward the end of the chapter, but for now, let's take a look at support for this API.

Supporting the API in a Browser

One of the key pitfalls we need to be need to be aware of is support in a browser – the CanIUse site indicates that support is still not 100%, as indicated in Figure 10-7:

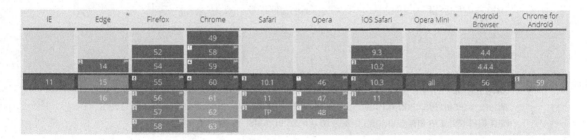

Figure 10-7. *Support for the Payment Request API*

I can see what the next question is going to be – why are we talking about something that is not fully supported across all browsers? It is a valid question: taking payments is one subject where our solution must be perfect. There are some advantages to using this API though, which are worthy of consideration:

- It is designed to work on both mobile and desktop – support is improving for it, although Apple has yet to add support for iOS, and follows their own standard.

- It has a consistent look and feel, which makes it easier to support.

- We can easily use a backup cart for those browsers that have yet to support the API; in the main, this is largely Safari and old IE, whereas Firefox, Chrome, and Opera already support, or will do once a flag is enabled.

- To get a minimum viable product working requires little code – we can then add more features as support improves.

Okay – enough theory for now; let's move on and get stuck into something more practical! For us to use the Payment Request API, we must work on secure web space; the API does not operate in unsecured web space. We can do this locally using a local web server if you have one installed, or it will work fine from the local file system using the `file://` protocol if this is your preferred choice.

Before we get stuck into the detail of setting up our payment option, Figure 10-8 shows a taster of how our finished cart will appear at the end of the upcoming exercise:

Figure 10-8. Our finished article

The cart won't look significantly different – we can see in Figure 10-9 that the real change comes when we hit the Proceed to payment button, and start to fill in our payment details:

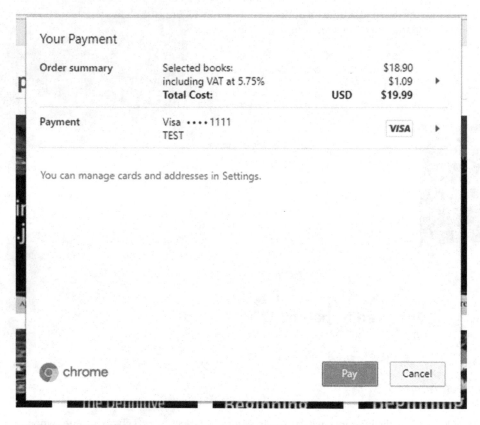

Figure 10-9. *The initial payment screen from the API*

If all of the details we've entered are correct, then on the point of pressing Pay, we will be prompted for the CVC number for our test card as shown in Figure 10-10:

←   Enter the CVC for Visa •••• 1111

Once you confirm, your card details will be shared with this site.

Figure 10-10. *The CVC entry screen*

A key point to note is that our cart will not contain any real details – once we have it up and running, we will simulate the process of sending details to a payment provider, before getting a response back to confirm successful payment has been made.

With this in mind, let's dive in and get started on our exercise.

Implementing a Solution

We've done the hard part building the cart – this next section will hopefully seem a lot easier in comparison!

It's at this stage where we can enable the Payment Request API – if we remember from *Supporting the API in a browser*, we can see that support needs to be enabled in the desktop versions of browsers, before we can make use of it. For this next part, I will assume Chrome is being used; you can use Firefox, Edge, or Opera if preferred, although you will need to alter the steps accordingly.

Please note – the Payment Request API is still classed as being experimental in Chrome; to get it working requires we enable some flags that are not on by default. Needless to say there is always an element of risk involved; our demo should not be used in a production capacity, without further development!

ENABLING PAYMENT REQUEST API

Leaving this aside for a moment, let's make a start:

1. Open a new browser session in Chrome, then enter `about://flags` in the address bar, and press Enter.

2. Scroll down until you see an entry marked Web Payments, as indicated in Figure 10-11:

Web Payments Mac, Windows, Linux, Chrome OS
Enable Web Payments API integration, a JavaScript API for merchants. #web-payments

```
Enabled  ▼
```

Figure 10-11. *Enabling Web Payments API*

3. Scroll to the bottom of the page and click on Relaunch Now to save the change and restart Chrome.

We can now begin to add code to our shop, so without further ado, let's get our text editor open and make a start:

IMPLEMENTING REQUEST PAYMENT API

1. We'll start by opening up `shop.js` from the js subfolder in our project area, and adding the following code blocks at the top of our file, leaving a line before the beginning of our Ractive code. This creates our payment request, but doesn't show the UI just yet:

```
function initPaymentRequest() {
  let networks = ['amex', 'diners', 'discover', 'jcb', 'mastercard', 'unionpay',
      'visa', 'mir'];
  let types = ['debit', 'credit', 'prepaid'];
  let supportedInstruments = [{
```

253

```
        supportedMethods: networks,
    }, {
        supportedMethods: ['basic-card'],
        data: {supportedNetworks: networks, supportedTypes: types},
    }];

    let tcost = $(".subtotal-number").text().replace("$", "").trim();
    let vat = tcost - (tcost / 1.0575).toFixed(2);
    let scost = (tcost - vat).toFixed(2);

    let details = {
        total: {label: 'Total Cost:', amount: {currency: 'USD', value: tcost}},
        displayItems: [{
            label: 'Selected books:',
            amount: {currency: 'USD', value: scost},
        },
        {
            label: 'including VAT at 5.75%',
            amount: {currency: 'USD', value: vat}
        }
        ],
    };

    return new PaymentRequest(supportedInstruments, details);
}
```

2. Next, leave a line after the code from step 1, and add in the following – this initiates the payment process:

```
function onBuyClicked(request) {
    request.show().then(function(instrumentResponse) {
        sendPaymentToServer(instrumentResponse);
    })
    .catch(function(err) {
        $("#buyButton").hide();
        $("#status").text(err);
    });
}
```

3. Once the payment has been sent, we'll simulate the time taken for a response to come back; it's at this point where we would send through the request if we were creating a live version:

```
function sendPaymentToServer(instrumentResponse) {
    window.setTimeout(function() {
        instrumentResponse.complete('success')
            .then(function() {
                $("#buyButton").hide();
                $("#result").text("Payment has been received - thankyou!")
            })
```

```
        .catch(function(err) {
          $("#status").text("err");
        });
    }, 2000);
}
```

4. We now need to add in the markup for our button – for this, go ahead and add the following code into the index.html file, immediately after the closing </li> of the subtotal section:

```
<span class="subtotal-number">$ {{subtotal}}</span>
  </li>

<div id="output" class="output">
  <div id="content">
    <div class="buy"><button id="buyButton">{{payment}}</button></div>
    <div id="result"></div>
  </div>
  <div id="status"></div>
  <pre id="log"></pre>
</div>
```

5. With our code added, all that remains is to adjust our styling to take account of our new feature. Go ahead and add the following rules into the shop.css style sheet, at the end of the file:

```
/********
 PAYMENT
*********/

#buyButton { width: 220px; margin-top: 15px; background: #ffcc00; border-radius:
5px; padding: 8px 20px; color: #000000; display: inline-block; font-weight: 700;
text-align: center; text-shadow: 1px 1px #ffffff; font-size: 18px; }
.buy { width: 220px; margin-left: auto; margin-right: auto; }
#result, #status { font-size: 17px; margin-left: auto; margin-right: auto;
margin-top: 15px; }
#result { width: 320px; }
#status { width: 230px; }
```

6. Save both shop.js and shop.css – if we preview the results of our marathon exercise, we should see an updated cart appear.

Go ahead and try it out – it's hard to imagine that only a few years ago (if that), we were forced to choose from the myriad of carts available. All offered different levels of support, and each required their own setup – what a pain!

Instead, we can use something that takes care of the look and feel for us, so that we can focus on providing the right functionality for our shop.

Understanding What Happened in Our Demo

Over the last few pages we've covered a sizable amount of code in our marathon exercise – if you managed to get this far, congratulations! Implementing a cart is not a quick process; we've only covered a fraction of what would need to be implemented for a cart within a live environment. However, our demo should show that we can produce a basic working example that forms a perfect basis for developing something more robust for future use. While you pause for a breather, let's go through what we've covered in more detail.

We kicked off by exploring how to enable the API – it's not enabled by default in some browsers, so for us to test it, we had to switch it on. Once enabled, we then started with adding support for our new cart – the first step is to construct a payment request that contains details such as the credit card number and amount. It's important to note that although we are creating the request, we're not showing the UI yet – this is handled by the #buyButton button at the end of the Ractive instance.

Once this has been clicked, we then simulate sending details to the payment server using the sendPaymentToServer function – it's at this point we would pass details to our payment provider, had this been a live environment. Assuming there hasn't been any issue, we return a simple "Payment has been received..." message that is rendered onscreen.

Pitfalls to Watch Out For

The Payment Request API is a great tool – it's hard to imagine that a core part of any e-commerce site can now be created from within the browser, without the need for extra libraries! Granted, we worked with localhost (or the file system), to get a demo working, but implementing SSL support would be essential if we were to use this API in a production environment.

Before we continue – I have a confession: when researching content for this chapter, I came across examples of our shopping cart that had been worked on by various people online, such as this example: https://codepen.io/shaoyu/pen/YyzyjV. Trouble is, many of these versions were for earlier versions of Ractive – the number of changes being made to the library meant that this example had fast become out of date!

It means that, although it's probably not obvious, the version of the cart we're using has been updated to use a more recent version (at the time of writing) – this chapter has become not only an exercise in creating our cart, but a useful opportunity to see how code has to be updated. The key to this is making use of the console part of our browser – Ractive will display debug messages to indicate if something should be updated. Once this has been completed, we can then add this line in to our script, to turn this debug off:

```
Ractive.DEBUG = /unminified/.test(function(){/*unminified*/});
```

Our example is simple and works well, but there are some considerations we still need to be aware of when using the API:

- Browser support is still somewhat experimental; Apple has yet to provide support for Safari, preferring to instead concentrate on its own implementation of Apple Pay. It means we would have to add in separate support for Safari, although there is an interface for Apple Pay from the API, which is available at https://github.com/GoogleChrome/appr-wrapper.

- Our demo doesn't touch on any security, such as the essential PCI legal requirement – this is something we would need to develop further, before we can release any solution into a production environment.

For more details on PCI, please refer to PCI standard – https://en.wikipedia.org/wiki/Payment_Card_Industry_Data_Security_Standard.

- The API is not supported in older browsers – it means that if we were to implement the API into a live environment, then we need to monitor browser traffic. If we find that older browsers are still being used (such as IE8), it will require us to consider if we support them (because the numbers are tiny), or if we have to implement an alternative basket until such time that these browsers are no longer an issue. At the point of writing, the older browsers that might cause issues would be Internet Explorer and Safari; Firefox and Opera will support it, but only when the appropriate browser flags have been enabled.

- Our demo doesn't include much in the way of error handling – most of this should be handled automatically within the API, but we should test all known scenarios to ensure our solution works correctly.

- Google (for now) is at pains to point out that this is an experimental API – they class it as sufficiently stable for use, but warn that features will change! To keep abreast of changes, they publish a blog at `https://developers.google.com/web/updates/2017/01/payment-request-updates`, with details of any changes to the API.

The key point though is that using the API will require discussions within your team or your customer – Google considers the API to be sufficiently stable for use, but is careful to point out that while it has yet to receive approval, features may change. Assuming that a decision is made to use the API, there are a host of options we can add to develop our cart even further – let's dive in and take a look.

Taking It Further

Throughout the course of this chapter, we've explored how Ractive can be used to create a simple shopping cart – the library is perfect for managing updates to our data automatically, allowing us to concentrate on adding the important features in our site. Our demo adds in enough to make a workable option for now, but there are a few ideas for improvement:

- Much of the code we're using in our demo, uses jQuery – there is a good opportunity to see if more can be implemented into a Ractive instance, or we can develop an adaptor to handle the information in a Ractive format, and pass it to the API.

- We've manually implemented the plus or minus options to adjust quantities – we may prefer to simply use a plugin such as ractive-stepper (from `https://github.com/JonDum/ractive-stepper`) instead.

- How about adding an option to cover shipping costs – either to vary the options based on location, or provide a simple flat-fee option?

- We've already touched on it, but we should consider implementing the wrapper that allows us to use Apple Pay within the API.

- We might need to get extra details such as telephone or email addresses – these shouldn't be collected without suitable justification though!

- We made mention of the issues around security – this needs to also include the fact that details are stored locally on a PC (for example within Chrome's settings, at chrome://settings/autofill). This isn't currently password protected, although this is more an issue with Chrome's autofill settings.

This is just a small selection of what is possible – we could of course use any cart with Ractive, but the Payment API is a more up-to-date, simpler option that makes it easier for us to link back into our Ractive instances. Much of what we do though will depend on circumstances surrounding each project, any limitations we have to work with, and whether the current experimental status of the API is not sufficient an issue for us to worry about in our projects.

Integrating the Cart into Our Site

We have a working demo for our cart, but what about integrating our shopping cart into the template from the previous chapter?

This is where I have a confession to make – integrating our cart won't work very well, unless we make some significant changes! At first this might seem a bit disappointing, but there is a good reason for this - the shopping cart we've developed in this next chapter is based on some existing designs from several years ago, but where we will update them to use a more current version of Ractive. Leaving aside the intricacies of how we might do this for a moment, Figure 10-12 gives a taster of how our design might look, in the template we developed in the previous chapter:

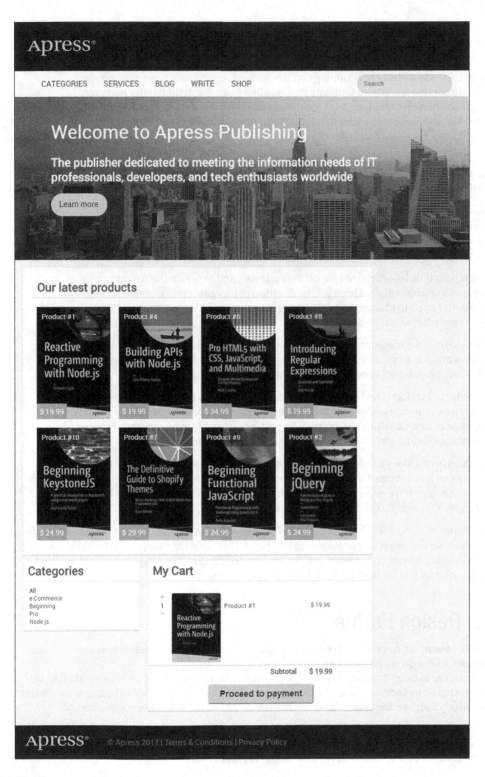

Figure 10-12. *Integrating a cart into our site*

For the purposes of this book, I should point out that this lack of compatibility wasn't planned - it nevertheless presents a useful opportunity to explore what we would need to do, before we can merge the code for our cart work with our new template design:

- Most of the code within the shopping cart sits within the template page; instead, we should turn it into a separate template that is called from the main Ractive instance. This has the benefit of making our container markup easier to read, and that our Ractive instance becomes easier to migrate to (or merged with) a new instance if required.

- The CSS style sheet needs reorganizing - some of the code should be optimized, and those styles that are used for what becomes individual components, be removed from the main style sheet.

- Some of the code used in Chapter 9 will conflict with Chapter 10 – for example, the use of <h1> tags, and how they have been styled differently between each chapter. These will need to be rationalized, as part of merging the code together and presenting a more consistent solution to our client.

- I think it would be beneficial to hive off the code we used to set up the payment pages into a separate file - at least for the duration of merging code together. This code doesn't need to change, so taking it out of the main file temporarily will make it easier to see what needs to be merged into the main code.

- We're not using a consistent version of JavaScript in our payment code - while this will still work, it isn't great that we're mixing styles; we should consider adjusting our code to use a consistent version, although this is only a minor issue.

- The `ProductList`, `Cart`, and `Categories` code are individual Ractive instances; this makes it harder to merge the code into our template. Instead, these should be turned into component files, which we can then import into a template page without having to worry about adding lots of extra code in our template page.

- We make use of jQuery in a handful of locations; it would be worth investigating if this code can be converted to a Ractive equivalent. This will help drop a dependency on using jQuery – if we need to use something, then plain JavaScript will be a better alternative, although this should not be necessary.

Although this doesn't seem much, I would nevertheless expect some radical changes need to be made to our cart code, before we can use it on our shopping cart page. This need for change is a risk that one must take when using an existing design - it is a good way to practice updating code so that our overall solution retains a consistent look and feel for both code and visual appearance.

Taking Our Design Further

Decisions, decisions – assuming our client likes the final design and that we've successfully merged our cart into the new template, where do we go from here?

Well – to quote an old saying, "the world is our oyster"; there are a multitude of ways we could take our design. A part of this should include an element of finessing the solution: there are some changes we should consider making, to help improve the code. These might include any of the following suggestions:

- We have a number of sections that have yet to be converted into components; these can then be hived off into separate files and a loader such as ractiveify (`https://github.com/norcalli/ractiveify`) used to import them into our project.

- The menu system reference each element directly; this would benefit from a conversion to use an `{{#each}}`...`{{/each}}` block.

- The CSS used throughout is already fairly tight, but I think it could benefit from some tweaking – in some places it feels a little code heavy, and that with some changes to surrounding content, some of the styles could be rationalized.

- We should consider using a preprocessor such as Sass to manage our styles – if we end up using a loader to import our components, then the compilation process can be added to the package.json file that would be required to manage these tasks. These are good examples of how we can automate parts of the processes, thereby saving us time and resources that would be better spent on other tasks.

- A minor tweak could be made to centralize the currency format used, and remove this from the price entries; this will make it easier to perform calculations if needed.

- We make use of images in the catalog – at present, the small numbers are manageable, but if we begin to increase the count, then we should investigate using lazy-loading to manage the rendering process. We can do this using the ractive-lazyload-img plugin, available from `https://github.com/TehShrike/ractive-lazyload-img`.

- We implemented a categories list on the front page, but what about hooking that up to the cart that we build in the next chapter, now that our cart has been built?

- Our layout was built from scratch, but this isn't always effective for production purposes – it may be worth investigating the use of a boilerplate type plugin such as create-ractive-app, from `https://www.npmjs.com/package/create-ractive-app`. This has the added benefit of including image optimization, a hook into using Gulp as a task runner, and the ractivefy plugin we mentioned as an earlier idea. (There isn't a strong preference on which task runner that should be used – this particular plugin uses Gulp, but a similar setup could be created using Grunt instead.)

- The only point we've not touched on in our design is the use of animation – in one regard this might not be seen as appropriate, but this doesn't always hold true. In this instance, a small amount of animation will help enhance the site – for example, we could put some on the hover action for the menu, or perhaps on the transition between categories that we will have in our shopping cart.

These are just some of the ideas that come to mind – I am sure there will be plenty more out there for us to consider. Ultimately though it is up to both us and our client to decide where we should take the site – much of our decisions should be based on feedback from customers, and research that will help determine the best route to success for our site.

Summary

Creating a shopping cart that works well takes a fair amount of effort – we can never say that a cart will ever be finished, as we should be able to evolve its look and feel over time. This said, there is a point where we can at least say we have a technical solution that works – over the course of this chapter we've explored the steps required to produce such an offering within Ractive, so let's take some time to review what we've learned.

We kicked off with an introduction to help set the scene for the cart as a continuation from the previous chapter, before preparing our work area. We then moved onto setting up the basic data used in our demo, before setting up the markup used on our catalog page. We then began to add code that created the basic functionality required to display our products and operate our shop. We then turned our attention to styling the cart, before adding the final code required to update the quantities required, and apply a selection filter based on categories of books in our store.

Next up came the payment option – we saw how this required a substantial set of steps to implement SSL, but understood that this is a necessary evil if we are to replicate what we see in a live environment. We then explored how to set up the Payment Request API, before using it to create a simple but effective cart for our demo. We then rounded out our demo by examining some of the pitfalls we may encounter when using this method, and some avenues we can explore to help develop our code for use in future projects.

Phew - we've now reached the end of our journey through the wonderful world of Ractive; I hope it has been as entertaining for you as it has been for me writing it. Here's hoping that you are now a convert to using the library and that to misquote that famous saying from *Hitchhiker's Guide to the Galaxy*, "the answer to life, universe and everything…isn't always 42" - Ractive may be smaller in size, but it is still a very capable library!

Ractive API

Over the course of this book, we've explored a wealth of options for configuring and using Ractive; to really get the best from the library, we should make use of its API. Ractive has over 50 methods, events, and properties we can use to tailor our code - throughout the course of this chapter, we will go through a summary of the options available for use within Ractive.

Mustaches

Ractive is a powerful tool that makes rendering and manipulating data onscreen a cinch - at the center of the toolkit is a group of tools we can use to implement mustaches, or placeholders, onscreen. These tools fall into one of two groups - miscellaneous and sections; let's take a look at the miscellaneous group first.

Miscellaneous

A key part of manipulating data within Ractive is the use of mustaches - we use these to position data onscreen, such as text or product details (as we saw back in Chapter 10, *Creating a Shopping Cart*). A summary of the options available is presented in Table A-1.

© Alex Libby 2017
A. Libby, *Beginning Ractive.js*, https://doi.org/10.1007/978-1-4842-3093-0

Table A-1. *List of features for working with Mustaches*

Feature / function	Purpose
Variables	`{{ }}`, `{{& }}` and `{{{ }}}` render a reference. For more details: `https://ractive.js.org/api/#mustaches`
In-template partials	`{{#partial }}` defines a partial that is scoped to the nearest enclosing element or the containing component if defined at the top level of the template. For more details: `https://ractive.js.org/api/#in-template-partials`
Static mustaches	`[[ ]]`, `[[& ]]` and `[[[ ]]]` render the reference only during the initial render. For more details: `https://ractive.js.org/api/#static-mustaches`
Expressions	Expressions in mustaches are evaluated, and its result is used as the referenced value. For more details: `https://ractive.js.org/api/#expressions`
Comments	`{{! }}` defines a template comment; these are ignored by the parser. For more details: `https://ractive.js.org/api/#comments`
Custom delimiters	`{{= =}}` defines custom delimiters. For more details: `https://ractive.js.org/api/#custom-delimiters`
Escaping mustaches	`\` prepended on a mustache interprets the mustache as literal text. For more details: `https://ractive.js.org/api/#escaping-mustaches`
Anchors	`<# />` define anchors, which are mounting points where instances can be mounted dynamically during runtime. For more details: `https://ractive.js.org/api/#escaping-mustaches`
`{{>content}}`	`{{>content}}` renders the inner HTML in the context of the component. For more details: `https://ractive.js.org/api/#content`
`{{yield}}`	`{{yield}}` renders the inner HTML in the context of the parent component. For more details: `https://ractive.js.org/api/#yield`

For a full listing and details of mustache options, please refer to `https://ractive.js.org/api/#mustaches`.

Sections

On occasion, we may want to render a block of text on-screen - we can do this using sections. Ractive contains a number of options to determine how these sections should be rendered; a summary is listed in Table A-2.

Table A-2. *Options for manipulating sections in Ractive*

Feature / function	Purpose
Sections	Sections render a block of markup depending on the value referenced. For more details: `https://ractive.js.org/api/#sections`
Inverted Sections	`{{^ }}` renders a block of markup if the reference is falsy or is an empty iterable. For more details: `https://ractive.js.org/api/#inverted-sections`
Optional section closing text	Regular (`{{# }}`) and inverted (`{{^ }}`) sections can be closed with optional closing text. For more details: `https://ractive.js.org/api/#optional-section-closing-text`
If sections	`{{#if }}` renders a block of markup if the reference is truthy or a non-empty iterable. For more details: `https://ractive.js.org/api/#if-sections`
Unless sections	`{{#unless }}` renders a block of markup if the reference is falsy or is an empty iterable. For more details: `https://ractive.js.org/api/#unless-sections`
Each sections	`{{#each }}` renders the block of markup for each item in the iterable. For more details: `https://ractive.js.org/api/#each-sections`
With sections	`{{#with }}` alters the current section's context by inserting a reference in front of the resolution order. For more details: `https://ractive.js.org/api/#with-sections`

Data Binding

We can use mustaches and sections to render content onscreen - what about managing elements such as radio buttons? No problem - we saw early in the book how Ractive makes managing them easy - a list of options is summarized in Table A-3.

Table A-3. *Data-Binding options in Ractive*

Feature / function	Purpose
Text inputs	Data can be bound to text inputs via the value directive. This includes text-like inputs such as password, email, color, tel, and date. For more details: `https://ractive.js.org/api/#text-inputs`
Number inputs	Numeric data can be bound to number inputs such as range, via the value directive. For more details: `https://ractive.js.org/api/#radio-buttons`
File Inputs	File data can be bound to file inputs via the value directive. The value from the input is an instance of FileList. For more details: `https://ractive.js.org/api/#file-inputs`
Checkboxes	Boolean data can be bound to checkboxes via the checked directive. For more details: `https://ractive.js.org/api/#checkboxes`
Radio buttons	Boolean data can be bound to radio buttons via the checked directive. For more details: `https://ractive.js.org/api/#radio-buttons`
Text areas	Data can be bound to text areas via the value directive. For more details: `https://ractive.js.org/api/#text-areas`
Select lists	Data can be bound to select lists via the value directive. For more details: `https://ractive.js.org/api/#select-lists`
contenteditable	Data can be bound to elements that have the contenteditable attribute via the value directive.

For a full listing and details of data binding options, please refer to `https://ractive.js.org/api/#style-42`.

Directives

When working with Ractive, there may be instances where we need to apply specific functions, such as event handlers, or set inline styling on our markup. We can do this using Ractive directives - a summary list of options is presented in Table A-4.

Table A-4. *A list of Directive options in Ractive*

Feature / function	Purpose
twoway	The element-specific directive form of twoway. For more details: https://ractive.js.org/api/#twoway
lazy	The element-specific directive form of lazy. For more details: For more details: https://ractive.js.org/api/#lazy
as-*	as-* directives augment the element with decorators. It accepts optional, comma-separated expressions as arguments to the decorator function. For more details: https://ractive.js.org/api/#as-42
class-*	class-* directives toggle individual class names based on the truthiness of its value. For more details: https://ractive.js.org/api/#class-42
on-*	on-* directives attach event handlers to DOM elements and components, using either a proxy or expression-based syntax. For more details: https://ractive.js.org/api/#on-42
*-in, *-out, *-in-out	*-in, *-out, and *-in-out directives apply transitions to the element. *-in specifies intro-only, *-out specifies outro-only, and *-in-out for both intro and outro. For more details: https://ractive.js.org/api/#42-in-42-out-42-in-out
style-*	style-* directives update individual style properties of the element. The part of the directive following style - will be used as the style property name. For more details: https://ractive.js.org/api/#style-42

For more details on directives, please head over to https://ractive.js.org/api/#directives.

Keypath Prefixes

When creating keypaths, we normally follow a specific routine. However, there may be occasions when we need to resolve a keypath to a specific data context, without using the normal resolution method. We can do this using keypath prefixes; these can be set to resolve to any data context specified, regardless of whether this context is valid. The full list of options are summarized in Table A-5.

Table A-5. *List of Keypath Prefix options*

Feature / function	Purpose
Current context	Resolves the keypath relative to the current data context. For more details: https://ractive.js.org/api/#current-context
Parent keypath	Resolves the keypath relative to the parent data. This prefix can be used more than once to reference ancestors. For more details: https://ractive.js.org/api/#parent-keypath
Parent context	Parent keypaths often work in the same manner as parent contexts, but in some scenarios can return different results. For more details: https://ractive.js.org/api/#parent-context
Instance root context	Resolves the keypath relative to the instance's root data context. For more details: https://ractive.js.org/api/#instance-root-context

For a full listing and details of keypath prefix options, please refer to https://ractive.js.org/api/#keypath-prefixes.

Special References

Special references are template keywords that act like data references but do not actually exist in your data. These references provide metadata such as the current instance, context, environment, and operation. A full list of options is summarized in Table A-6.

Table A-6. *A list of Special Reference options*

Feature / function	Purpose
this	The current data context. For more details: https://ractive.js.org/api/#this
@this	The current Ractive instance; we can also use its shorthand, which is @. For more details: https://ractive.js.org/api/#this_1
@index	The current iteration index of the containing repeated section. For more details: https://ractive.js.org/api/#index
@key	The current key name of the containing object iteration section. For more details: https://ractive.js.org/api/#key
@keypath	The keypath to the current data context relative to the instance's root data context. For more details: https://ractive.js.org/api/#keypath
@rootpath	The keypath to the current data context relative to the originating instance's root data context. For more details: For more details: https://ractive.js.org/api/#rootpath
@global	The global object of the current environment. For browsers, it references the window object. For Node.js, it references the global object.
@shared	@shared is a Ractive-global model similar to @global but not subject to interference from outside of Ractive. For more details: https://ractive.js.org/api/#shared
@context	The context object associated with the current context. For more details: https://ractive.js.org/api/#context
@event	The DOM event that is triggering an event directive. For more details: https://ractive.js.org/api/#event
@node	The DOM node associated with an event directive. This reference is only available to event directive expressions. For more details: https://ractive.js.org/api/#node
@local	Special context-local storage associated with the current context. For more details: https://ractive.js.org/api/#local
$n	$n is a reference available when handing events using the expression syntax that points to a specific argument passed by the event. For more details: https://ractive.js.org/api/#n
arguments	arguments is a reference available when handling events using the expression syntax that points to an array of arguments passed by the event. For more details: https://ractive.js.org/api/#arguments

For a full listing and details of special reference options, please refer to https://ractive.js.org/api/#special-references.

Initialization Options

Ractive has a comprehensive list of initialization options that can be passed to either Ractive() or Ractive. extend(). Extra properties passed as options that are not initialization options are added as properties or methods of the instance. A summary of these options is listed in Table A-7.

Table A-7. *Initialization options in Ractive*

Feature / function	Purpose
adapt	An array of adaptors to use. Values can either be names of registered adaptors or an adaptor definition. For more details: https://ractive.js.org/api/#adapt
adaptors	A map of adaptors where the key is the adaptor name and the value is an adaptor definition. For more details: https://ractive.js.org/api/#adaptors
append	Controls how the instance is attached to el. For more details: https://ractive.js.org/api/#append
attributes	An array of optional attributes or a map of optional and required attributes. For more details: For more details: https://ractive.js.org/api/#attributes
components	A map of components where the key is the component name and the value is a component name that has been statically defined or retuned dynamically. For more details: https://ractive.js.org/api/#components
computed	A map of computed properties where the key is the name of the computed property and the value is either a computed property expression, a function that returns a value, or an object that has get and set functions. For more details: https://ractive.js.org/api/#computed
csp	Determines if inline functions for expressions should be added after parsing. Defaults to false. For more details: For more details: https://ractive.js.org/api/#csp
css	Scoped CSS for a component and its descendants.
data	The data for an instance, or default data for a component. For more details: https://ractive.js.org/api/#data
decorators	A map of decorators where the key is the decorator name and the value is a decorator definition. For more details: https://ractive.js.org/api/#decorators
delegate	Determines if automatic event delegation for iterative sections should be enabled within an element. For more details: https://ractive.js.org/api/#delegate
delimiters	Sets the template delimiters. For more details: https://ractive.js.org/api/#delimiters
easing	A map of easing functions where the key is the easing function name and the value is the easing function. For more details: https://ractive.js.org/api/#easing
el	The element against which an instance should be rendered. For more details: https://ractive.js.org/api/#easing

(continued)

Table A-7. (*continued*)

Feature / function	Purpose
enhance	Determines if progressive enhancement should be applied by inspecting the contents of el and try to reuse as much of the existing tree as possible. For more details: https://ractive.js.org/api/#enhance
events	A map of events where the key is the event name and value is an event definition. For more details: https://ractive.js.org/api/#events
isolated	Controls whether the component will try to resolve data and plugins on its ancestors. Relevant only to Components. For more details: https://ractive.js.org/api/#isolated
lazy	Whether or not to update data using late-firing DOM events (i.e., change, blur) instead of events that fire immediately on interaction (i.e., keyup, keydown). For more details: https://ractive.js.org/api/#lazy_1
nestedTransitions	Whether or not to allow transitions to fire if they are already downstream from a transitioning element. For more details: https://ractive.js.org/api/#nestedtransitions
noCssTransform	Prevents component CSS from being transformed with scoping guids. For more details: https://ractive.js.org/api/#nocsstransform
noIntro	Determines if intro transitions should be skipped on initial render. For more details: https://ractive.js.org/api/#nointro
noOutro	Determine if outro transitions should be skipped during an instance unrender. For more details: https://ractive.js.org/api/#nooutro
observe	A hash of observers to subscribe during initialization and unsubscribe during teardown. For more details: https://ractive.js.org/api/#observe
partials	A map of partials where the key is the partial name and the value is either a template string, a parsed template object, or a function that returns any of the previous options. For more details: https://ractive.js.org/api/#partials
preserveWhitespace	Determine if whitespace should be preserved in templates when parsing. For more details: https://ractive.js.org/api/#preservewhitespace
resolveInstanceMembers	Whether or not to include members of the Ractive instance at the end of the reference resolution process. Defaults to true. For more details: https://ractive.js.org/api/#resolveinstancemembers
sanitize	Whether or not certain elements will be stripped from the template during parsing. For more details: https://ractive.js.org/api/#sanitize
staticDelimiters	Sets the static (one-time binding) delimiters. Defaults to ['[[', ']]']. For more details: https://ractive.js.org/api/#staticdelimiters
staticTripleDelimiters	Sets the static (one-time binding) triple delimiters. Defaults to ['[[[', ']]]']. For more details: https://ractive.js.org/api/#statictripledelimiters

(*continued*)

Table A-7. (*continued*)

Feature / function	Purpose
stripComments	Determines if comments should be removed in templates when parsing. For more details: https://ractive.js.org/api/#stripcomments
syncComputedChildren	Determine if the dependencies of an expression should be invalidated when child keypaths of the expression are updated. For more details: https://ractive.js.org/api/#synccomputedchildren
target	An alias for el.
template	The template to use.
transitions	A map of transitions where the key is the name of the transition and the value is a transition definition.
transitionsEnabled	Works out if transitions are enabled.
tripleDelimiters	Sets the triple delimiters - this defaults to ['{{{', '}}}']. For more details: https://ractive.js.org/api/#tripledelimiters
twoway	Determines whether or not two-way binding is enabled. For more details: https://ractive.js.org/api/#twoway_1
warnAboutAmbiguity	Whether or not to warn about references that don't resolve to their immediate context. For more details: https://ractive.js.org/api/#warnaboutambiguity

For a full listing and details of initialization options, please refer to https://ractive.js.org/api/#initialization-options.

Initialization Methods

A subset of the options available for initializing a Ractive instance includes a set of methods – these are listed in Table A-8.

Table A-8. *Initialization methods*

Feature / function	Purpose
on	A hash of event listeners to subscribe during initialization and unsubscribe during teardown. For more details: `https://ractive.js.org/api/#on`
oncomplete	A lifecycle event that is called when the instance is rendered and all the transitions have completed.
onconfig	A lifecycle event that is called when an instance is constructed and all initialization options have been processed.
onconstruct	A lifecycle event that is called when an instance is constructed but before any initialization option has been processed.
ondestruct	A lifecycle event that is called when an instance is torn down and any associated transitions are complete.
ondetach	A lifecycle event that is called whenever `ractive.detach()` is called.
oninit	A lifecycle event that is called when an instance is constructed and is ready to be rendered.
oninsert	A lifecycle event that is called when `ractive.insert()` is called.
onrender	A lifecycle event that is called when the instance is rendered but *before* transitions start.
onteardown	A lifecycle event that is called when the instance is being torn down.
onunrender	A lifecycle event that is called when the instance is being unrendered.
onupdate	A lifecycle event that is called when `ractive.update()` is called.

Static Properties

When working with any instance of Ractive, we will need to set and manipulate individual properties that belong to all instances; Ractive provides various registries to store these properties. The details of each registry are summarized in Table A-9.

Table A-9. *Static Properties*

Feature / function	Purpose
Ractive.adaptors	The registry of globally available adaptors.
Ractive.components	The registry of globally available component definitions.
Ractive.DEBUG	Determines if Ractive should be in debug mode.
Ractive.DEBUG_PROMISES	Tells Ractive to log errors thrown inside promises.
Ractive.decorators	The registry of globally available decorators.
Ractive.defaults	Global defaults for initialization options with the exception of plugin registries.
Ractive.easing	The global registry of easing functions. The easing functions are used by the ractive.animate method and by transitions. Four are included by default: linear, easeIn, easeOut, and easeInOut.
Ractive.events	The global registry of custom event plugins.
Ractive.interpolators	A key-value hash of interpolators use by ractive.animate() or non-CSS transitions.
Ractive.partials	The global registry of partial templates.
Ractive.svg	Indicates whether or not the browser supports SVG.
Ractive.transitions	The global registry of transition functions.
Ractive.VERSION	The version of the currently loaded Ractive.

For a full listing and details of static property options, please refer to https://ractive.js.org/api/#static-properties.

Static Methods

The Ractive library has a healthy selection of API methods, which fall into two categories - those that can be used to manipulate a specific instance, or those that can be used in any Ractive instance. Let's take a look at the group that makes up static methods that can be applied to all instances (as shown in Table A-10), in more detail:

Table A-10. *Static Methods*

Feature / function	Purpose
Ractive.escapeKey()	Escapes the given key so that it can be concatenated with a keypath string. For more details: https://ractive.js.org/api/#ractiveescapekey
Ractive.extend()	Creates a "subclass" of the Ractive constructor or a subclass constructor. For more details: https://ractive.js.org/api/#ractiveextend
Ractive.extendWith()	Creates a "subclass" of the Ractive constructor or a subclass constructor using an existing constructor. For more details: https://ractive.js.org/api/#ractiveextendwith
Ractive.getCSS()	Returns the scoped CSS from Ractive subclasses defined in the call. For more details: https://ractive.js.org/api/#ractivegetcss
Ractive.getContext()	Accepts a node and returns a Context object containing details of the Ractive instance the node is associated to. For more details: https://ractive.js.org/api/#ractivegetcontext
Ractive.joinKeys()	Joins the given keys into a properly escaped keypath. For more details: https://ractive.js.org/api/#ractivejoinkeys
Ractive.parse()	Parses the template into an abstract syntax tree that Ractive can use. For more details: https://ractive.js.org/api/#ractiveparse
Ractive.splitKeypath()	Splits the given keypath into an array of unescaped keys. For more details: https://ractive.js.org/api/#ractivesplitkeypath

For a full listing and details of static method options, please refer to https://ractive.js.org/api/#static-methods.

Instance Properties

When working with a specific instance of Ractive, we will need to set and manipulate individual properties that belong to that instance; Ractive provides various registries to store these properties. The details of each registry are summarized in Table A-11.

Table A-11. *List of Instance properties*

Feature / function	Purpose
ractive.adaptors	The instance-only registry of adaptors. For more details: https://ractive.js.org/api/#ractiveadaptors_1
ractive.components	The instance-only registry of components. For more details: https://ractive.js.org/api/#ractivecomponents_1
ractive.container	Each component instance that is in a yielded fragment has a container instance that is accessible using this.container. For more details: https://ractive.js.org/api/#ractivecontainer
ractive.decorators	The instance-only registry of decorators. For more details: https://ractive.js.org/api/#ractivecontainer
ractive.easing	The instance-only registry of easing functions. For more details: https://ractive.js.org/api/#ractiveeasing_1
ractive.events	The instance-only registry of custom event plugins. For more details: https://ractive.js.org/api/#ractiveevents_1
ractive.interpolators	A key-value hash of interpolators use by ractive.animate() or non-CSS transitions. For more details: https://ractive.js.org/api/#ractiveinterpolators_1
ractive.parent	Each component instance can access its parent using this.parent.
ractive.partials	The instance-only registry of partials. For more details: https://ractive.js.org/api/#ractiveinterpolators_1
ractive.root	Each component instance can access its root Ractive instance using this.root. For more details: https://ractive.js.org/api/#ractiveroot
ractive.transitions	The instance-only registry of transitions. For more details: https://ractive.js.org/api/#ractivetransitions_1

For a full listing and details of instance property options, please refer to https://ractive.js.org/api/#instance-properties.

Instance Methods

The Ractive library has a healthy selection of API methods, which fall into two categories - those that can be used to manipulate a specific instance, or those that can be used in any Ractive instance.

Let's take a look at the group that makes up instance methods in more detail, which are summarized in Table A-12:

Table A-12. *Instance Methods*

Feature / function	Purpose
ractive._super()	Calls the parent method from a child method of the same name. For more details: https://ractive.js.org/api/#ractive95super
ractive.add()	Increments the selected keypath. For more details: https://ractive.js.org/api/#ractiveadd
ractive.animate()	Similar to ractive.set(), this will update the data and re-render any affected mustaches and notify observers. For more details: https://ractive.js.org/api/#ractiveanimate
ractive.attachChild()	Creates a parent-child relationship between two Ractive instances. For more details: https://ractive.js.org/api/#ractiveattachchild
ractive.detach()	Detaches the instance from the DOM, returning a document fragment. For more details: https://ractive.js.org/api/#ractivedetach
ractive.detachChild()	Detaches a child from an instance when it was previously attached with ractive.attachChild(). For more details: https://ractive.js.org/api/#ractivedetachchild
ractive.find()	Returns the first element inside a given Ractive instance matching a CSS selector. For more details: https://ractive.js.org/api/#ractivefind
ractive.findAll()	This method is similar to ractive.find(), with an important difference - it returns a list of elements matching the selector, rather than a single node. For more details: https://ractive.js.org/api/#ractivefindall
ractive.findAllComponents()	Returns all components inside a given Ractive instance with the given name (or all components of any kind if no name is given). For more details: https://ractive.js.org/api/#ractivefindallcomponents
ractive.findComponent()	Returns the first component inside a given Ractive instance with the given name (or the first component of any kind if no name is given). For more details: https://ractive.js.org/api/#ractivefindcomponent
ractive.findContainer()	Returns the first container of this component instance with the given name. For more details: https://ractive.js.org/api/#ractivefindcontainer
ractive.findParent()	Returns the first parent of this component instance with the given name. For more details: https://ractive.js.org/api/#ractivefindparent

(continued)

Table A-12. (*continued*)

Feature / function	Purpose
ractive.fire()	Fires an event, which will be received by handlers that were bound using the ractive.on method. For more details: https://ractive.js.org/api/#ractivefire
ractive.get()	Returns the value at keypath. For more details: https://ractive.js.org/api/#ractiveget
ractive.getContext()	This is a version of Ractive.getContext() specific to an instance, that will only search the local instance DOM for a matching node when a selector is given. For more details: https://ractive.js.org/api/#ractivegetcontext_1
ractive.insert()	Inserts the instance to a different location. For more details: https://ractive.js.org/api/#ractiveinsert
ractive.link()	Creates a link between two keypaths that keeps them in sync. For more details: https://ractive.js.org/api/#ractivelink
ractive.observe()	Observes the data at a particular keypath. For more details: https://ractive.js.org/api/#ractiveobserve
ractive.observeOnce()	Observes the data at a particular keypath until the first change. For more details: https://ractive.js.org/api/#ractiveobserveonce
ractive.off()	Removes an event handler, several event handlers, or all event handlers. For more details: https://ractive.js.org/api/#ractiveoff
ractive.on()	Subscribe to events. For more details: https://ractive.js.org/api/#ractiveon
ractive.once()	Subscribe to an event for a single firing. For more details: https://ractive.js.org/api/#ractiveonce
ractive.pop()	The Ractive equivalent to Array.pop that removes an element from the end of the array at the given keypath and triggers an update event. For more details: https://ractive.js.org/api/#ractivepop
ractive.push()	The Ractive equivalent to Array.push that appends one or more elements to the array at the given keypath and triggers an update event. For more details: https://ractive.js.org/api/#ractivepush
ractive.readLink()	Gets the source keypath and instance for a link. For more details: https://ractive.js.org/api/#ractivereadlink
ractive.render()	Renders the component into a DOM element. For more details: https://ractive.js.org/api/#ractiverender
ractive.reset()	Resets the entire ractive.data object and updates the DOM. For more details: https://ractive.js.org/api/#ractivereset
ractive.resetPartial()	Resets a partial and re-renders all of its use sites, including in any components that have inherited it. For more details: https://ractive.js.org/api/#ractiveresetpartial

(*continued*)

Table A-12. (*continued*)

Feature / function	Purpose
ractive.reverse()	The Ractive equivalent to Array.reverse reverses the array at the given keypath and triggers an update event. For more details: https://ractive.js.org/api/#ractivereverse
ractive.set()	Updates data and triggers a re-render of any mustaches that are affected (directly or indirectly) by the change. For more details: https://ractive.js.org/api/#ractiveset
ractive.shift()	The Ractive equivalent to Array.shift that removes an element from the beginning of the array at the given keypath and triggers an update event. For more details: https://ractive.js.org/api/#ractiveshift
ractive.sort()	The Ractive equivalent to Array.sort sorts the array at the given keypath and triggers update event. For more details: https://ractive.js.org/api/#ractivesort
ractive.splice()	The Ractive equivalent to Array.splice that can add new elements to the array while removing existing elements. For more details: https://ractive.js.org/api/#ractivesplice
ractive.subtract()	Decrements the selected keypath. For more details: https://ractive.js.org/api/#ractivesubtract
ractive.teardown()	Unrenders this Ractive instance, removing any event handlers that were bound automatically by Ractive. For more details: https://ractive.js.org/api/#ractiveteardown
ractive.toCSS()	Returns the scoped CSS of the current instance and its descendants. For more details: https://ractive.js.org/api/#ractivetocss
ractive.toHTML()	Returns a chunk of HTML representing the current state of the instance. For more details: https://ractive.js.org/api/#ractivetohtml
ractive.toggle()	Toggles the selected keypath. For more details: https://ractive.js.org/api/#ractivetoggle
ractive.transition()	Triggers a transition on a node managed by this Ractive instance. For more details: https://ractive.js.org/api/#ractivetransition
ractive.unlink()	Removes a link set up by ractive.link(). For more details: https://ractive.js.org/api/#ractiveunlink
ractive.unrender()	Unrenders this Ractive instance, throwing away any DOM nodes associated with this instance. For more details: https://ractive.js.org/api/#ractiveunrender
ractive.unshift()	The Ractive equivalent to Array.unshift that prepends one or more elements to the array at the given keypath and triggers an update event. For more details: https://ractive.js.org/api/#ractiveunshift
ractive.update()	"Dirty checks" everything that depends directly or indirectly on the specified keypath. For more details: https://ractive.js.org/api/#ractiveupdate
ractive.updateModel()	Used to force a resync when manipulating inputs and other elements programmatically, that have two-way binding set up. For more details: https://ractive.js.org/api/#ractiveupdatemodel

For a full listing and details of instance method options, please refer to https://ractive.js.org/api/#instance-methods.

Context Object

When working with Ractive, there are occasions where knowing the current context will affect the outcome of a given operation. To facilitate this, Ractive provides a .getContext() method; this provides a number of properties and methods that allow us to obtain information about the Ractive instance and its surrounding context. These are listed in summary in Table A-13.

Please note – a number of these methods and properties share similarities with instance methods available in Ractive; I would recommend consulting the appropriate methods and properties as listed in Table A-7.

Table A-13. *List of Context Object properties and methods*

Feature / function	Purpose
context.add()	See ractive.add().
context.animate()	See ractive.animate().
context.decorators	A map of decorator name to decorator return object for all of the decorators on the node associated with the context.
context.event	The original event for contexts supplied to event directives.
context.get()	See ractive.get().
context.getBinding(), context.getBindingPath()	Returns the value or path of the binding if the node represented by this info object has a two-way binding.
context.isBound()	Returns true if the node represented by this info object has a two-way binding.
context.link()	See ractive.link().
context.listen()	Subscribes an event listener either directly on the node associated with the context or as a delegate if appropriate.
context.node	The node associated with the context.
context.observe()	See ractive.observe().
context.observeOnce()	See ractive.observeOnce().
context.original	The original DOM event object.
context.pop()	See ractive.pop().
context.push()	See ractive.push().
context.ractive	This property holds a reference to the Ractive instance that controls the node represented by this info object.
context.raise()	Triggers the nearest matching event directive relative to the context. For more details: https://ractive.js.org/api/#contextraise

(continued)

Table A-13. (*continued*)

Feature / function	Purpose
context.readLink()	See ractive.readLink().
context.resolve()	Resolves the given keypath to a full keypath. For more details: https://ractive.js.org/api/#contextresolve
context.reverse()	See ractive.reverse().
context.set()	See ractive.set().
context.setBinding()	Sets the binding of the node represented by this info object to the specified value. For more details: https://ractive.js.org/api/#contextsetbinding
context.shift()	See ractive.shift().
context.splice()	See ractive.splice().
context.sort()	See ractive.sort().
context.subtract()	See ractive.subtract().
context.toggle()	See ractive.toggle().
context.unlink()	See ractive.unlink().
context.unlisten()	Unsubscribe an event listener that was subscribed with listen.
context.unshift()	See ractive.unshift().
context.update()	See ractive.update().
context.updateModel()	See ractive.updateModel().

For a full listing and details of context object options, please refer to https://ractive.js.org/api/#context-object.

Parse Object

The parse object is an object you receive as the second argument in function templates. This helper object provides you with essential functions to dissect markup before turning over the template for use. Table A-14 details the list of methods available for use with the Parse Object:

Table A-14. *Methods available with the Parse Object*

Feature / function	Purpose
p.fromId()	Retrieves the template from the DOM <script> tag specified by id.
p.isParsed()	Tests if the supplied template is already parsed and is in its object form.
p.parse()	Parses the template using Ractive.parse(). Full Ractive runtime must be loaded.

For a full listing and details of parse object options, please refer to https://ractive.js.org/api/#parse-object.

Transition Object

The transition object is an object we receive when writing transitions; it has a few properties and methods designed to simplify the creation of transitions. Table A-15 shows the methods available for use with this object:

Table A-15. *Methods available with the Transiton Object*

Feature / function	Purpose
t.animateStyle()	Animates CSS properties to a certain value.
t.complete()	Signals Ractive that the transition is complete.
t.getStyle()	Retrieve a CSS property value from t.node.
t.isIntro	Works out if our transition is entering the DOM.
t.name	The name of the transition.
t.processParams()	Builds a map of parameters whose values are taken from the provided arguments.
t.setStyle()	Sets a CSS property on t.node to a value.

For a full listing and details of transition object options, please refer to `https://ractive.js.org/api/#transition-object`.

Index

© Alex Libby 2017
A. Libby, *Beginning Ractive.js*, https://doi.org/10.1007/978-1-4842-3093-0

Get the eBook for only $5!

Why limit yourself?

With most of our titles available in both PDF and ePUB format, you can access your content wherever and however you wish—on your PC, phone, tablet, or reader.

Since you've purchased this print book, we are happy to offer you the eBook for just $5.

To learn more, go to http://www.apress.com/companion or contact support@apress.com.

Apress®

All Apress eBooks are subject to copyright. All rights are reserved by the Publisher, whether the whole or part of the material is concerned, specifically the rights of translation, reprinting, reuse of illustrations, recitation, broadcasting, reproduction on microfilms or in any other physical way, and transmission or information storage and retrieval, electronic adaptation, computer software, or by similar or dissimilar methodology now known or hereafter developed. Exempted from this legal reservation are brief excerpts in connection with reviews or scholarly analysis or material supplied specifically for the purpose of being entered and executed on a computer system, for exclusive use by the purchaser of the work. Duplication of this publication or parts thereof is permitted only under the provisions of the Copyright Law of the Publisher's location, in its current version, and permission for use must always be obtained from Springer. Permissions for use may be obtained through RightsLink at the Copyright Clearance Center. Violations are liable to prosecution under the respective Copyright Law.

Printed in the United States
By Bookmasters

Printed in the United States
By Bookmasters